THE
WARSAW
PACT

Center for International Studies, Massachusetts Institute of Technology

Studies in Communism, Revisionism, and Revolution
(formerly *Studies in International Communism*)
William E. Griffith, general editor

1. Albania and the Sino-Soviet Rift
   William E. Griffith (1963)

2. Communism in North Vietnam
   P. J. Honey (1964)

3. The Sino-Soviet Rift
   William E. Griffith (1964)

4. Communism in Europe, Vol. 1
   William E. Griffith, ed. (1964)

5. Nationalism and Communism in Chile
   Ernst Halperin (1965)

6. Communism in Europe, Vol. 2
   William E. Griffith, ed. (1966)

7. Viet Cong: The Organization and Techniques of the
   National Liberation Front of South Vietnam
   Douglas Pike (1966)

8. Sino-Soviet Relations, 1964–1965
   William E. Griffith (1967)

9. The French Communist Party and the Crisis of International Communism
   François Fejtö (1967)

10. The New Rumania: From People's Democracy to Socialist Republic
    Stephen Fischer-Galati (1967)

11. Economic Development in Communist Rumania
    John Michael Montias (1967)

12. Cuba: Castroism and Communism, 1959–1966
    Andrés Suárez (1967)

13. Unity in Diversity: Italian Communism and the Communist World
    Donald L. M. Blackmer (1967)

14. Winter in Prague: Documents on Czechoslovak Communism in Crisis
    Robin Alison Remington, ed. (1969)

15. The Angolan Rebellion, Vol. I: The Anatomy of an Explosion (1950–1962)
    John A. Marcum (1969)

16. Radical Politics in West Bengal
    Marcus F. Franda (1971)

17. The Warsaw Pact: Case Studies in Communism Conflict Resolution
    Robin Alison Remington (1971)

THE WARSAW PACT

Case Studies
in Communist Conflict
Resolution

ROBIN ALISON REMINGTON

The MIT Press

Cambridge, Massachusetts, and London, England

To all those who work for a peace that is more than an absence of war and understand that waiting for the barbarians is not a solution.

Why have our two consuls and the praetors come out
today in their red, embroidered togas;
why do they wear amethyst-studded bracelets,
and rings with brilliant glittering emeralds;
why are they carrying costly canes today,
superbly carved with silver and gold?

Because the barbarians are to arrive today,
and such things dazzle the barbarians.

Why don't the worthy orators come as usual
to make their speeches, to have their say?

Because the barbarians are to arrive today;
and they get bored with eloquence and orations.

Why this sudden unrest and confusion?
(How solemn their faces have become.)
Why are the streets and squares clearing quickly,
and all return to their homes, so deep in thought?

Because night is here but the barbarians have not come.
Some people arrived from the frontiers,
and they said that there are no longer any barbarians.

And now what shall become of us without any barbarians?
Those people were a kind of solution.

"Expecting the Barbarians"
C. P. Cavafy

CONTENTS

DOCUMENTS

LIST OF
TABLES AND
CHARTS

PREFACE

RESEARCH on this book began ten years ago when, after struggling with a comparative analysis of international regional organizations for a graduate seminar at Indiana University, I decided that nothing worth reading had been written in English on the Warsaw Pact. Since that time some excellent but scattered articles have appeared along with brief chapters in broader studies of Soviet–East European relations. However, the sparseness of information on Communist coalition politics remained. There are volumes written on NATO. Fewer works, but still a substantial number, are devoted to the Organization of American States. A handful of well-researched studies have appeared on the Arab League and the Organization of African Unity. Therefore this book has been written to help fill a gap. It is not a definitive study. It is, I hope, a modest step in the right direction. It was written for general students of international relations as well as for students of communism in a style intended to be readable. I may not always have succeeded, but I wrote with the firm conviction that it is an author's responsibility to present material so that it can be understood by any reader who regularly keeps informed on world affairs, rather than the reader's responsibility to figure things out.

My research was based on the assumption that efficiency in the operation of any political alliance, indeed any institution, whether it be a school board, the US Supreme Court, the United Nations, or the Catholic Church, depends upon an accurate assessment of the adjustments that must be made and the ability to make them. There is always a struggle between the cost of adjustment and the cost of attempting to alter the environment in order to make adjustment unnecessary. There is always a lag between perceiving the changes that must be responded to and the ability to respond. This is a study of how a Communist regional defense alliance responded to conflict among its member states. It has been written with an awareness that, given the nature of Communist ideology, much of the relationship between Communist states depends upon party activities rather than joint institutions. Yet this does not make it impossible to analyze such institutions. Both party and state relations among Communist states respond to the same external phenomena.

Nor do I subscribe to the theory that there is not enough data available on Soviet–East European organizations to be meaningful. There is, in fact, almost too much information to handle, most of it unfortunately not in English. In this sense, I have been extremely lucky. First, this is true because the bulk of my research was done in Cambridge, Massachusetts, which meant that I had the files of Massachusetts Institute of Technology Center for International Studies Project on Communism, Revisionism, and Revolution in the next room and the Harvard Russian Research Center library fifteen minutes away. Second, I was able to work with assistants who knew Albanian, Czech, German, Polish, and Rumanian.

Any book that involves so many countries and languages is of necessity a collective effort. Thus my acknowledgments are long. I am grateful to William E. Griffith, director of the M.I.T. Project on Communism, Revisionism, and Revolution, both for his encouragement and his comments on the draft manuscript. I greatly benefited from conversations with Walter Clemens, Stephen Fischer-Galati, Michael Gamarnikow, Robert Hunter, Malcom Mackintosh, Peter R. Prifti, Stanley Riveles, William Zimmerman, and a number of Czech and Slovak scholars who because of the unhappy events of August 1968 must remain anonymous. Albanian materials were checked in the original by Peter R. Prifti, Czech and Slovak by Michael Berman, German and Rumanian by Rodica Saidman, Hungarian by László Urban, Polish and Russian by Irena Mauber Skibinski. My writing was made much easier by the general research assistance of Mary Patricia Grady. The manuscript was typed by Mrs. Lila Fernandez and prepared for press by Mrs. Elizabeth G. Whitney, who tirelessly retrieves documents from M.I.T. project archives.

I am appreciative of the aid and comfort given by the Harvard Russian Research Center during the early phases of my research, 1961–1963, and to the Belgrade Institute of International Politics and Economics, where I am currently on an academic exchange, and to the Institute of Strategic Studies in London, for assisting in the revisions inevitable after August 1970.

Finally I am grateful to the Center for International Studies and to its late director Max F. Millikan, and its present director, Everett Hagen, for their support in this study. Its publication has been made possible by a generous grant to M.I.T. by the Ford Foundation for research and teaching in international affairs. However, neither the center, the foundation, nor any of those whose suggestions or assistance contributed to this book is responsible for the book's contents or errors. That responsibility is mine alone.

Robin Alison Remington

Belgrade, Yugoslavia
April 1, 1971

CHRONOLOGY OF
WARSAW PACT MEETINGS
1955–1970

May 11–14, 1955	Warsaw	Founding conference
January 27–28, 1956	Prague	Political Consultative Committee (PCC)
May 24, 1958	Moscow	PCC
April 27–28, 1959	Warsaw	Meeting of foreign ministers of Warsaw Treaty states and China
February 4, 1960	Moscow	PCC
March 28–29, 1961	Moscow	PCC
August 3–5, 1961	Moscow	Conference of first secretaries of the central committees of Communist and Workers' parties of Warsaw Treaty member states
September 8–9, 1961	Warsaw	Conference of defense ministers
January 30–February 1, 1962	Prague	Conference of defense ministers
June 7, 1962	Moscow	PCC
February 28, 1963	Warsaw	Conference of defense ministers
July 25, 1963	Moscow	Heads of government and first secretaries of Warsaw Pact states
July 26, 1963	Moscow	PCC
1964		No publicized meeting occurred

January 19–20, 1965	Warsaw	PCC
May 10–18, 1965	Sub-Carpathian region of USSR	Meeting of "joint high command" (ministers of defense, chiefs-of-staff, and heads of political departments)
September 26, 1965	Dresden	Meeting of "military leaders"
November 24–25, 1965	Warsaw	Deputy ministers of defense and other military leaders
December 13–14, 1965	Dresden	Representatives of joint supreme command
May 27, 1966	Moscow	Warsaw Pact defense ministers
June 6–18, 1966	Moscow	Meeting of foreign ministers of Warsaw Treaty countries
July 5–9, 1966	Bucharest	PCC
November 14–17, 1966	Bucharest	Meeting of military delegations from Warsaw Treaty member states with Grechko
February 8–10, 1967	Warsaw	Conference of foreign ministers of Warsaw Treaty countries
February 26–27, 1968	East Berlin	Deputy ministers of foreign affairs
March 6–7, 1968	Sofia	PCC
October 29–30, 1968	Moscow	Meeting of defense ministers
March 17, 1969	Budapest	PCC
May 12–16, 1969	Warsaw	Chiefs of Staff
May 20–21, 1969	East Berlin	Conference of ministers of foreign affairs
October 30–31, 1969	Prague	Consultation of ministers of foreign affairs
October 30–November 3, 1969	Prague	Consultation of leaders of the armed forces
December 3–4, 1969	Moscow	Meeting of heads of parties and governments
December 9–10, 1969	Moscow	Session of the military council
December 22–23, 1969	Moscow	Meeting of committee of defense ministers

January 26–27, 1970	Sofia	Meeting of deputy ministers of defense
April 27–28, 1970	Budapest	Meeting of military council
May 21–22, 1970	Sofia	Meeting of defense ministers
June 21–22, 1970	Budapest	Meeting of ministers of foreign affairs
August 20, 1970	Moscow	PCC
October 27–30, 1970	Varna	Meeting of military council
December 2, 1970	East Berlin	PCC

THE
WARSAW
PACT

1
INTRODUCTION

FOR EUROPE, 1970 was a year of hope, when times did indeed seem to be changing. Shock at the Soviet invasion of Czechoslovakia had faded. The brief return to cold war rhetoric following that act of repression soon ended under continued pressure for détente. Brandt's Social Democrat coalition in West Germany had intensified its *Ostpolitik* and improved Bonn's changes for better relations with East Europe by signing the nuclear nonproliferation treaty. Optimism generated by the Soviet–West German Treaty on Renunciation of Force and hopes for progress in Soviet–United States Strategic Arms Talks created a political climate in which a European Security Conference seemed a real possibility. By August the Western press had stopped treating Warsaw Pact appeals for such a conference as only propaganda ploys. Despite differences in approach, "authoritative sources" in NATO were reported as regarding an ESC "quite likely" in 1971.

That timetable is still possible. But at the end of April 1971, the prospect seems less likely. The snail's pace of the Four-Power negotiations on Berlin and East–West German talks, Washington's apparent concern that West German *Ostpolitik* might go too far, fluctuating hopes for SALT, and the potential impact of upheaval in Poland on Moscow's European priorities have not been entirely good omens.

Whether or not the predicted European Security Conference occurs, however, the seriousness of efforts in that direction has added to the importance of the Warsaw Pact on three levels: (1) as a consideration in Soviet–East European relations; (2) as a part of Soviet policy toward Europe; and (3) as an actor in European politics. As Karl Deutsch said:

3

Most real-life situations tend to differ from formalized games in their greater range of possibilities for change in the rules and even in the very units of competition.[1]

Given the situation in Europe as it exists today, there is more reason than ever before to look closely at such units of competition. That is what I have tried to do with respect to the military-political alliance between the Soviet Union and the Communist states in Eastern Europe. What is the Warsaw Pact? Why was it established? How does it function? Has it changed? These are simple questions, but the answers are not simple. In part because of the nature of Communist esoteric communication, much of the relevant data is indirect. There is not as much hard fact as one would like in any language. There is no easy pattern or single set of priorities. And there are certain facts that have to be kept in mind.

First, like its Western counterparts the North Atlantic Treaty Organization (NATO) and the Organization of American States (OAS), the Warsaw Treaty Organization (WTO) is composed of states, limited in membership (despite its officially open-ended membership policy) and embodied in a separate organizational machinery.

Second, unlike NATO and the OAS, Warsaw Treaty members have undergone similar revolutions, i.e., fundamental changes in political organization, social institutions, economic control, and myth structure. This is not a discussion of whether that was good or bad. The discrete fact is that it happened, and for my purposes, it makes no difference that the Russian revolution came in 1917 whereas most East European revolutions were exported on the coattails of the Red Army after World War II. Rather I am trying to understand how the fact that Warsaw Treaty members have a common ideological orientation as well as similar social, economic, and political systems modifies the rules of the game in Communist coalition politics.

Warsaw Pact states share

> . . . that ensemble of norms, standards and values which is current in the Communist system, common to party members and separating them from non-members: "reactionaries," "capitalists," "imperialists," and the like. This culture is embodied in its own prolific literature, has

[1] Karl Deutsch, "The Growth of Nations: Some Recurrent Patterns of Political and Social Integrations," *World Politics* 2 (January 1953): 181.

its own distinct language and symbols, its own history and its own heroes, villains, and martyrs, and its own special ritual behavior. . . .[2]

This does not refer to the myth of a monolithic Communist foreign policy but rather to the perception of Communist states themselves of their separateness from non-Communist states, i.e., their sense of belonging to a "family of socialist nations" within which rules apply that do not yet maintain on the outside. Thus Warsaw Treaty members consider relations among Communist states (say the USSR and Poland) to have special characteristics that distinguish them from relations among non-Communist states (India and the United States) and from those among Communist and non-Communist states (Rumania and France).[3] Concrete expectations of behavior on the part of the in-group exist and differ from the behavior expected of non-Communist states.

As one Soviet author put it:

The development of cooperation, including of military cooperation, of the countries of socialism, is based on the fact that they have a uniform social and government structure, a unified ideology, i.e., the Marxist-Leninist concept, and a common goal, namely the building of communist society and its defense against the feeble impulses of internal and external counterrevolution. They have a common enemy, namely international imperialism led by the U.S. who is waging a struggle against socialism . . . [by] attempting to activate a common front to coordinate the direction of its attacks. The primary factor of close solidarity of the peaceful system of socialism is the leading role of the communist and working parties in all spheres of social life in our countries, and the firm observance by them of the principles of proletarian internationalism.[4]

Although there are certain ambiguities, particularly on the nature of proletarian internationalism, this is as clear a statement of the organizational principle (if not always practice) underlying the Warsaw Treaty as one is likely to get. And it should not be discounted, for even if the im-

---

[2] George Modelski, *The Communist International System* (Princeton University: Center for International Studies Monograph, 1960), p. 45.

[3] Communist states have typically assumed that they should have a community, if not an identity of interests, as well as common tactics in coping with a common enemy. That the "community of interests" has obviously broken down in a series of instances ranging from the Soviet-Yugoslav dispute through the current Sino-Soviet split to Soviet-Rumanian "differences" does not detract from the feeling among Communists in and out of power that there is a "right" course at any given time which can and must be found.

[4] M. Monin, "Ukreplenie voennogo sotrudnichestva—internatsional'nyi dolg bratskikh marksistsko-leninskikh partii," *Kommunist Vooruzhennykh sil* 9 (May 1969): 9–17, quoted from JPRS, no. 48287, June 25, 1969, p. 26.

portance of ideology among Communist states has been somewhat eroded as the number of its interpreters has grown, ideological purity as defined by Moscow has functioned as an unwritten criterion for participation in the Warsaw Pact. That the member states sanctioned Soviet prevention of Hungary's unilateral abrogation of the Warsaw Treaty by force, that Soviet-Albanian differences led to *de facto* exclusion of Albania from WTO meetings, and that Rumanian representatives were conspicuously absent from multilateral discussions on Czechoslovakia throughout 1968 all underline the rigidity of that criterion.

Third, despite this ideological symmetry, today the Warsaw Pact provides formal underpinning of coalition increasingly subject to conflicts of interest. For contrary to postwar prediction, there is no Soviet empire in Eastern Europe,[5] the invasion of Czechoslovakia notwithstanding. East European Communist states have retained their national identities, have resisted extensive economic integration, and have kept national control of their armed forces.[6] These states are tied to a national base, and govern peoples with a memory of pre-Communist national history. The high level of diversity they have maintained throughout the past decade is an explicit reminder that such memories frequently cut across ideological considerations. Consequently, the Warsaw Treaty Organization is faced with differing interpretations of the common interest, springing from the specific historical pressures and national interests of the countries involved.

Throughout the 1960's, the world Communist movement underwent drastic change. It was torn by interparty polemics and influenced by changing Soviet priorities in foreign policy. The Sino-Soviet dispute has split the image of a monolithic Communist unity almost beyond repair. That process continues while in 1970 Soviet bilateral negotiations with

[5] Brzezinski has well documented the quantities of "satellite" literature prior to the late 1950s; Z. K. Brzezinski, *The Soviet Bloc: Unity and Conflict,* 3rd ed. (Cambridge, Mass.: Harvard University Press, 1967). For some of earlier reassessments of Soviet-East European relations, see J. F. Brown, *The New Eastern Europe* (New York: Praeger, 1966); Herbert S. Dinerstein, "The Transformation of Alliance Systems," *The American Political Science Review* 59, no. 3 (September 1965); Barry Farrell, "Foreign Policy Formation in the Communist Countries of Eastern Europe," *East European Quarterly* 1, no. 1 (March 1967); William E. Griffith, ed., *Communism in Europe,* Volumes I and II (Cambridge, Mass.: The M.I.T. Press, 1964 and 1966), sections dealing with Eastern Europe; and Ghita Ionescu, *The Break-up of the Soviet Empire in Eastern Europe* (Baltimore, Md.: A Penguin Special, 1965).

[6] For an interesting account of current developments along these lines, see R. Waring Herrick, "Warsaw Pact Restructuring Strengthens Principle of National Control," Radio Liberty Research Bulletin, no. 10 (2540), March 11, 1970.

such capitalist countries as the United States and West Germany have added substance to discussions of peaceful coexistence and détente.

Now it is not far-fetched to speculate that the Italian concept of polycentrism, rather than falling on the "rubbish heap of history" with the Soviets' rebuke of Togliatti in 1956, may accurately depict future trends. In these circumstances the Soviet Union is subjected to multiple pressures and Moscow's attitude toward the Warsaw Treaty Organization has become more complex. Desire for support against the Chinese has made any attempt to consolidate Soviet economic and military influence in East Europe without consideration for East European sensitivities more difficult. Hence there has been a consistent tendency to upgrade the Warsaw Pact as an already legitimate instrument through which Soviet power can be manifested. The very fact of greater emphasis on its importance, in turn, has made increasingly remote the hypothetical possibility (at one time often mentioned if not seriously considered) of the Russians deciding to scrap the Warsaw Treaty for East-West objectives such as a collective security treaty.[7]

Rumanian resistance to "perfecting" the Warsaw Pact notwithstanding, Bucharest's intra-alliance diplomacy has reinforced Soviet perception of the value of the pact ever since the mid-1960s. For example, former Rumanian party leader Gheorghiu-Dej attended the January 1965 political consultative committee meeting after having been conspicuously absent from other Communist meetings in 1964. He did not go to the March 1965 "consultative" meeting of Communist parties. Renewed Rumanian military participation within the Warsaw Pact followed Bucharest's independent recognition of West Germany and nonalignment in the Middle East Crisis. Thus in August 1967, Rumanian troops took part in joint military exercises for the first time in three years.[8] The same pattern

---

[7] From the beginning members of the Warsaw Pact stressed that the WTO was a transitional organization which they hoped would soon be replaced by an all-European collective security treaty. As West German *Ostpolitik* became more pronounced in 1967, however, references to the eventual dissolution of the Warsaw Pact almost disappeared (with the exception of Rumania). Emphasis shifted to the importance of nonaggression pacts between the two blocs that would by implication leave both NATO and the Warsaw Pact intact. Subsequently, despite formal repetition of willingness to see the pact go, its departure has been securely tied to creation of a collective security system in Europe—i.e., something more elaborate than an all-European treaty. See I. Yakubovsky, "Bastion mira i bezopasnosti narodov," *Voenno-istoricheskii zhurnal* 3 (March 1971): 20–31.

[8] *Pravda*, August 29, 1967; also Bucharest Domestic Service in Rumanian, 0500 GMT, August 28, 1967. For Western analysis, *The New York Times*, August 29, 1967. Also, Yugoslav observers attended Warsaw Pact exercises (a logical extension of Soviet-Yugoslav cooperation with respect to the Arab-Israeli conflict).

of organizational concessions to balance foreign policy initiatives recurred during the Czechoslovak crisis of 1968. Bucharest sharply condemned the senseless repression of the Prague spring but participated in postinvasion Warsaw Pact activities including the 1969 joint military exercises in Bulgaria.

In short, if the handling of Soviet-Rumanian differences could be considered a model for future tensions,[9] by 1967 the Warsaw Pact appeared to be evolving into an important channel for communication or even conflict resolution among European Communist states. On the face of it, Moscow's decision to use Soviet and East European troops to force Czechoslovak "socialism with a human face" back into a more orthodox mold cut short that process. Still, there is not a little evidence that the very multilateral nature of that invasion as well as some of its complicated after-effects increased rather than diminished Soviet need of the Warsaw Pact.

These possibilities are not irrelevant in analyzing either the nature of Communist East Europe or the options open for all European cooperation. In studying them I am not attempting to chronicle postwar Soviet policy toward Eastern Europe or to write a history of Soviet-East European relations.[10] Rather my purpose is to analyze the impact of internecine strife on European Communist coalition politics using data relevant to the working of a Communist regional defense alliance—the Warsaw Pact. In trying to determine the limits of diversity within that institution, I have focused on three cases of intra-alliance conflict between the USSR and an East European member state: Rumania, Czechoslovakia, and East Germany. Soviet-Rumanian, and more recently Soviet-East German differences have been contained to date without resort to force. What went

---

[9] Certainly Colonel Tykociński's revelations indicated awareness of similar opportunities for increasing Polish autonomy among high-level party and government officials. (Tyko-cinski was head of the Polish Military Mission in West Berlin who defected in May 1965.) "Poland's Plan for the 'Northern Tier,' " an interview with Władysław Tykociński, *East Europe* 15, no. 11 (November 1966). For an early Czechoslovak viewpoint, see Václav Kotyk, "Některé otázky dějin vztahů socialistických zemí" (Some Aspects of the History of Relations Among Socialist Countries), *Československý časopis historický* 4 (1967), in *RFE Czechoslovak Press Survey*, no. 1973 (233), October 30, 1967, p. 14.

[10] Readers interested in more general or exhaustive treatment of this topic should see Kurt London, ed., *Eastern Europe in Transition* (Baltimore, Md.: Johns Hopkins Press, 1966); H. Gordon Skilling, *The Governments of Communist East Europe* (New York: Crowell, 1966); and Thomas W. Wolfe, *Soviet Power and Europe: 1945–1970* (Baltimore, Md.: Johns Hopkins Press, 1970).

wrong in Czechoslovakia? Also, since the Warsaw Treaty Organization offers as yet unexplored possibilities for comparison of the functioning of different sociopolitical systems at the international level, I have framed the core questions so that they could be applied to non-Communist coalitions as well.

Specifically:

1. In what way was the institution of the coalition itself involved in these instances of conflict among its member states?

2. Did this differ from the role played during earlier crises? In the cases in question, how did Rumanian-Soviet maneuvering, subsequent Soviet–East German disagreements and the resort to multilateral use of force against Czechoslovakia in 1968 differ from the Polish October of 1956, the Hungarian "counterrevolution" of that same year, and Albanian defiance dating from 1960?

3. What effect did such conflict have on the superpowers' perception of the coalition? Did it change the nature of the obligations or expectations of the smaller members?

4. Did actual changes in the institutional form of the alliance result?

However, as became painfully obvious during the Czech crisis of 1968, the opportunity for Rumanian and East German maneuvering has in itself been contingent upon Moscow's perception of the role played by the Warsaw Pact in Soviet-East European relations. Therefore an understanding of fluctuations in the Soviet attitude toward the alliance is fundamental in assessing its potential, and in Chapter I on the origin of the pact, I am most concerned with one problem: What did the Russians have in mind?

2
ORIGIN OF THE
WARSAW PACT

ANY ATTEMPT to use behavior in conflict situations as an index of attitude
change must begin with the original attitude. Thus it is necessary to
describe the starting point. The Soviet Union had already signed bilateral
treaties of Friendship, Cooperation, and Mutual Assistance with all the
East European Communist states except East Germany and Albania.
Why the multilateral alliance? What purposes did it serve for Moscow?
What was the relation to domestic developments in the USSR?

On the international level the Soviet explanation is both straight-
forward and correct. The Warsaw Treaty was rooted in Soviet and East
European fears of a rearmed Germany. Specifically it grew out of Moscow's campaign to prevent West German membership in the West European Union (WEU), which was the way Bonn came to participate in
NATO.

On November 13, 1954, the USSR sent a note directed against ratification of the Paris Agreements to the governments of twenty-three other
European countries and the United States inviting them to take part in
an all-European security conference to be held in either Moscow or Paris
in November. It condemned the October 23, 1954, Agreements for resur-
recting German militarism in violation of previous international agreements and made plain that German unity would be the price of including
West Germany in the WEU. The key passage warned:

> The plans drawn up at the London and Paris conferences for resurrecting
> German militarism and incorporating the remilitarized Western Germany
> in military alignments cannot but complicate the situation in Europe.
> Realization of these plans will inevitably strain relations between the
> European nations. It will therefore be natural if the peace-loving Euro-

pean nations find themselves obliged to adopt new measures for safe-guarding their security.[1]

However, although fear of a reviving German militarism provided impetus for the Warsaw Pact, Soviet internal developments strongly colored Moscow's perception of its purpose.

The Importance of the CPSU Innerparty Struggle

Throughout 1955, the innerparty struggle among Stalin's successors had had wide repercussions. Much of that conflict hinged on differing views of the "correct" foreign policy and military doctrine, both vital matters for Soviet evaluation of the Warsaw Treaty Organization.

In brief, Malenkov, who had been associated both with Soviet commitment to détente and with the theory that nuclear war could mean "the destruction of world civilization," [2] was forced to resign the premiership on February 8, 1955. Within the Soviet Politburo, Khrushchev, Molotov, Bulganin, and Voroshilov had been opposed to Malenkov. In foreign policy matters this opposition demanded sustained "vigilance" and the full development of Soviet defense in order to combat the innate aggressiveness of imperialists. The anti-Malenkov group viewed steps to reduce international tension with suspicion and considered constant struggle to isolate imperialism more important than détente. At the Moscow conference of future Warsaw Pact members in November–December 1954, Molotov, Minister of Foreign Affairs, had presented the Soviet interpretation of the situation facing the participants of the conference. His speech was blunt, militant, and harsh.

> Inasmuch as Western Germany is now not only being remilitarized but is also being involved in military alignments directed against other European countries, the evil consequence of this should not be minimized. What is taking place in the sight of all is a direct compact between the German militarists and revanchists believe, and not without

---

[1] *Pravda*, November 14, 1954, quoted from "Note of the Soviet Government to the Governments of Europe and the U.S.A.," *New Times* 46 (November 13, 1954): 3. For strongly worded Soviet views on the Paris agreements see G. I. Tunkin, "Parizskie soglasheniia i mezhdunarodnoe pravo," *Sovetskoe gosudarstvo i pravo* 2 (1955) and "New Measures for Security of Peace-Loving Countries," *International Affairs* 5 (May 1955). Subsequent Soviet interpretations continue to rely heavily on the importance of the Paris Agreements in necessitating the Warsaw Treaty. See G. P. Zhukov, *Varshavskii dogovor i voprosy mezhdunarodnoi bezopasnosti* (Moscow: Cotsekgiz, 1961).

[2] *Pravda*, March 13, 1954. See also H. S. Dinerstein, *War and the Soviet Union: Nuclear Weapons and the Revolution in Soviet Military and Political Thinking* (New York: Praeger, 1959), pp. 70–74.

reason, that, with the resources of Western Germany at their disposal, and with the support of the Western Powers, and primarily of the aggressive element in America, they will in the very near future secure military preponderance in Western Europe, with the help of which they will be able again to trample underfoot all agreements restricting their action.[3]

According to Molotov, this threat required not only "special vigilance" but also "practical measures" to safeguard socialist security.

Nor had his tone softened in his February 8 report on the international situation:

> The attitude of the Soviet Union to the Paris Agreements is perfectly clear. It leaves no room for misconstruction.
>
> It is obvious to us that if the Paris Agreements are ratified, Western Germany will proceed to revive militarism and will, in fact, fall under control of the German revanchists. . . .
>
> This fact cannot be disregarded by the Soviet Union and the People's Democracies, against whom the Paris Agreements are spearheaded. The Soviet people and their army sincerely desire peace and, at the same time, are deeply imbued with a consciousness of, and a determination to, defend their socialist achievements. . . .
>
> In view of the new situation arising in Europe, the Soviet Union and the other peaceable states against whom the Paris Agreements are directed will not sit with folded arms. They will have to adopt appropriate measures for the more effective safeguarding of their security and protection of peace in Europe.[4]

Yet with the defeat of Malenkov's domestic program in late 1954 and

---

[3] V. M. Molotov, Statement to the 1954 Moscow Conference, New Times 49 (December 4, 1954), supplement, "Conference of European Countries on Safeguarding European Peace and Security," p. 11. Text, speeches, communiqués, and declaration are included in Moskovskoe soveshchanie evropeiskikh stran po obespecheniu mira i bezopastnosti v Evrope (Moscow: Gospolitizdat, 1954). For English versions see New Times 49 (December 4, 1954). Although the Declaration used more Communist terminology than the preceding speeches, in many portions it paraphrased the Soviet delegate's opening speech.

[4] Molotov Report on the International Situation, February 8, 1955; V. M. Molotov, Pravda, February 9, 1955; quoted from NEWS, Supplement 4 (February 16, 1955): 10. Hereafter cited as Molotov Report on the International Situation, February 8, 1955. In this speech, Molotov specified for the first time that a treaty of friendship, cooperation, and mutual assistance among the 8 Moscow conference countries was among the "appropriate measures" the Soviets had in mind to counter West German entry into NATO. He spoke of consultations concerning such a treaty as "already in progress." [For a detailed analysis of the report, see the section on internal struggles and Soviet foreign policy in Uri Ra'anan, The USSR Arms the Third World: Case Studies in Soviet Foreign Policy (Cambridge, Mass.: The MIT Press, 1969), pp. 102–122.] Then on March 22 the Soviet Ministry of Foreign Affairs tersely announced "complete agreement" among the participants of the Moscow Conference on the need for a united command and indicated that China took part in the consultations. (Pravda, March 22, 1955).

"Bravo, I like your way of thinking." Reprinted from Informatia Bucurestiului
(*Bucharest*), *June 22, 1967.*

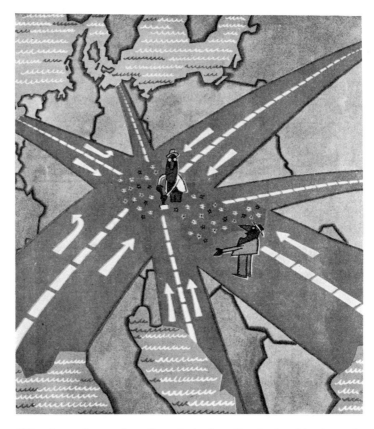

"It's nice to know that all roads lead to Czechoslovakia, but why were we chosen for this honor?" Reprinted from Nedele *(Prague), no. 21 (1968).*

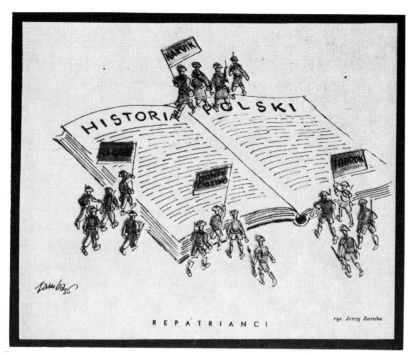

The Gomulka regime has "rehabilitated" Polish soldiers who fought with the West during World War II. This cartoon shows them marching back into the pages of Polish history— from which they had been ejected. Reprinted from Szpilki (Warsaw), Jan. 13, 1957.

"Hush!" The small figure at the left is Sir Leslie Munro talking on the Hungarian question at the UN General Assembly; the rest of the world is shown focusing on Soviet Premier Khrushchev as he addresses the Hungarian Party Congress. Reprinted from Nepszabadsag (Budapest), Dec. 2, 1959.

Reprinted from Ylli *(Tirana) 5, no. 8 (Aug. 1964).*

January 1955, Bulganin took over the premiership and Molotov became isolated in a collective leadership bent on moving away from a hard-line approach to foreign relations. This first took the form of renewed emphasis on "normalization" of relations, which meant, in effect, Soviet concessions with respect to Austria and stepped-up moves toward a Soviet-Yugoslav rapprochement. That Molotov's position was weakening was dramatically underlined when *Pravda* and *Izvestia* published Tito's criticism of his February 8 analysis of the improvement in Soviet-Yugoslav relations as made possible by the Yugoslav abandonment of previous positions.[5] The next day *Pravda* announced the new Soviet concessions on the Austrian question.[6] Reportedly these developments were followed by a presidium meeting at which Molotov attempted to block both the establishment of party relations with Yugoslavia and implementation of concessions on Austria.[7] He failed.

The extent to which Molotov had been downgraded became apparent in his reduced role at the Warsaw Treaty conference in early May. He went to Warsaw, but Bulganin spoke for the Soviet government. And the Soviet Premier's speech[8] differed markedly from that of Molotov at the preceding Moscow Conference. Bulganin began by stating that "the unalterable principle of Soviet foreign policy is Lenin's principle of co-existence of different social systems." Whereas Molotov had spoken at length both on the threat to peace inherent in the Paris Agreements and the aggressive nature of the Western powers, Bulganin balanced continued hostility to the Paris Agreements and "aggressive military blocs" with conciliatory gestures. Molotov's emphasis had been on "the aggressive plans and military and political machinations of the three Western

---

[5] *Pravda* and *Izvestia*, March 11, 1955; CDSP 7, no. 8 (April 6, 1955): 11. Significantly, it was in early 1955 that the review of Soviet military doctrine had concluded with renewed emphasis on the importance of surprise nuclear attack and preemption: *Voennaia mysl'* 2 (February 1955), cited by Dinerstein, *War and the Soviet Union*, p. 186.

[6] *Pravda*, March 12, 1955.

[7] See Committee of the Judiciary, US Senate, 84th Cong. 2nd sess., Internal Security Subcommittee Hearings, part 29, June 8–29, 1956; "Scope of Soviet Activity in the U.S." (Washington, D.C.: Government Printing Office, 1957), pp. 1155–1174 and the testimony of Seweryn Bialer, pp. 1190–1191; David J. Dallin, *Soviet Foreign Policy After Stalin* (Philadelphia: Lippincott, 1961), pp. 227–233, and Wolfgang Leonard, *The Kremlin Since Stalin* (New York: Praeger, 1962), p. 103. Certainly Molotov's hostility to concessions on Austria had been apparent in his February 8 report where he carefully balanced indications of Soviet willingness to negotiate by tightly tying the Austrian issue to the German question and pointedly stating that "it must be borne in mind that ratification of the Paris Agreements" would create a "serious threat" to Austrian independence.

[8] Statement of N. A. Bulganin, *New Times* 21 (May 21, 1955): 6–15.

powers." Bulganin stressed the Soviet commitment to peace, the Austrian settlement, and the new Soviet disarmament proposals.

Nor was the degree of hostility toward the West the only difference between Molotov's speech to the Moscow conference and the Bulganin statement. Bulganin's references to the future East European members of the Warsaw Treaty underlined the equality of these countries in contrast to Molotov's categorical assertion that:

> The peoples of the Soviet Union, Poland, Czechoslovakia, Hungary, Rumania, Bulgaria, Albania, and the German Democratic Republic, whose governments are represented at this Conference, know that the present plans of the Western imperialist powers call not only for special vigilance but also for practical measures to safeguard their security. . . . This requires that the countries represented at this conference *shall take joint measures* in the sphere of organization of their armed forces and their command, as well as other measures, so as to reliably protect the peaceful labors of their peoples, to guarantee the inviolability of their frontiers, and to provide defense against possible aggression.[9] [Italics mine.]

Rather Bulganin stressed that the "consultations" held by the participants of the Moscow conference "revealed full unanimity of views" concerning need for a Treaty of Friendship, Cooperation and Mutual Assistance, that "relations among our countries are based on the principles of equality, respect for one another's national sovereignty, and noninterference in one another's internal affairs," and continued:

> The relations between our countries are an embodiment of the noble principles of socialist internationalism, of the noble idea of fraternal friendship between free and equal Nations.

This was Bulganin's[10] single reference to the socialist nature of the Warsaw Treaty states. It represented a decided weakening of Molotov's assertion:

> One would think that it should have been realized long ago that no threats can scare the Soviet people and the democratic countries in which the power is wielded by working class in alliance with the laboring peasants, and which are making effective headway in the building of socialism. If such attempts ended in fiasco in the past, still more hopeless are all aggressive plans of this nature today, when the great Soviet Union and the People's Democracies are more than ever confident in

---

[9] Molotov statement to 1954 Moscow Conference, p. 15.
[10] Statement of N. A. Bulganin, p. 14.

themselves and in their continued success in building socialism. There is no power on earth that can turn back the wheel of history.[11]

This was an expedient omission. In May 1955, the keynote of Soviet East-West policy was one of peace, disarmament, détente. Bulganin reiterated the Soviet disarmament proposals of May 10 in his speech to the Warsaw Treaty conference. The Austrian Treaty was about to be concluded. And despite a strong condemnation of the Paris agreements and West German militarism, the Soviet premier spoke favorably of a summit conference. It was not the time to remind the West that socialism advanced via "the wheel of history." (Table 1)

Treaty Text and Organizational Structure

The language of the Warsaw treaty itself reflected international priorities of the Khrushchev-Bulganin leadership. The treaty consisted of eleven articles defining the member-states' relationship to one another, particularly in the event of aggression, to the United Nations, and to nonmember states. The majority of its clauses dealt with relations among member states. Basing the treaty on the "principle of respect for independence and sovereignty of others and noninterference in internal affairs" (Article VIII), the members agreed: (1) to settle all disputes peacefully (Article I); (2) to consult on all international issues affecting their common interests; (3) to consult immediately in the event that one of the treaty partners were threatened with armed attack so as to "ensure joint defense" (Article III); (4) to establish a joint command (Article V) and a political consultative committee (Article VI); and (5) to promote economic and cultural intercourse within the group (Article VIII). With respect to the United Nations, the treaty specified that it was in accordance with the UN Charter (Article I) and that measures of joint defense would be taken under Article 51 of that charter (Article IV).[12] As for nonmember

[11] Molotov Statement to 1954 Moscow Conference, p. 12. That Molotov's formulation had been repeated almost word for word in the concluding declaration to the Moscow Conference indicated the extent of his influence in December 1954. Moscow Declaration, *New Times* 49 (December 4, 1954), Supplement: 72.

[12] Both the North Atlantic Treaty and the Warsaw Pact refer specifically to Article 51 rather than to those articles of the charter directly concerned with regional arrangements. Article 51 is not included within the chapter of the United Nations Charter devoted to regional arrangements or agencies, nor is it considered to refer to regional arrangements by Leland M. Goodrich and Edvard Hambro, *Charter of the United Nations: Commentary and Documents* (Boston: World Peace Foundation, 2nd rev. ed., 1949).

The difficulty was, in part, that neither Soviet nor US policymakers wanted the organizations involved to be subject to the authority of the UN Security Council as are regional

TABLE I

CHRONOLOGY OF EVENTS SURROUNDING THE ORIGIN OF THE WARSAW PACT

October 23, 1954	Paris Agreements signed.
November 13, 1954	Soviet note calling for an all European Security Conference.
December 1954	Moscow Conference: USSR and East European states agree to take joint measures if Paris Agreements are ratified.
February 8, 1955	Malenkov resigns; Bulganin becomes premier.
	Molotov's Report on the International Situation calls for "appropriate measures in self-defense."
March 11, 1955	Soviet newspapers publish Tito's criticism of Molotov February 8 report.
March 12, 1955	Soviet concessions on Austria announced.
March 22, 1955	TASS announcement of agreement among Moscow Conference members to conclude Warsaw Pact should Paris Agreements be ratified.
March 23, 1955	Eisenhower press conference: Call for summit meeting.
March 26, 1955	Bulganin responds favorably to US suggestion of summit talks.
April 12–15, 1955	Soviet-Austrian negotiations.
May 5, 1955	Paris Agreements are ratified.
	Long article by GDR leader Walter Ulbricht in *Pravda* calls for joint measures.
May 6–7, 1955	Soviets denounce Anglo-Soviet Treaty of 1942 and Franco-Soviet Treaty of 1943.
May 10, 1955	Soviet disarmament proposal.
May 11, 1955	Warsaw Treaty conference opens in Poland.
May 14, 1955	Warsaw Treaty signed.
May 15, 1955	Austrian State Treaty signed.
May 1955	Khrushchev goes to Belgrade to further Soviet-Yugoslav rapprochement.
July 4, 1955	CPSU presidium meeting at which Molotov unsuccessfully attacks policy toward Yugoslavia and Austria.
July 18–23, 1955	Geneva Summit Conference.

states, "all European" states were invited to join the treaty if they agreed with its aims "irrespective of their social and political systems" (Article IX).[13] The treaty partners pledged to take part in international activities designed to safeguard the peace (Article II) and, conversely, not to join any coalitions or alliances or make any agreements in conflict with the Warsaw Treaty (Article VII). The duration of the treaty was made contingent on the realization of a General European Treaty of collective security and thus dependent upon an action of members and nonmembers alike.[14]

Little is known of the institutional structure set up by the Warsaw Treaty. The treaty itself referred only to a political consultative committee with the power to appoint auxiliary bodies. Member states were to be represented on this committee by a member of their respective governments or by other specifically authorized delegates. Further organizational details were worked out in closed session during the January 1956 political consultative committee meeting at which it was decided that the PCC should meet not less than twice a year with chairmanship of the meetings to rotate among members. At that time two auxiliary institutions were created: (1) a standing commission to work out recommendations on questions of foreign policy, and (2) a joint secretariat which was to be staffed by representatives of all the treaty members. Both bodies were to be located in Moscow. From 1956 until recently organizational decisions among Warsaw Treaty members were not made public; nor

---

organizations according to Article 53 of the UN Charter. However, the Soviets were quite frank that China was limited to observer status solely because China was not a European country; see M. Lachs, "Varshavskii dogovor i problema kollektivnoi bezopasnosti v Evrope," *Mezhdunarodnaya zhizn'* 10 (1955), and G. I. Tunkin, "O nekotorykh voprosakh mezhdunarodnogo dogovora v sviazi s varshavskim dogovorom," *Sovietskoe gosudarstvo i pravo* 1 (1956).

[13] In hailing the Warsaw Treaty as a new high point in international relations the Soviets point particularly to this clause and contrast NATO's rejection of the Soviet Union's request for membership in March 1954. "Genuine Concern for European Peace and Security," *New Times* 20 (May 14, 1955): 1–3; M. Lachs, "O varshavskom dogovore i severoatlanticheskom pakte," *Mezhdunarodnaya zhizn'* 2 (1956): 113; and *Voprosy vneshei politiki, stran sotsialisticheskogo lageriia* (Moscow: Izd-vo mezhdunarodnykh otnoshenii, 1958), pp. 15–16. Nevertheless membership has remained limited to the Soviet Union and East European Communist states and there is evidence to suggest that, in fact, Moscow considers this necessary in terms of any workable arrangement.

[14] For the text of the Warsaw Treaty, see Document 1, p. 201. Should a general European treaty of collective security not be signed, the Warsaw Treaty was to remain in force for twenty years.

was there any further mention of the activity of either the standing policy commission or the joint secretariat.[15]

From a political point of view the minimal nature of that structure was not particularly important in Moscow. For at that time the Warsaw Treaty was designed to be primarily a prop for Soviet strategy at the Four Power Geneva Conference in July. The second stage envisaged by the USSR draft European collective security treaty assumed that the North Atlantic Treaty, the Paris Agreements, and the Warsaw Treaty would simultaneously cease to operate, to be replaced by an all-European collective security system.[16] This was Moscow's maximum goal: One which the Soviets obviously did not expect to achieve at that time. Bulganin had hedged the suggestion by making such a move contingent upon an agreement in armament reduction and the withdrawal of foreign troops from the territory of European countries,[17] an agreement the United States Congress could be counted upon to refuse.

As an alternative, the Soviets proposed that states party to the North Atlantic Treaty and the West European Union, on the one hand, and states party to the Warsaw Treaty, on the other conclude a treaty promising not to employ armed force against each other and providing for consultation in the event of disputes that might threaten the peace.[18]

No concrete steps were taken, and both suggestions were reserved for further consideration at the October Foreign Ministers' meeting. At that time *Mezhdunarodnaia zhizn'* printed a long Polish article insisting that the results of the Geneva Conference indisputably proved the significance

[15] See *Zasedania politicheskogo konsul'tativnogo komiteta, uchrezdennogo v sootvestvii s varshavskim dogovorom* (Moscow: Gospoltizdat, 1956). For Western analyses: J. F. Brown, *The New Eastern Europe* (New York: Praeger, 1966); D. Andre Loeber, "The Legal Structure of the Communist Bloc," *Social Research* 27, no. 2 (Summer 1960); Z. K. Brzezinski, "Organization of the Communist Camp," *World Politics* 23, no. 2 (January 1961), reprinted as an appendix to the 3rd edition of *The Soviet Bloc*; the section dealing with the Warsaw Treaty in Kazimierz Gryzbowski, *The Socialist Commonwealth of Nations: Organizations and Institutions* (New Haven: Yale University Press, 1964), and Robin Alison Remington, "The Growth of Communist Regional Organization, 1949–1962," Ph. D. dissertation, Indiana University, April 1966. Brief coverage of PCC meetings may be found in the journal *International Organization*.

[16] Draft of the USSR Delegation, "General European Treaty of Collective Security in Europe," Article 14, *New Times* 31 (July 28, 1955): 8–9.

[17] "Statement by Bulganin, Chairman of the Council of Ministers of the USSR," *New Times* 30 (July 21, 1955): 17. See also "Na puti koslableniu mezhdunarodnoi napriazhennosti," *Kommunist* 32, no. 11 (July 1955): 44.

[18] "Basic Principles of a Treaty Between the Alignments of States Existing in Europe" (Proposed by the USSR Delegation), *New Times* 31 (July 28, 1955): 13.

of the Warsaw Treaty.[19] The foreign ministers, however, continued to disagree. Moscow blamed recalcitrant circles in the West for this situation,[20] and references to the Warsaw Treaty disappeared from the Soviet press until the first political consultative committee meeting in January 1956.

Military Considerations

The Warsaw Pact primarily symbolized a buffer between West Germany and the Soviets. Practically speaking, it also extended Soviet military involvement in Eastern Europe for the Warsaw Treaty legalized Soviet troops that otherwise should have been withdrawn from Hungary and Rumania after the Austrian State Treaty. Albania, with whom Moscow had no bilateral military assistance pact, was included. Yet there is little evidence that initially the Warsaw Treaty was needed or seriously expected to serve as a channel by which to speed up military integration of Soviet and East European armed forces.

During the national front coalition period of the people's democracies (1945–1947), the Communists had consolidated control of the political departments of East European armed forces as well as the special security forces and the police. Even before Communist regimes were firmly in power, they had begun to repress potential opposition. By 1947 local Communists began to replace non-Communist ministers of defense. Emil Bodnaras became Minister of Defense in Rumania in 1948. Marshal Konstantin Rokossovski, a Polish national and Russian officer, was made Minister of National Defense in Poland in November 1949; and Alexej Čepička, the son-in-law of President Gottwald, became Defense Minister of Czechoslovakia in April 1950.[21]

With Communists sitting at the top of the military hierarchies, the

[19] M. Lachs, "Varshavskii dogovor i problema kollektivnoi bezopasnosti v Evrope," p. 61. Certainly some reference to GDR membership in the Warsaw Treaty Organization could have been expected with the signing of the bilateral Soviet–East German treaty in September 1955. This omission seems to support the assumption that, at least initially, the Warsaw Treaty had a largely propagandistic significance related to Soviet East-West maneuvering. "Treaty on Relations between the Union of Soviet Socialist Republics and the German Democratic Republic," *United Nations Treaty Series* (hereafter cited UNTS) 266, no. 3114:201.

[20] See L. Bezymensky, "The Geneva Conference," *New Times* 45 (November 1955): 7–11.

[21] Ithiel de Sola Pool, *et al., Satellite Generals: A Study of Military Elites in the Soviet Sphere* (Stanford, Calif.: Hoover Institution Studies, Stanford University Press, 1955).

elimination of potentially disloyal, restless, or incompetent elements within the East European armed forces accelerated. There was intensive political indoctrination. All high officers were required to take courses at political-military institutes, and many East European officers were sent to the Soviet Union for political as well as technical training. In some cases, the officers of the East European armies were in fact Russians.[22] Technical, nonmilitary matters were coordinated with Soviet usages such as style of uniforms, marching, and drill.[23]

Thus, by and large a copy of the Soviet pattern had been imposed on East European armed forces by 1950. The age of service had dropped to twenty years, while the term was extended to two years, often three years for the air forces and security troops. Rapid physical build-up based on Soviet tanks, motorized weapons, and airplanes paralleled the drive for education, expansion, and modernization on all levels. In sum, even prior to the Warsaw Pact, the Soviets had remolded the armed forces of the people's democracies into a separate yet subordinate arm of the USSR army.

Under the Warsaw Treaty, a joint command of Soviet and East European armed forces was set up.[24] Soviet Marshal I. S. Konev[25] was appointed commander-in-chief of the joint armed forces. He was to be assisted by the ministers of defense of the other member states as deputy-commanders-in-chief. Each such deputy commander was to have charge of the armed forces contributed by his home state. A staff of the joint armed forces including permanent members from the East European general staffs was to be located in Moscow; disposition of the joint forces

---

[22] Hans von Krannhals, "Command Integration Within the Warsaw Pact," *Military Review* 41, no. 5 (May 1961); and "The Military Establishments II," *East Europe* 5, no. 7 (May 1958).

[23] For a comment on the reaction of the Hungarian army to the Russian uniform, see Ferenc A. Váli, *Rift and Revolt in Hungary* (Cambridge, Mass.: Harvard University Press, 1961), p. 73.

[24] The reasoning that went into establishing the joint command is still a matter of conjecture, for Soviet General Antonov spoke to the Warsaw Treaty Conference on these questions in closed session, while other published speeches of that conference referred only to the "defensive nature" of the treaty.

[25] For a brief biographical sketch of Konev, see Michel Garder, *Histoire de l'armée soviétique* (Paris: 1959), p. 289, and the *Biographic Directory of the USSR*, Institute for the Study of the USSR, Munich, Germany (New York: Scarecrow Press, Inc., 1958), pp. 291–293. Given his position as inspector of coordination of the satellite armies since April 1950, Konev was the logical choice for Commander-in-Chief of the Joint Armed Forces. His chief of staff, A. I. Antonov, had served as the Soviet chief of the general staff from February 1945 until after the Soviet war with Japan, *ibid.*, p. 32.

on the territories of member states to be covered by (presumably separate) agreements among the states as the requirements of their mutual defense might indicate.[26]

Whether or not such a reorganization of forces actually resulted from the creation of a joint command is unknown. In the West it has been generally accepted that, apart from a further standardization of weapons, the Warsaw Treaty Organization simply continued earlier arrangements whereby East Europe served largely as an extension of the Soviet early warning and air defense system.[27]

Yet the possibility that Moscow weighed the value of the Warsaw Pact at least partially in terms of tightening Soviet military control within Eastern Europe should not be entirely discounted. Soviet references to Moscow's military expectations were phrased in the most vague and general terms.[28] There is an interesting account, although impossible to

[26] "Establishment of a Joint Command of the Armed Forces of the Signatories to the Treaty of Friendship, Cooperation, and Mutual Assistance," *New Times* 21 (May 21, 1955): 68.

[27] In the West, the Warsaw Pact was considered of negligible military importance before the joint maneuvers began in the fall of 1961. For example, H. S. Dinerstein, *War and the Soviet Union,* does not mention the Warsaw Treaty Organization, although he does refer to the November 1954 note stressing the necessity for joint measures should West Germany join the WEU. Nor does Raymond L. Garthoff, *Soviet Strategy in the Nuclear Age* (rev. ed., New York: Praeger, 1962) consider the Warsaw Treaty Organization as other than one aspect of Soviet field forces—an aspect which he makes no attempt to evaluate.

For more recent reassessments see J. F. Brown, *The New Eastern Europe,* Walter C. Clemens, Jr., "The Future of the Warsaw Pact," *Orbis* 11, no. 4 (Winter 1968); Robin Remington, *The Changing Soviet Perception of the Warsaw Pact* (M.I.T.: Center for International Studies C/67-24, November 1967); Patricia Haigh, "Reflections on the Warsaw Pact," *World Today* 24, no. 4 (April 1968); Roman Kolkowicz, ed., *The Warsaw Pact: Report on a Conference on the Warsaw Treaty Organization Held at the Institute for Defense Analysis May 17-19, 1967* (IDA, Research Paper P-496, March 1969); and "The Warsaw Pact: Entangling Alliance" *Survey* 70/71 (Winter/Spring 1969); Malcolm Mackintosh, "The Evolution of the Warsaw Pact," *Adelphi Papers,* no. 58 (London: ISS, June 1969); Richard F. Staar, "The East European Alliance," *United States Naval Institute Proceedings* 90, no. 9 (September 1964) and *The Communist Regimes of Eastern Europe: An Introduction* (Stanford, Calif.: Hoover Institution on War, Revolution, and Peace, 1967), pp. 259-280; Thomas W. Wolfe, *Soviet Power and Europe,* pp. 312-331; *The Warsaw Pact: Its Role in Soviet Bloc Affairs,* a report of the Subcommittee on National Security and International Operations to the Committee on Government Operations, United States Senate, 89th Congress, 2nd Session (Washington, D.C.: U.S. Government Printing Office, 1966).

[28] As noted, the Soviets emphasized only the defensive nature of the treaty. At the 1954 Moscow Conference Molotov spoke of "joint measures in the sphere of organization of armed forces" and even the military coverage of the Warsaw meeting referred only to the "bases for guaranteeing the security of peace-loving peoples," *Krasnaya zvezda,* May 15, 1955.

verify,[29] of the scheduled reorganization of Hungarian armed forces that indicates at least projected developments prior to the 1956 Hungarian uprising. According to this information, a special Supreme Command was to be set up in Hungary directly under Marshal Konev. Only the most politically reliable and best-trained officers could be assigned to the general headquarters of the reorganized army. Sixty-five per cent of them were required to be party members with general staff qualifications. Only generals and staff officers trained at the Frunze military academy and able to speak fluent Russian were considered eligible for Konev's staff. For the time being Hungary was to put two divisions at the disposal of the Warsaw Pact Supreme Command. These divisions were not to be under the command of the Hungarian general headquarters, but immediately under Marshal Konev. One division was slated to be stationed in Czechoslovakia, the other in Rumania.

Active military service was to last for four years. Standardized equipment and weapons like that supplied to the other people's democracies would come from the USSR. All Warsaw Treaty states were to reserve a territory within their country for the common army group. This was to be used by a "foreign formation" under the command of Konev. By this plan, Hungarian forces would have been supplied with modern weapons after 1956, its personnel purged of otherwise unsuitable elements by the summer of 1957, and total reorganization completed by the end of 1957.[30]

[29] "Reorganization of the Hungarian People's Army under Provisions of the Warsaw Pact," October 1956 (translated August 1958). This document also included a circular that allegedly passed to various party personnel under elaborate secrecy precautions, describing in detail a meeting of the party active of the Kalocsa 12th Division in July 1956 devoted to the Warsaw Pact and the changes to be made in the Hungarian forces, the resolutions passed at that meeting, and joint Soviet-Hungarian troop maneuvers, also said to have been held in July 1956. The maneuvers, which ostensibly lasted four weeks, were described as being canceled by saying that the operation had not achieved its aim. The history of this document is obscure and even if the information could be considered reliable for the period covered, events in the fall of 1956 sharply interrupted any such planned reorganization. I have discussed it in some detail, however, because it is the only available concrete description of the intended influence of the Warsaw Treaty upon the armed forces of one of the East European member states. And if accurate this would mean that Moscow maximally intended the joint command set up under the Warsaw Treaty to further integration of Soviet-East European armed forces at a rapid pace paralleled by ever increasing Soviet control.

[30] That the Soviet Union intended to keep direct control of the Warsaw Treaty Command hierarchy is supported by the statement of the Polish defector Pawel Monat that the "real" military orders go directly from Moscow to the general staffs of the East European armies. Pawel Monat with John Dille, *Spy in the US* (New York: Harper and Row, 1961), pp. 188–189. As Monat was a Polish military attaché in the United States and then in charge of Polish military attachés throughout the world, he was in a position to

As to the decision-making involved, although the political consultative committee was empowered both to examine and to decide general questions relating to strengthening the joint armed forces and organization of those forces, there is no evidence that a direct connection existed between the PCC and any initial military reorganization that may have taken place under the Warsaw Treaty. Indeed, if reorganization of Hungarian forces was to have begun in June 1955, it would have been impossible for the committee to have considered it on other than an ex post facto basis, for the first PCC meeting took place in January 1956.

PCC Prague Meeting

Held in Prague, this meeting was another move in Moscow's campaign to formalize the division of Germany. The committee accepted East German participation in the joint command and gave the GDR equal status with the other East European member states by allowing the East German minister of defense to serve as one of the deputy commanders-in-chief of the united arms forces.[31]

---

have more accurate information on these matters than even relatively high-placed Polish party cadres. As of 1958, he credits the Soviet general staff with specifically deciding such questions as "where each division is stationed, how many tanks the Czechs will produce, how many guns and planes the Poles will build, how many trucks the Hungarians must provide and which army gets them." (p. 189). With respect to the staffing of Warsaw Pact headquarters in Moscow, he recorded that the smaller pact members have only one officer permanently stationed at Pact headquarters, to which he comments that "only Bulgaria seems to have enough generals on hand to waste one in Moscow," (*ibid.*). Király has strongly implied that the Warsaw Treaty Organization simply meant a continuation of Soviet control and infiltration of East European forces [General Béla Király, "Hungary's Army Under the Soviets," *East Europe* 7, no. 3 (March 1958)]. However this is a disputed point. For example, Mackintosh considers the Warsaw Treaty as militarily valuable to the Soviets, at least in the sense of facilitating reorganization and redeployment. As an example, he notes that each Warsaw Pact ally received a new Soviet military mission in 1955 headed by a senior general. J. M. Mackintosh, *Strategy and Tactics of Soviet Foreign Policy* (London: Oxford University Press, 1963).

[31] There is little doubt of Soviet initiative in the changed East German status. Although no distinctions were made with respect to GDR membership in the Warsaw Treaty text, East German participation in the Joint Command had been carefully postponed and both Soviet and GDR spokesmen emphasized the possibility of East Germany withdrawing from the WTO into a united Germany. Thus in speaking to the Warsaw Treaty Conference Grotewohl emphasized that "The Warsaw Treaty leaves the German Democratic Republic complete freedom to negotiate for peaceful reunification," *New Times* 21 (May 21, 1955): 36. Then in 1958 a Soviet review of Ludwik Gelberg's book, *Układ warszawski* (Warsaw: 1957), strongly criticized the Polish author for omitting this point but ignored his conclusion that Soviet troops did not enter Hungary to fulfill their obligations under the Warsaw Pact; see G. Zhukov, "Part of Peace and Security," *International Affairs* 3 (March 1958): 111–113. Moreover, GDR contingents were accepted into the united command only

Moscow must have realized that such a step would be highly unpalatable in the West. In both the documents of the Prague meeting and general Soviet statements concerning the "international significance" of the political consultative committee decisions, it was carefully balanced by conciliatory gestures. The Declaration of States Participating in the Warsaw Treaty took a moderate tone. Whereas the meeting's concluding communiqué accepted GDR contingents into the joint command, no mention of support for the infant GDR armed forces appeared in the declaration. Rather the declaration reiterated the willingness of member states to examine proposals leading to an all-European collective security system, proposed a zone of limited armaments in Europe (to include both Germanies), suggested that Warsaw Treaty states and North Atlantic Treaty states agree to settle all disputes by peaceful means, and advocated "the establishment of good relations . . . between countries irrespective of whether they may be associated at the present time with one or another military alliance." [32]

The single *Pravda* editorial devoted to the Prague meeting related that the PCC had "accepted the suggestion of the joint command and also the delegation of the German Democratic Republic" that after creation of the GDR "national peoples army" its contingents be included in the joint command.[33] This brief, factual reference appeared after a column and a half of evidence detailing the peace initiatives of the "states of the socialist camp . . . participants in the Warsaw Treaty." It followed strongly worded praise for Bulganin's letter to Eisenhower proposing a treaty of friendship and cooperation between the USSR and the USA.[34]

Clearly Soviet internal dissensions continued to affect the Kremlin's

---

after the bilateral Soviet-East German treaty in which Moscow recognized the East German regime as being free to make decisions on all questions of its domestic and foreign policy, thereby purporting to give the GDR the same status that the Western allies had granted Bonn in the May 26, 1952, agreement which ended the occupied status of West Germany. In this sense integration of GDR forces into the joint command was a part of the Soviet policy of insisting that East Germany be treated as a sovereign state.

[32] *Pravda,* January 29, 1956; quoted from "Declaration of the States Participating in the Warsaw Treaty of Friendship, Cooperation and Mutual Assistance," Supplement to *New Times* 6 (February 2, 1956): 36.

[33] *Pravda,* January 30, 1956.

[34] *Pravda,* January 29, 1956, featured the Declaration and Bulganin's message side by side on page 1, while an editorial in *New Times* presented the Prague Meeting and Bulganin's letter as dual prongs of a socialist peace initiative; "In the Interests of Universal Peace and Security," *New Times* 6 (February 2, 1956): 1–3.

conception of the Warsaw Pact. Despite the July Plenum and Molotov's self-criticism of September 1955,[35] the innerparty conflict was unresolved. This intense struggle gave a strangely divided cast to Moscow's response to the Prague meeting.

Molotov had spoken for the Soviets. His speech was briefer than the speeches of either the East European delegates or the Chinese observer. For Molotov the tone was moderate; yet he included a sharp warning against the aggressive nature of imperialists, strongly supported the new GDR armed forces, and warned that "the peoples of our countries, confident in their own strength, inspired by great victories in the construction of socialism, cannot be confused," [36] a warning in all likelihood not only directed to "imperialists."

Pravda printed the text of Molotov's speech without comment. Molotov was not mentioned either in the editorial on the significance of the PCC meeting or in the reports of *Pravda*'s special correspondents L. Tolkunov and B. Tarasov.[37] Instead the Prague gathering was described as stemming from the vital questions raised by Khrushchev in his recent speech to the Supreme Soviet of the USSR.[38] Emphasis was on peace, cooperation, détente. The socialist nature of the member states received only token reference.[39]

Unlike its coverage of the original Warsaw Conference, the tone of the military newspaper *Krasnaya zvezda* (*Red Star*) contrasted sharply to that of *Pravda*. *Krasnaya zvezda* sent its own special correspondent, Colonel S. Zykov to Prague. Zykov focused on the socialist nature of the

---

[35] *Kommunist* 14 (September 1955), p. 127. For analysis see Myron Rush, *The Rise of Khrushchev* (Washington, D.C.: Public Affairs Press, 1958).

[36] *Pravda*, January 29, 1956.

[37] Coverage by L. Tolkunov and B. Tarasov, *Pravda*, January 28, 1956; also *Pravda*, January 29, 1956.

[38] "Speech by N. S. Khrushchev," *New Times* 2 (January 5, 1956): 24–31.

[39] According to Tolkunov and Tarasov, the Prague meeting showed "complete unity" of view on the question of the international situation and all speeches "underlined the necessity for further joint activity in the struggle for peace, against war, to strengthen the economic and defensive power of the countries of the socialist camp," *Pravda*, January 28, 1956. This was a weaker formulation than that of the concluding declaration, which despite its generally conciliatory tone, echoed Molotov:

"The peoples of our countries, confident in their strength and inspired by their achievements in building socialism, are not to be frightened or deceived. Relying on the irrepressible desire of all peoples for peace, and on their combined and growing might, they will continue to pursue their peaceful constructive policy. . . ."

Declaration, Moskovskoe soveshchanie . . . , p. 35.

states participating in the PCC meeting. His reporting was staunchly hostile toward "aggressive imperialists," analyzing the committee's declaration in decidedly militant terms:

> The forces of reaction and war, in spite of the will of the peoples, want to hinder cooperation between states. The countries of the great camp of democracy and socialism are firmly resolved to rebuff the lovers of aggression and to prevent war.[40]

Like Molotov, he enthusiastically supported the decision to admit East Germany to the joint command as well as "decisions on other organizational questions" and concluded by stressing that the importance of the Prague meeting was "first of all" that it mobilized the Warsaw Treaty countries so that they would "not for one minute weaken defenses, [but] be always prepared to rise to the defense of their historic victories."[41]

The editorial following Zykov's articles was less strongly worded but nonetheless quoted Molotov's speech warning of the dangers of aggressive military blocs, of the revival of German militarism.[42] There was no mention of Khrushchev in any of the military reporting of the Prague meeting. Then on February 10, a second *Krasnaya zvezda* editorial—entitled "Growing Power of the Socialist Camp"—described the PPC Prague meeting as demonstrating the peaceful intentions of the socialist camp in a situation where the participating states had realized the need for "wide coordination of their efforts to heighten their own defensive capacity."[43]

These were not minor differences. *Pravda* had emphasized détente and given Khrushchev credit for an analysis of the European situation fundamental to the political consultative committee declaration. *Krasnaya zvezda* ignored Khrushchev, repeating Molotov's warning of the need for building up one's defenses in a hostile world. Two images of the world within which the Warsaw Treaty Organization would operate existed in Moscow. Each image entailed its own preconception of the purpose and function of the political consultative committee and the joint command. For Khrushchev the importance of the Warsaw Pact focused outside itself; a reflection of his drive toward détente with the West. It was intended not to fight but to gain another asset in the cold war. For

---

[40] *Krasnaya zvezda,* January 29, 1956.
[41] *Ibid.,* January 27, 28, 1956.
[42] *Ibid.,* January 31, 1956.
[43] *Ibid.,* February 10, 1956.

Molotov the Warsaw Pact was a vehicle for socialist consolidation, military preparedness, defense.

Thus it is not strange that many, and conflicting, Soviet policies were reflected both in the early documents of the Warsaw Treaty Organization and in Moscow's analysis of its importance—détente, defense of the socialist camp, disarmament, threat of imperialist aggression. This was a consequence of the pitched, still largely submerged struggle for power that dominated all aspects of Soviet political life.

Molotov lost. Relegated to Outer Mongolia, he has seen the pressure of events outmaneuver his rival as well. For the Warsaw Pact, born of Moscow's attempt to block the rearming of West Germany, modeled on NATO and the OAS, has acquired substance largely in relation to Soviet policy toward East Europe and the socialist commonwealth.

3
HUNGARY AND ALBANIA:
INVASION
VERSUS EXCLUSION

ALTHOUGH SOVIET TANKS cut off the Hungarian revolution and Albania faced economic sanctions and violent polemical attacks for its defiance, Rumanian maneuvering within the Warsaw Pact found decision-makers in Moscow much further along the force-persuasion continuum than had these earlier challenges to Soviet authority. Indeed, the Russians systematically worked to contain Soviet-Rumanian differences within the existing institutional framework. In analyzing why it is necessary to go back to 1956. For in each instance Soviet response to intra-Communist conflict in Eastern Europe imposed its own future limitations.

The Impact of De-Stalinization

The Warsaw Treaty Organization had barely acquired organizational roots when the CPSU 20th Congress demolished the myth of Stalin within the international Communist movement. Khrushchev's secret speech informed the party elite that the leader they had venerated was a tyrant, murderer, military incompetent with a "mania for greatness" and no respect for Lenin's memory.[1] It was a critical move in the innerparty struggle. In becoming the architect of de-Stalinization, Khrushchev conveniently implicated his rivals in Stalin's crimes. Molotov and Kaganovich were held partly responsible for the appointment of Yezhov, thereby indirectly blamed for the purge. Malenkov was pictured as Stalin's confidante, by implication his accomplice.[2]

---

[1] "Secret Speech of Khrushchev Concerning the "Cult of the Individual" delivered at the Twentieth Congress of the Communist Party of the Soviet Union," February 25, 1956; *The Anti-Stalin Campaign and International Communism: A Selection of Documents* (New York: Columbia University Press, 1956), pp. 1–90.

[2] *Ibid.*, p. 52. For analysis see Wolfgang Leonhard, *The Kremlin Since Stalin* (New York: Praeger, 1962), pp. 167–192.

Although the Soviets attacked Stalin for domestic reasons, the repercussions of that attack were international. In particular, East European Communists could hardly afford the luxury of de-Stalinization. Too much had been done in the name of Stalin. Memories were too raw. Worse, the practical result of rehabilitation would be to free a large, obviously hostile element into already festering populations. The anguish of the party leadership evident in attempts to stem disillusionment among the membership in Czechoslovakia was not atypical.

> Much has happened this year. Much that was dear to us has been smashed. . . . Our souls are full of pain because strings have suddenly been touched which we thought inviolable and feelings which were dear to us. Side by side with joy about recent rapid developments many old Communists will feel sadness. He may even feel bitter.
>
> We too feel in the same way, comrades, but one is unthinkable without the other. And if we believe in the Party we believe in it firmly! Only a Party for which revolutionary truth is everything is in a position to plunge the knife of self-criticism so deeply into its own flesh. . . .[3]

Absorbed in its own succession struggle, Moscow's perception of Soviet-East European relationships continued much in the Stalinist mold. East European leaders were expected to imitate the permutations of the "New Course" much as they had imitated former Stalinist policies. In a sense, although a key actor was gone, the psychology was the same. Soviet statements still had an aura of infallibility, and when Khrushchev decided to woo Yugoslavia back into the Communist bloc in 1955 he demanded a chorus of approval from the smaller Communist states. In April 1956, the Cominform was dissolved as a prelude to a broadened Soviet-Yugoslav rapprochement, the barometer of Soviet faith in "different roads to socialism."

The Polish October

On June 28, eight days after the Declaration on Relations between the League of Yugoslav Communists and the Communist Party of the Soviet Union, a strike in Poznań flared into an uprising. Polish troops fired on the workers. This was the escalation of tensions that led to reshuffling of the Polish Central Committee in October.[4] (Table 2) It brought about

---

[3] *Rudé právo,* May 1, 1956; quoted from Leonhard, *ibid.,* p. 203.

[4] For detailed analysis of the Polish October, see Adam Bromke, *Poland's Politics: Idealism vs. Realism* (Cambridge, Mass.: Harvard University Press, 1967); Z. K. Brzezinski, *The Soviet Bloc: Unity and Conflict,* 3rd ed. (Cambridge, Mass.: Harvard University Press,

TABLE 2

CHRONOLOGY OF EVENTS: POLAND AND HUNGARY, 1956

Events Prior to Soviet Military Intervention

February	CPSU 20th Party Congress: Khrushchev's secret speech attacking Stalin.
March	Petofi Circle (focus of Communist intellectual criticism of the party) founded in Hungary.
April	Cominform disbanded.
June 20	Declaration on Relations Between the League of Yugoslav Communists and the CPSU.
June 28	Riots in Poznań, Poland.
July 18	Dismissal of Rákosi in Hungary.
October 6	Reburial of purged Hungarian party leader Rajk; massive public demonstration.
October 17	Polish leadership refuses to go to Moscow for consultations.
October 19	High-level Soviet party delegation arrives in Poland.
October 21	Soviet-Polish communiqué: Gomułka has returned to Polish leadership
October 23	Demonstration in Hungary honoring General Bem, a hero of both the Polish Revolution of 1830 and the Hungarian revolution of 1948.
	Demands presented to radio station
	• restoration of Nagy to government
	• return to his New Course of 1953
	• readjustment of political and economic relations with Soviet Union to respect Hungarian sovereignty.

---

a sharp rise in Soviet concern for the internal stability of the East European regimes.

Thus, Bulganin flatly corrected the Polish interpretation of Poznań, retreating to the Stalinist concept of "enemy agents" and "mad plans of international reactionary elements." [5] *Pravda* demanded heavy punish-

---

1967), pp. 230 ff.; and M. K. Dziewanowski, *The Communist Party of Poland: An Outline of History* (Cambridge, Mass., Harvard University Press, 1959).

[5] Leonhard, *The Kremlin Since Stalin: Unity and Conflict* (Cambridge, Mass.: Harvard University Press, 3rd ed., 1967) pp. 218 ff. The Poles had stressed the importance of exploring the social causes of the revolt rather than concentrating upon "foreign agents" as an explanation.

TABLE 2 (*continued*)

	Secret police fire on people at radio station and the revolt begins.
October 24	Soviet politburo members Mikoyan and Suslov arrive in Budapest.
	First Soviet Military Intervention
October 26	Gerö flees; Nagy forms government.
October 28	*Pravda* editorial admitting past mistakes.
	Nagy declares he will begin negotiations for the withdrawal of Soviet troops.
October 30	Soviet Declaration on Principles of Development and Further Strengthening Friendship and Cooperation between the Soviet Union and Other Socialist States heavily emphasizes role of the Warsaw Pact.
	Suez crisis begins with Anglo-French-Israeli attack on Egypt.
October 30	Soviet troops begin to move toward Budapest.
October 31	Soviet-Hungarian talks; reportedly Mikoyan "agreed to everything."
November 1	Nagy forms a new government, announced by Kádár who then disappears.
	Hungary abrogates the Warsaw Pact and declares its neutrality.
November 2	Hungarian political and military delegations begin talks with Soviets.
November 3	Hungarian negotiators have last contact with their governments, are arrested by Soviets, and are not heard from again.
	Kádár announces formation of his pro-Soviet government.
November 4	Second Soviet military intervention.

ments for the accused. But Soviet control over political development in Eastern Europe had slipped. The Polish regime first delayed and then quietly released or acquitted the majority of the striking workers.

By mid-October the Soviets had decided to intervene directly. On October 17, the Soviet ambassador in Warsaw formally invited the Poles to Moscow for consultations.[6] The Polish leadership declined. Two days later, October 19, an uninvited Soviet delegation arrived in Warsaw.

[6] Ochab, *Nowe drogi* 10 (1956): 18, cited by Brzezinski, *The Soviet Bloc*, p. 257. For the Chinese claim that they indeed prevented the Soviet intervention, see the later section of this chapter dealing with the Soviet-Albanian break.

Simultaneously Soviet troops stationed in Poland under postwar agreements and the Warsaw Treaty began to move toward the Polish capital. At this time there was no declared state of emergency requiring use of Soviet troops on Polish territory, and in the Soviet Press no mention was made either of the troop movements or that a delegation including such important leaders as Khrushchev, Kaganovich,[7] Mikoyan, and Molotov had flown to Warsaw.[8] The composition of this delegation showed yet another shift in the fluctuating balance of power in Moscow.

The Polish Central Committee Plenum suspended its session to consult with the Soviets.[9] These negotiations were not made public. Although reportedly "sincere, difficult, and bitter," [10] they concluded with a brief Polish-Soviet communiqué noting that Gomułka took part in the debates which "centered on problems of current interest" to the two parties and took place in an atmosphere of "Party-like and friendly sincerity." [11]

Hungarian Uprising and the Declaration of October 30, 1956

In Hungary, with news of Soviet concessions to Polish autonomy serving as a catalyst, popular demands rapidly slipped beyond Communist Party control. The Hungarian uprising has been analyzed in detail elsewhere.[12]

[7] That the Stalinist faction had recouped some of its losses was unmistakable when Kaganovich, who had been dismissed from his government post in June, was appointed Minister of the Building Materials Industry on September 22, 1956.

[8] *Pravda's* coverage of events in Poland at this time was pointedly sparse. On October 17 there was a brief announcement of the coming Polish plenum and of Gomułka's scheduled participation; on October 18, an equally brief note on the resolutions to be considered at the plenum; on October 19 nothing at all. On October 20, a lengthy story on "The Anti-Soviet Speeches on the Pages of the Polish Press" refrained from attacking the Polish Party directly; then on October 21 the Polish-Soviet communiqué appeared without comment.

[9] According to Ochab, the Soviets had neglected to inform the Poles of their decision to send the delegation. See Brzezinski, *The Soviet Bloc*, p. 256.

[10] *Ibid.*, p. 257.

[11] *Pravda*, October 21, 1965. For English translation from the Polish source, see Paul E. Zinner, ed., *National Communism and Popular Revolt in Eastern Europe: A Selection of Documents on Events in Poland and Hungary February to November 1956* (New York: Columbia University Press, 1956), p. 196.

[12] See Brzezinski, *The Soviet Bloc*, pp. 210 ff.; Francois Fejtö, *Behind the Rape of Hungary* (New York: McKay, 1957); Paul Kecskemeti, *The Unexpected Revolution* (Stanford, Calif.; Stanford University Press, 1961); Melvin J. Lasky, *The Hungarian Revolution* (New York: Praeger, 1957); Ference A. Váli, *Rift and Revolt in Hungary* (Cambridge, Mass.: Harvard University Press, 1961); and Paul E. Zinner, *Revolution in Hungary* (New York: Columbia University Press, 1962).

Here it is important for the resulting clarification of relations among Warsaw member states.

Despite the use of Soviet forces, Moscow's initial reaction was far from resolute. Two members of the Soviet presidium, Mikoyan and Suslov, arrived in Budapest the afternoon of the first Soviet intervention (October 24). At Party headquarters they must have found complete chaos. The Hungarian Communist Party verged on disintegration. By October 26, Gerö, the remaining prop of the Rákosi regime, had fled—leaving Nagy free to form a government. He did so. Communist and non-Communist ministers were invited to participate, and the Central Committee of the Hungarian Communist Party announced impending negotiations for the immediate withdrawal of Soviet forces. Two days later Nagy called for a ceasefire.

Mikoyan and Suslov's report to Moscow seems to have led to the conclusion that as many Hungarian demands as possible should be met within the framework of maintaining Communist power in Hungary. Along this line the *Pravda* editorial of October 28 referred to "serious past mistakes" of Hungarian Communists as contributing to the difficulties in Hungary,[13] and the "Soviet Government Declaration on the Principles of Development and Further Strengthening of Friendship and Cooperation Between the Soviet Union and Other Socialist States" confessed:

> In the process of the rise of the new system [of the People's Democracies in Eastern Europe] and the deep revolutionary changes in social relations, there have been many difficulties, unresolved problems, and down-right mistakes, including mistakes in the mutual relations among the socialist countries—violations and errors which demeaned the principle of equality among the socialist states.[14]

The Soviet government declared that it was ready to discuss both economic and military grievances with the governments of the other socialist states. The sections referring to military matters largely concerned the Warsaw Treaty. Reiterating that Soviet forces in Rumania and Hungary were there in accordance with the Warsaw Treaty and other

---

[13] *Pravda,* October 28, 1956; English translation in Zinner, *National Communism and Popular Revolt in Eastern Europe,* p. 435. The editorial was careful to blame the subversive activity of the imperialist powers for igniting the situation, however.

[14] *Pravda,* October 31, 1956, quoted from Zinner, *ibid.,* p. 486.

unspecified and hitherto unpublicized governmental agreements,[15] it announced:

> For the purpose of assuring mutual security of the socialist countries, the Soviet Government is prepared to review with the other socialist countries which are members of the Warsaw Treaty the question of Soviet troops stationed on the territory of the above mentioned countries. In so doing the Soviet Government proceeds from the general principle that stationing the troops of one state or another which is a member of the Treaty on the territory of another state which is a member of the Treaty is done by agreement *among all its members* and only with the consent of the state on the territory of which and at the request of which troops are stationed or it is planned to station them.[16] [Italics mine.]

In effect, this statement promised an extension of the Warsaw Treaty which said nothing at all about the decision-making process in such cases. It was, in fact, a potentially unilateral extension of the treaty by means of Soviet interpretation in that the January 1956 meeting of the political consultative committee had not—at least publicly—reached the conclusion that withdrawal of Soviet forces stationed in East European states required the collective agreement of Warsaw Treaty member states. Moreover, the later withdrawal of Soviet troops from Rumania and the partial withdrawal from Hungary received only ex post facto sanction of Warsaw Treaty members.[17]

The declaration also contained the Soviet government's official interpretation of the situation in Hungary. It recognized, as did the October 28 *Pravda* editorial, the importance of the popular discontent growing from the desire to eliminate economic evils, improve the standard of living, and combat "bureaucratic distortions." But the declaration added that "black reaction and counterrevolution" had taken over the move-

---

[15] Since the Soviets subsequently felt it necessary to conclude treaties specifically on the subject of Soviet forces with the countries involved, it is doubtful if the previous "governmental agreements" amounted to much more than verbal recognition of the inevitable on the part of East European leaders.

[16] The Declaration of October 30, *ibid.*, p. 487.

[17] *Pravda*, May 28, 1958. It has been reported that on October 30 Mikoyan and Suslov —with the authorization of Khrushchev—signed an agreement promising that Soviet troops would leave Hungary. (Király, "Hungary's Army: Its Part in the Revolt," p. 15.) That no general consultation involving other Warsaw Treaty member states took place concerning the use of Soviet troops on Hungarian territory during the 1956 uprising would seem to be confirmed by Albania's flat statement that "as regards the Hungarian question, "the Soviet comrades do not bother in the least to inform our leadership about what is happening, about what measures they intend to take." Enver Hoxha's speech at the Moscow November 1960 meeting, in *Rruga e Partisë* 17, no. 8 (August 1970): 3–42, at 33.

ment in an attempt to undermine socialism in Hungary. Under the circumstances, "the sacred duty" of the workers, peasants, intelligentsia, of all the Hungarian working people "at the present moment" was "to guard the socialist achievements of the people's democratic Hungary." This set the outermost limit of what Moscow would sanction: a more responsive but solidly Communist Hungary.

Initiatives from Peking

Interestingly enough, the first concrete statement other than the Declaration of October 30 explaining the relationship of the Warsaw Treaty to the Hungarian revolt came not from Moscow but from Peking. Soviet announcements had been limited to maintaining that Soviet troops "stationed in Hungary in accordance with the Warsaw Treaty" had come forward at the request of the Hungarian government to help restore order.[18] On November 4, however, *Pravda* printed a long Chinese article which, in effect, redefined the functions of the Warsaw Pact in East Europe. That the article appeared in the Soviet press at all indicates that Moscow at least considered adopting its interpretations.[19]

The Chinese article stressed the importance of the Warsaw Treaty in strengthening the camp of socialism:

> The Warsaw Treaty guarantees a situation in which the countries of the socialist camp in Europe can build their own happy lives in security without risking being left helpless in the face of the aggressive forces of Western imperialism and also guarantees that the countries of the socialist camp will not be destroyed one by one by Western imperialist and counterrevolutionary forces of different countries, which are always the enemies of socialism and constantly attempt to overthrow socialist countries and to reestablish in these countries capitalist and fascist counterrevolutionary regimes. . . . The Warsaw Treaty must exist while the Atlantic Pact— directed toward preparing for war by Western imperialists—operates.
>
> The imperialists try to make the socialist states of Eastern Europe forget both their debt to and need for the USSR. . . . They attempt to

---

[18] *Pravda,* November 4, 1956. It has been established, however, that even in the first Soviet intervention, Soviet troops were brought in from Rumania and the USSR proper. See *UN Report Supplement of the Special Committee on the Problem of Hungary,* General Assembly Records: 11th Session, supplement 18 (A/3592) (New York, 1954), p. 24. Hereafter cited UN Report.

[19] This seems particularly likely in that the bulk of the first paragraph quoted above is repeated almost word for word in an editorial of the CPSU theoretical journal, *Kommunist*: "Velikoe edinstvo sotsialisticheskich stran nerushimo," *Kommunist* 16 (November 1956 [passed for the press November 16]):3–13.

destroy the fraternal friendship between socialist countries and liquidate the Warsaw Treaty. This counterrevolutionary plan of the imperialist aggressors, parallel to their attack on Egypt, represents a serious threat to the peace.[20]

On the next day, *Pravda* featured a long unsigned Soviet account entitled "The Hungarian Working People Defend Their Own Socialist Achievements."[21] The article cited the Proclamation of the Hungarian Workers' and Peasants' Government (Kádár's newly formed administration) requesting the commander of Soviet troops to help defeat the forces of reaction and establish order, and reiterated that after order was reestablished the Kádár government would negotiate with the USSR and other Warsaw Treaty members on the question of removing Soviet troops from Hungarian territory.[22] A supporting article from Peking in the same issue went on to explain the difference between recent events in Poland and Hungary; according to its interpretation, Poland had not given way to reaction and, indeed, had continued to support the Warsaw Treaty and to maintain a policy of friendship with the Soviet Union. The government of Nagy, on the other hand, had announced withdrawal from the Warsaw Treaty, causing even Poland to declare that it considered the reactionary forces in Hungary "a huge misfortune."[23]

Soviet Rationale

Whether or not the Hungarian desire to withdraw from the Warsaw Pact precipitated Soviet intervention, the use of Russian troops to put down the Hungarian rebellion directly violated the text of the Warsaw Treaty. The treaty refers only to aiding a member state threatened by aggression on the part of another state (Article V). It makes no mention of what to do in case of civil war. Nor could the use of Soviet forces be considered the peaceful settlement of disputes called for in Article I. There is no significant evidence that consultation (Article III) other than of a bilateral nature took place prior to or during the Soviet intervention,

---

[20] *Pravda*, November 4, 1956.

[21] *Pravda*, November 5, 1956.

[22] These negotiations have been conducted in private, and although one Soviet division did withdraw in 1958, sizable Soviet forces remain in Hungary to date. In fact, Kádár felt it necessary to deny rumors that Soviet forces would leave in 1964 after the nineteenth anniversary of the liberation of Hungary from Nazi occupation. In doing so he tied withdrawal of Soviet troops from Hungary to that of NATO forces from West Germany. See *The New York Times*, March 20, 1964.

[23] *Pravda*, November 5, 1956.

and the political consultative committee—which had agreed to convene twice a year—did not meet until May 1958, more than two years from the date of its last meeting.

Yet, in retrospect, the events in the autumn of 1956 increased the importance of the Warsaw Pact while underlining its initial impotence. In the October 30 Declaration Moscow had admitted mistakes and agreed to renegotiate its military arrangements within the framework of the Warsaw Pact.

The slogan of the early years of the people's democracies, "many roads to socialism," was revived; the importance of specific historical conditions emphasized. This further increased the vulnerability of Soviet ideological control, for it was one thing to admit diversity as a necessity before consolidating power and quite another thing to legitimize such diversity once the Communists had seized control in the individual countries. Therefore despite some Soviet backtracking, Khrushchev's later attempts to substitute economic and military ties for the weakening bonds of ideology were a direct result of the situation in which he found himself. The revival of CMEA and increased military integration under the Warsaw Pact were a logical consequence.

Ex post facto justifications of the military intervention in Hungary consistently emphasized Soviet obligations under the Warsaw Treaty.[24] This was so to the extent that by 1958 the Soviets bluntly contended that the "active strength of the Warsaw Treaty manifested itself in the days of the counterrevolutionary events in Hungary." [25] As for the activities of the WTO joint command during the Hungarian uprising, Khrushchev spoke of Hungary as having given "the necessary rebuff to international reaction and Hungarian counterrevolutionaries with the help of the socialist camp," [26] a euphemism for Soviet troops.

Moreover, under the pressure of the Hungarian uprising, the original Soviet assertion that the Warsaw Pact was a collective self-defense agree-

[24] For Soviet reasoning see the UN Report Supplement, pp. 13–20; "Velikoe edinstvo sotsialisticheskich stran nerushimo," interview with G. P. Zodorozhny in The Hungarian Situation and the Rule of Law (The Hague: International Commission of Jurists, 1957), pp. 19–20; E. Korovin, "Law of the Jungle Versus the Law of Nations," New Times 11 (January 1, 1957).

[25] F. T. Konstantinov, ed., Sodruzhestvo stran sotsializma (Moscow: Akad. nauk, 1958), p. 149. See also Colonel S. Lesnevskii, "Voevoe sodruzhestvo vooruzhennykh sil sotsialisticheskikh stran," Kommunist vooruzhennykh sil 10 (May 1963): 73.

[26] Pravda, May 27, 1958. Kádár went a step further to claim that Soviet troops acting under the Warsaw Treaty had "saved" Hungary from a NATO conspiracy. There is no evidence that forces from any other East European country fought alongside of the Soviets.

ment in accordance with Article 51 of the UN Charter, made a 180-degree turn. Soviet attempts to bar UN consideration of the Hungarian question rested on the claim that "the Warsaw Treaty was concluded in full accordance with the UN Charter as a regional agreement for the maintenance of international peace and security,"[27] thus making the events in Hungary the exclusive affair of the Hungarians, Soviets, and the other Warsaw Treaty states.

The Bilateral Treaties

But more important than Moscow's rationalizations, the Polish and Hungarian events of 1956 resulted in both an extension and clarification of the Warsaw Treaty. Legally, the treaty was extended by four bilateral treaties covering the stationing of Soviet troops on East European territory. The first such agreement, which was with Poland,[28] stated unqualifiedly that the presence of Soviet troops should in no way impair the sovereignty of the Polish state and that Soviet troops were not to interfere in Poland's internal affairs. It further provided for special agreements: (1) to define the number of Soviet troops in Poland and their location; (2) to regulate legal aid with regard to the prosecution of crimes and misdemeanors; and (3) to determine the communication lines, time limits, procedures, and terms of payment for transit of Soviet troops and military property as well as military shipments through Polish territory. The crux of the treaty was that it made Polish consent mandatory for troop movement, training and maneuvers outside the base area. A joint Soviet-Polish commission was set up in Warsaw to settle any disputes arising under the treaty.

Similar treaties were signed with the German Democratic Republic[29] (March 12, 1957), Rumania[30] (April 15, 1957) and Hungary[31] (May 27,

[27] E. Korovin in *The Hungarian Situation and the Rule of Law*, p. 25; cited from Radio Moscow as monitored by the BBC Summary of World Broadcasts, Part I, no. 782, November 30, 1956, p. 1. See also Kuznetsov's statement in *Pravda*, November 11, 1956.

[28] "Treaty Between the Government of the Union of Soviet Socialist Republics and the Government of the Polish People's Republic Concerning the Legal Status of Soviet Forces Temporarily Stationed in Poland," *Pravda*, December 18, 1956; *United Nations Treaty Series (UNTS)* 266, no. 3830, pp. 179–207.

[29] "Agreement on Questions Relating to the Temporary Presence of Soviet Forces in the Territory of the German Democratic Republic," *Izvestia*, March 14, 1957; *UNTS*, 285, no. 4150, pp. 105–133.

[30] "Agreement Concerning the Legal Status of Soviet Forces Temporarily Stationed in the Territory of the Rumanian People's Republic," *Izvestia*, April 17, 1957; *UNTS*, 274, no. 3964, pp. 143–171.

[31] "Agreement between the Government of the Hungarian People's Republic and the

1957). These treaties together with the 1964 Soviet–East German Treaty of Friendship, Mutual Assistance, and Cooperation, substantially similar pacts, form one of the concrete extensions of the Warsaw Treaty. In Poland, Rumania, and Hungary, Soviet troop movements require the consent (soglasiia) of the smaller member country involved.[32] However, in the case of the GDR Moscow agreed only to "consult" with the East German government regarding troop movements.[33]

In fact, Chinese emphasis on the Warsaw Treaty as a safeguard for the internal construction of socialism amounted to a further extension. In this respect, Hungary may be considered a test case. For the Chinese only described a political reality. Soviet troops had been used to "save socialism" (as defined by Moscow) in Hungary. This use of Soviet forces had been sanctioned by the Soviets as their "duty" under the Warsaw Treaty and seconded individually if not jointly by the other treaty members. It now became clear to all concerned that unilateral withdrawal from the Warsaw Treaty would not be tolerated in circumstances where Moscow could prevent it, a lesson not lost on the Rumanians.

WTO Reaction

As for the response of the Warsaw Treaty Organization to the events of 1956, the WTO took no action whatsoever. Nagy's charge that the Soviets had violated the Warsaw Pact was ignored. The organization as such did nothing to cope with or contain this conflict among its member states. However, the Warsaw Pact did contain the impact of the conflict upon itself.

The political consultative committee did not meet in 1956 or in 1957. When such meetings resumed, they did not degenerate into a stream of

Government of the USSR on the Legal Status of Soviet Forces Temporarily Stationed on the Territory of the Hungarian People's Republic," *Izvestia*, May 28, 1957; *UN Report Supplement*, Annex A, pp. 60–62.

[32] Two minor indications of Poland's stronger bargaining position in December 1956 marked the Polish-Soviet Treaty text. Only Poland retained control over the entry and exit procedures to be followed by Soviet forces (Article 5) and only in Poland were the Soviets required to return such facilities as barracks, airfields, and training grounds "in good condition" (Article 8). The Polish Embassy version of the treaty reprinted in *The American Journal of International Law* 52, no. 1 (January 1958) tersely described the requirement as that of returning such facilities in "a state fit for use." Moreover, according to "The Military Establishments II," *East Europe* 17 (May 1958), only in Poland did the actual character of the armed forces show a significant liberalization in such matters as a reduction of Soviet officers in command posts. Not only was Rokossovsky replaced by General Marian Spychalski as Polish Minister of Defense but hundreds of lower-echelon Soviet officers went home.

[33] Soviet-GDR Agreement, Article II.

abuse against either the new Polish leadership or the Hungarian "counter-revolutionaries." It is true that since the Soviets had come to terms with Gomułka, in all probability no action was demanded or, for that matter, required of the committee, save to accept the result. With respect to Hungary, the situation was not so clear.

All the individual East European Communist regimes, some more, some less, enthusiastically had endorsed the Soviet interventions in Hungary. The Warsaw Treaty political consultative committee met in May 1958. At that time the committee issued a declaration which did not mention the Soviet interpretation of the USSR's legal and political position, although Khrushchev's speech to the committee had cited the defeat of "counterrevolution" in Hungary as a victory for the camp of socialism brought about by the "rising of the Hungarian people with the aid of the socialist countries." Rather, the declaration praised Soviet troop withdrawal from Rumania and the cutback of Soviet military strength in Hungary. The changes in Poland were ignored. In general the declaration stressed the peace-loving nature of the Warsaw Treaty states, supported a nonaggression treaty between the WTO and NATO, and hailed the Soviet initiative for a summit meeting that would not interfere in the internal affairs of the East European Communist regimes by discussing their legitimacy. It was more significant for what it did not say than for what it did. Moreover, the speeches to the May 1958 meeting expressed considerable diversity; thereby continuing the initial WTO egalitarian trends.

Content Analysis of Warsaw Pact Documents, 1955–1958

Although even superficial content analysis of speeches to the founding Warsaw Treaty Conference and to the 1956 and 1958 political consultative committee meetings shows that Soviet policy initiatives did occupy a large place on Soviet disarmament proposals and Moscow's summit diplomacy, it is also true that these speeches were far from uniform. Specific issues of interest to various East European members, such as the Polish western territories, Albanian internal development, and peace in the Balkans, received varying degrees of attention from the smaller member states. The similarity of Albanian and Chinese speeches was marked, and even as early as 1955 the Rumanians were claiming at least partial credit for the victory against German fascism.

Charts 1 through 5 were designed to reveal the similarities and differences in these speeches in five areas: (1) attitude toward the treaty itself; (2) support for Soviet policy initiatives; (3) attitude toward the West; (4) stress on issues of East European national interest; and (5) attitude toward the Soviet Union and the socialist camp. The categories—weak, positive, and emphatic—refer to both the frequency and the context of given statements. For example, at the Warsaw Treaty Conference in 1955 the Albanian delegate referred to the "camp of peace and socialism headed by the Soviet Union" three times and mentioned disarmament only once. At each mention of the camp headed by the Soviet Union there was a simultaneous reference to "indestructible unity," "complete unity," or "iron unity" combined with references to guarantees against aggression, "insuperable barriers" against aggression, "watching the moves of our enemies" or "strengthening the defensive power of our countries." Thus the Albanian reference to Soviet leadership was considered emphatic, to disarmament weak, particularly since it was followed by accusations that the United States obstructed Soviet proposals.

These charts are valuable only as a sign that differences of emphasis existed among WTO member states from the beginning. For, despite a concerted effort to remain consistent, they rely heavily upon individual interpretation. Second, the texts of speeches at political consultative committee meetings were published only for the first two meetings—a small, if perhaps indicative sample.

Comparison with the Cominform

Certainly the 1958 PCC reticence to completely support Moscow's interpretation was a sharp contrast to the results of the first Soviet-Yugoslav dispute upon the earlier forms of intra-Communist organization. The cominform had expelled Yugoslavia. Its newspaper *For a Lasting Peace, For a People's Democracy* conducted a campaign of bitter denunciation against the Yugoslavs, and the total life of the cominform became warped to the ends of Soviet conflict. All its members joined the Soviet Union in unilaterally renouncing their bilateral treaties of friendship, cooperation, and mutual assistance with Yugoslavia, while hurling extreme insults against the Yugoslav leaders. Yugoslav sources have accused CMEA of simultaneously directing an economic boycott designed to weaken Tito's regime.

Indeed, there are signs that Moscow looked back to the cominform nostalgically in 1957. Undoubtedly one approach to containing diversity

CHART I

ATTITUDES TOWARD THE WARSAW TREATY, 1955–1958

	USSR	China	Albania	Bulgaria	Rumania	Hungary	East Germany	Poland	Czechoslovakia	Declaration
1955										
Chinese support		a	b	c		c		c	c	
Defensive nature	b	a	a	a	a	a	a	a	a	a
Conforms to UN principles	c		c		c	c		c	c	b
Open membership	c				c	c		c	c	b
Purpose										
Serves to strengthen the camp of peace	c				c			c	a	
Serves to strengthen the USSR and People's Democracy									c	
Serves to strengthen the socialist camp	b	a	a	c		c			c	
Serves specific national interests	c	c	c	b	c	c	a	a	b	
1956										
Peaceful nature	b	c	b	a	b	a	c	a	a	a
Need for joint defense measures	a	b	c	b	c	b	a	b	c	b
Proposed nonaggression treaty with NATO										b
Importance of Chinese support	a	a		b						
Leading role of the USSR				b		a				
Equate aims with those of the socialist camp		a	a				b		c	
Aids internal struggle for socialism			a							c
1958										
Peaceful nature	a	b	b	a	a	a	b	a	a	a
Warsaw Treaty troop cuts; USSR withdrawal from Rumania	b		c	c	b	c	c		a	a
Polish suggestion of atom-free zone	a		c	c	c	c	c	a		a
Socialist nature	a	a	c	b	a	b	c	a	a	a
WTO-NATO nonaggression pact	a	c	b	a	c	c	b	b	c	a

a emphatic
b positive
c weak

CHART 2
SUPPORT FOR SOVIET INITIATIVES, 1955–1958

	USSR	China	Albania	Bulgaria	Rumania	Hungary	East Germany	Poland	Czechoslovakia	Declaration
1955										
United Germany	a		c	b	b	c	a	c	c	
European Collective Security System	b	c	c	c	b	c	b	c	b	b
Disarmament	a		c	b	c	b		b	c	b
Negotiated Settlement	c			b	c	c	c	c	c	b
Austrian Treaty	c		c	c	c	a	c	c	c	
1956										
United Germany	b	c	a	c	c	c	a	c	c	c
with specific recognition of two German states	a				b		a	c		
European Collective Security System	c		c		c	b	a	b	a	a
Disarmament	c		c	a	a	b		c	a	b
Praise Geneva Conference	c	c	c	c	b	c	b	b	c	b
Peaceful coexistence	a	c	c		c		c	a	c	c
1958										
Summit diplomacy	a		b	c	c	c	b	b	b	a
Specific reference that summit meeting must not interfere in East European affairs	b		a			b	b	b	a	a
Disarmament: end nuclear testing	a		c	c	a	b	a	a	a	a
The German question	b		c	b	c	a	b	a	a	a
Peaceful coexistence	a		c	c	b			a	a	a

CHART 3

ITEMS OF EAST EUROPEAN NATIONAL INTEREST, 1955–1958

	USSR	China	Albania	Bulgaria	Rumania	Hungary	East Germany	Poland	Czechoslovakia	Declaration
1955										
Condemn German militarism	a	b	a	a	a	a	a	a	a	a
Relations based on sovereignty, independence, noninterference in internal affairs	b		c	c	b	c	c	c	c	b
German unity	a		c	b	b	c	c	c	c	
Polish Oder-Neisse boundary								a		
1956										
Condemn German militarism	a	b	a	a	b	a	a	a	a	a
East European membership in the UN			a	a	a	a		a		
Peace in the Balkans			b	a	b					
Polish Oder-Neisse boundary								a		
German unity	b	c	a	c	c		a	c	c	c
Support GDR army	a	a	c	b			a	a	b	c
1958										
Peace in the Balkans			b	a	b					
Summit must not interfere in EE affairs	b		a			b	b	b	a	a
German unity	a		c			b	c	a	a	a
Polish Oder-Neisse boundary								a		

CHART 4
ATTITUDE TOWARD THE WEST, 1955–1958

	USSR	China	Albania	Bulgaria	Rumania	Hungary	East Germany	Poland	Czechoslovakia	Declaration
1955										
1. Condemn Paris Agreements as revival of German militarism	a	b	a	a	a	a	a	a	a	b
2. Specifically anti-US	a	a	a	b	b	b	a	a	a	
1956										
Condemn aggressive, imperialist blocs	a	a	a	b	a	a	b	a	a	a
Specifically anti-US	c	a	a			c		c	b	
Emphasize 1955 NATO nuclear decision	a					c	a	c		b
Remilitarization of West Germany	a	b	a	a	b	a	a	a	a	a
Importance of widening diplomatic, cultural, economic bonds			c	b	a	c	a		b	c
1958										
Condemn US aggression	a	a	a	a	a	b	a	b	c	a
Condemn aggressive military blocs	a	c	a	c	a	c	a	a	a	a

CHART 5
ATTITUDE TOWARD THE USSR AND THE SOCIALIST CAMP, 1955–1958

	USSR	China	Albania	Bulgaria	Rumania	Hungary	East Germany	Poland	Czechoslovakia	Declaration
1955										
Stress socialist nature of the camp	c	a	a			b	c	c	c	
Stress camp of peace and democracy	b	c	c	c		b	c	a	c	
Soviet leadership		a	a	c			a		b	
Importance of internal socialist construction		a	a		c	c	b	c	a	
Praise of the USSR										
1. Bulwark of peace	a	c	a	a	b	b	a	c	a	
2. Soviet liberation			b		c	a		c	b	
3. Fraternal aid					c	c			c	
1956										
Peaceful aims of the camp	c		b		c	a	c	c	c	b
Significance of cooperation within the camp			c		c	a	c		c	
Importance of internal socialist construction	b		a							c
Leading role of the USSR			a		b		a			
Praise of the USSR										
1. Bulwark of peace	b	a	a	a	c	b	b	b	a	
2. International significance of the five-year plan	c		b							
3. 20th party congress			c	c						
4. Khrushchev-Bulganin trip to Asia and Africa					c		c	c		
5. Initiative in Austrian treaty					b		c			
1958										
Identification with the socialist camp	c	a	a	b	a	a	b	a	b	c
Growth of the camp strengthens forces for peace	b	c	c	b	b	a		a	b	
Unity of the camp	c	a	a	c	a	a		a		
Moscow 1957 conference		a	a	b						
Role of the socialist camp in the Hungarian Revolution	a		b			a				
Soviet leadership			a	c	c	b	c			
Importance of internal socialist construction	a	a	a	b	b	a		c	b	b

within Eastern Europe would have been the revival of an interparty organization along similar lines. Such an organization had obvious advantages for Soviet control, as well as the more subtle advantage of being identified as the successor of the comintern and the cominform, organizations within which a dominant-subordinate relationship had existed between the Soviet Union and the other members, thereby placing the East European Communist leaders at a psychological disadvantage despite their objectively increased power. As with the cominform, the initiative ostensibly came from outside the Soviet party. *Tvorba,* a Czechoslovak Party weekly, suggested that: "It would seem that for the sake of firm unity of international Communism roughly the same contacts should be promoted as existed when the cominform was in existence." [34] The Czechoslovak Party plenum in July 1957 again stressed the need for at least an interparty journal and perhaps a commission for political and economic problems.[35]

The objective political situation had changed radically in the ten years since 1947, however. That the November 1957 meeting of Communist and Workers' Parties did not establish any form of interparty organization testified to that change. The 1957 Moscow declaration limited itself to saying:

> After exchanging views, the participants in the meeting arrived at the conclusion that in present conditions in addition to bilateral meetings of leading personnel and exchange of information, it is expedient to hold as the need arises, more representative conferences of Communist and Workers' Parties to discuss current problems, share experience, study each other's views and attitudes and concert action in the joint struggle for common goals—peace, democracy, and socialism.[36]

In Communist terms "exchanging views" has become increasingly synonymous with "discussed and disagreed." The planned interparty journal was not again mentioned at that time, although the conference had agreed to such a journal "in principle." [37]

---

[34] *Tvorba* 3 (1957: 1; see Brzezinski, *The Soviet Bloc,* pp. 290–291.

[35] *Ibid.* That the Czechoslovak statement was reprinted in *Pravda,* June 21, 1957, indicates Soviet support for the proposal.

[36] The 1957 Moscow Declaration; cited from the translated text in G. F. Hudson, Richard Lowenthal, and Roderick MacFarquhar, *The Sino-Soviet Dispute* (New York: Praeger, 1961), p. 56.

[37] This journal, *Problems of Peace and Socialism,* was established in March 1958. See J. C. Clews, *Communist Propaganda Techniques* (New York: Praeger, 1964), pp. 72–74. Later at the 1960 Conference of Communist and Workers' Parties, the issue came up again

The Soviet-Albanian Break

Indeed, by 1960 Soviet-Albanian polemics could hardly have contributed to East European enthusiasm for a revived cominform. For viewed in perspective the Soviet-Albanian dispute had much in common with the Soviet-Yugoslav conflict of 1948, and the role of that organization in the Soviet-Yugoslav split was an all too recent and painful part of interparty history.

By the February 1960 meeting of the political consultative committee, it was obvious that despite the committee's claim that exchange of opinion showed complete agreement on international questions, conflict existed among the member states, while the Chinese observer's militant speech contrasted sharply with the moderate tone of the official PCC declaration. This marked yet another phase in the development of the Warsaw Treaty Organization: namely, that in which tacit approval for the Soviet formulations amounted to taking part in the conflict between the Soviet Union and Albania, a conflict in which Albania ultimately received open Chinese support.

The Soviet-Albanian conflict was qualitatively different from the 1956 events in either Poland or Hungary. First, although the impact of Khrushchev's de-Stalinization program helped to precipitate all three crises, Stalinists retained control of the Albanian Party and Hoxha's leadership was never effectively challenged.[38] Second, Soviet-Albanian relations deteriorated gradually; and with memories of Poland and Hungary still relatively fresh, the Soviets never found a convenient moment to intervene. Third, nonmember states played a vital role in this conflict in that tension increased in proportion to improvement in Soviet-Yugoslav relations, with China providing an alternative source of support within the

---

as a proposal for a "permanent committee or secretariat." The French Communist Party (a generally accurate reflection of Soviet preferences at that time) condemned this suggestion as "going back to some form of information bureau . . . which is no longer adapted to present conditions in our movement. Declaration of the Delegation of the French Communist Party to the November 1960 Meeting. JPRS translation 14, 610 (July 26, 1962): 33. Given Soviet bitterness over Chinese fractional activities within existing Communist organizations, it is hardly surprising if Moscow took a dim view of a reorganized "secretariat" by 1960. See Edward Crankshaw's account of the Moscow 1960 meeting in *The New Cold War: Moscow v. Peking* (Baltimore, Md.: Penguin Special, 1963), pp. 111–136.

[38] Both Khrushchev's denunciation of Albania at the CPSU Twenty-Second Party Congress and later Albanian polemics indicate that the Soviets attempted to support (or perhaps even to create) an alternative, pro-Soviet Albanian leadership. See *Pravda*, October 18 and 29, 1961, and Hoxha's November 8 speech in W. E. Griffith, *Albania and the Sino-Soviet Rift* (Cambridge, Mass.: The MIT Press, 1963), pp. 334–346.

socialist camp. Such Chinese support had been lacking in 1956, despite temporary hopes on the part of the Poles.[39] With respect to Albania, however, Chinese support for the Albanians was hardly surprising, as from the beginning Albanian defiance was in large part a reflection of Sino-Soviet differences.

When Khrushchev and Hoxha met in Moscow at the November Conference of Communist Parties, the Albanians were condemned for anti-Soviet policies. Hoxha replied by attacking Khrushchev for interfering in the affairs of fraternal parties, mishandling the situation in Hungary in 1956, factionalism, and applying economic pressure to bring Albania into line with Soviet policies.[40] He accused Soviet Marshal Malinovsky of attacking Albania during a meeting of Warsaw Pact chiefs-of-staff, and the commander of the Warsaw Pact joint armed forces, Marshal Grechko, of threatening to exclude Albania from the Pact.[41]

Unfortunately, it is impossible to tell exactly what meeting Hoxha was referring to. It could not have been *before* the February 4, 1960 PCC meeting because it was at that time that Grechko replaced Konev as commander-in-chief of the joint armed forces. Certainly Malinovsky had been present at the February 1960 session as had the other ministers of defense; although it was not formally a military meeting. Therefore, Hoxha may have been speaking of an *unpublicized* gathering in conjunction with the February 1960 meeting. Yet from the chronology of the summary of Hoxha's speech he appears to be talking about Soviet pressure sometime after August 1960. First, he discussed the Albanian plea for moderation in Soviet attacks on the Chinese at the Bucharest meeting (June 1960) and then a secret letter that the Soviets allegedly sent to Tirana in August asking the Albanians to form part of an anti-China bloc. Albania refused. The threat to exclude Albania from the Warsaw Pact is included in what seems to be a series of Soviet attempts to force the Albanian leaders to change their minds. In answering the Albanian charges, November 23, Khrushchev ignored the reference to the Warsaw Pact. As for Hoxha's claim that the Soviet-Yugoslav rapprochement in 1955 had been carried out without consulting the Albani-

[39] Brzezinski, *The Soviet Bloc*, p. 296.
[40] BBC Summary of Hoxha's Speech to the November 1960 Moscow Conference of Communist Parties; for analysis, see W. E. Griffith, "The November 1960 Meeting: A Preliminary Reconstruction," *The China Quarterly* 11 (July–September, 1962): 48 and *Albania and the Sino-Soviet Rift*.
[41] BBC Summary of Hoxha's speech.

ans, the Soviet leader insisted that the Albanian party wrote to Moscow
on June 21, 1954, giving its complete agreement.[42] Subsequently, Soviet-
Albanian polemics affected first Albanian military then political cooperation within the Warsaw Pact. Soviet submarines were withdrawn.

By the August meeting of first secretaries of Communist and Workers
Parties of the Warsaw Treaty states, Soviet-Albanian relations had deteriorated to the point of no return. For the first time a list of participants
was missing from the communiqué of a Warsaw Pact Meeting.[43] Clearly
Hoxha did not attend and during the meeting Radio Tirana broad-
casted a separate Albanian statement on the German question.[44] In
August 1961, the Soviet Ambassador left Albania.

Like the joint communiqué, the Albanian declaration praised the proposed German peace treaty as a guarantee of European peace and security.
The Albanians, however, went further. They stressed that such a treaty
would also act to strengthen the socialist camp, thereby striking a blow
at West Germany and its Atlantic Pact partners. On the whole, the
Albanian statement—at least three times as long as the Warsaw Treaty
Organization's official communiqué—was more extreme, more anti-
American, and much more concerned with advancing the cause of socialism than was the brief formal communiqué.

Tirana's separate declaration on the German question in August 1961
was remarkable primarily in its very existence. At that time, this was the
only separate statement ever issued by one of the smaller treaty members
on a topic of joint discussion and there is at least the possibility that its
distribution, along with several other documents by the Albanian embassy
in Moscow, caused the Soviets to sever diplomatic relations.

Virtual exclusion of Albania from Warsaw Treaty consultation followed. There was no public Soviet response to the Albanian declaration.[45] However, it is likely that the Albanians did not attend the

---

[42] Much later it was revealed that of the twelve Soviet submarines involved the Albanians
kept four. See Leo Heinman, "Peking's Adriatic Stronghold," *East Europe* 13, no. 4 (April
1964). The Albanians later formally accused the Soviets of "tearing up" the bilateral agreements related to Moscow's obligations under the Warsaw Pact for equipping the Albanian
army and "stealing" eight submarines which were undergoing repairs at the Soviet port
of Sevastopol. "Letter from the Albanian Government to the Participants of the 19 January
Warsaw Pact Meeting," *Zëri i popullit*, February 2, 1965. The charge was repeated in an
attack on Malinovsky, *Zëri i popullit*, May 22, 1965, and *Le Monde*, May 26, 1965.

[43] *Pravda*, August 6, 1961.

[44] Published in *Zëri i popullit*, August 8, 1961.

[45] This was typical of Moscow's policy prior to the fall of 1961. Thus, although Soviet-
Albanian differences had begun affecting Albanian representation at Warsaw Treaty meetings

September meeting of Warsaw Pact defense ministers. The announcement of that meeting referred only to "the chiefs of the general staffs of
armed forces of Warsaw Treaty countries and their defense ministers." [46]
Certainly no Albanian troops took part in the joint maneuvers of Warsaw Pact forces during October and November. [47]

The CPSU 22nd Congress and Thereafter

Then at the 22nd CPSU congress, Khrushchev openly attacked Albania
for purging Soviet sympathizers within the Albanian party, for refusing
to consult with the Soviets concerning their differences, for dogmatism,
sectarianism, narrow nationalism, and revisionism. [48] In short, the charges
made were remarkably reminiscent of Soviet accusations leveled at Yugoslavia in the late forties. Rather than yielding, the Albanians—supported
by the Chinese—claimed that bringing the issue up in open forum violated
the Moscow 1960 agreement for handling interparty differences. [49] Khrushchev then demanded that the Albanian leadership be punished for
their Stalinist crimes. [50] The Albanians responded with a series of violent
denunciations of Khrushchev, many of which are included in William
E. Griffith's study. [51] Most important with respect to the Warsaw Treaty
Organization, the Albanian embassy in Moscow proceeded to distribute
key Albanian documents relating to the dispute, thereby providing the
official cause for the Soviet rupture of diplomatic relations. It has been

---

by March 1961, there was no indication of this in Zhukov's detailed analysis of the Warsaw
Treaty. Obviously writing after the March meeting, he avoided any mention of attendance.
In fact, the only sign of coolness in Soviet-Albanian relations was that when illustrating
his points the Soviet author used examples from all the other member states, none from
Albania. He referred to Albania only once, when listing the original signatories of the
Warsaw Treaty. Zhukov, *Varshavski dogovor i voprosy mezhdunarodnoi bezopasnosti*, p.
11.

[46] *Krasnaya zvezda*, September 10, 1961.

[47] See Raymond L. Garthtoff, "The Military Establishment," p. 14.

[48] *Pravda*, October 18, 1961.

[49] "Declaration of the Central Committee of the Albanian Party of Labor," *Zëri i popullit*, October 21, 1961; complete text in Griffith, *Albania*, Document 9. See also Chou En-lai's
speech to the Twenty-second Party Congress, *Peking Review* 4, no. 43 (October 27, 1961):
9.

[50] *Pravda*, October 29, 1961. Once again the attack had the same overtones as had Stalin's
and subsequently the Cominform's denunciations of the Yugoslav leaders.

[51] See particularly "Marxism-Leninism Will Triumph," *Zëri i popullit*, November 1,
1961, and Griffith, *Albania and the Sino-Soviet Rift*, p. 236; "The Name and Deeds of
J. V. Stalin Will Continue to Live for Centuries to Come," *Zëri i popullit*, November 2,
1961 and Griffith, *ibid.*, p. 240; and Hoxha's November 8 speech, excerpts in Griffith, *ibid.*,
p. 242.

reported that those documents included a unilateral Albanian declaration concerning a Warsaw Pact meeting.[52] There is some confusion, however, both as to exactly what documents and which Warsaw Treaty meeting were involved. The Soviets specified only the declaration of the Albanian Communist Party on October 20, 1961 and Hoxha's speech of November 1961.[53] If, in fact, an Albanian declaration was passed out accusing Khrushchev of injuring the international Communist movement by not signing a separate German peace treaty as called for by the August 1961 Warsaw Pact meeting, it would have been the second separate Albanian statement on the German question, which is unlikely.[54]

However, if in view of the Soviet position of August 1961 it was not clear that the Albanian Declaration implicitly accused Khrushchev of sacrificing East German interests by equivocating on the question of a German peace treaty, distribution of such a statement in November would have left little room for doubt, particularly if it were distributed in conjunction with Hoxha's speech.

De Facto Exclusion, 1962–1963

By the June 1962 political consultative committee meeting, Albania, although in theory retaining membership in organizations set up under the Warsaw Treaty, had been effectively excluded from participating in the Warsaw Pact.

Tirana protested, declaring:

> The meeting of the Political Consultative Committee of the Warsaw Pact, held in Moscow on June 7, 1962, without the participation of the Albanian People's Republic, and any other meeting which may be held in

[52] Griffith, *Albania and the Sino-Soviet Rift* cites a Moscow Agence France Press dispatch from the *Neue Zürcher Zeitung* of November 24, 1961 to this effect. *Ibid.*, p. 113.

[53] *Pravda,* December 12, 1961. In addition to the two documents cited, the Soviet note mentioned only "other materials filled with lies and foul slanders against our party, the Soviet government, and the decisions of the 22nd CPSU Congress."

[54] There is also the possibility that it was the first Albanian Central Committee declaration on the German question that was distributed, although that declaration did not specifically accuse Khrushchev of injuring the international Communist movement by refusing to sign a separate German peace treaty on schedule. It could not have, for the Warsaw Treaty states' communiqué specified only that such a treaty should be signed by the end of the year and the first Albanian declaration appeared August 8. Yet, Hoxha's November 8 speech both alluded to Soviet foot-dragging in this respect and accused Khrushchev of injuring the international Communist movement. It is not inconceivable that the AFP dispatch jumbled these documents together, for according to Peter Prifti, who follows the Albanian press at the MIT Center for International Studies, no second Albanian declaration on the German question has appeared and the Albanians have not been reticent in much more violent denunciations of Khrushchev.

the future within the framework of the Warsaw Pact without the participation of the Albanian People's Republic, to be illegal because it is in flagrant contradiction to the Warsaw Pact itself and also to the principles of the relations among socialist states. It is a grave act, consciously and maliciously carried out not only against the Albanian People's Republic, but also against the interests of the Warsaw Pact Organization itself and the entire socialist camp. The responsibility for this most grave action and the decisions taken at the separate Moscow meeting rests with its organizers and with the governments which participated in the meeting.[55]

Moscow had already openly accused the Albanians of not attending both the March and August 1961 meetings so as not to have to discuss the "misunderstandings" which had grown up between them and their Soviet comrades.[56]

Throughout 1962 and early 1963 the Soviets continued attacking Albania at a series of European Communist party congresses. By this time, open Sino-Soviet polemics progressed parallel to the attacks on Albania, while the charges leveled against Tirana made clear that Albania's primary sin was alignment with China against Soviet positions within the international Communist movement. Albanian membership in the Warsaw Pact was largely ignored, although at the East German party congress, Hermann Matern did accuse the Albanians of violating their obligations under the Warsaw Treaty.[57]

The similarities with Stalin's method of trying to control Yugoslavia are inescapable. Nevertheless the Soviets did not resort to use of force, and the effect of the Soviet-Albanian dispute upon the Warsaw Pact institutionally was limited.

Although de facto exclusion of Albanian representatives from the Warsaw Treaty Organization resulted, Albania was never formally expelled.[58]

---

[55] "Albanian Governmental Statement on the Warsaw Pact Meeting," *Zëri i popullit*, June 13, 1962; complete text in Griffith, *Albania and the Sino-Soviet Rift*, Document 29, pp. 355–356. The Chinese observer was also absent.

[56] See Griffith, *ibid.*, Document 23, p. 319 for translation of Leonid Sergeyev commentary, "Albanian Leaders' Refusal to Discuss Differences," Radio Moscow, February 8, 1962. Subsequently, the Albanians claimed that the Soviet government forced de facto exclusion of Albania from the Warsaw Pact in 1961. "Letter from the Albanian Government to the Participants of the 19 January Warsaw Pact Meeting," *Zëri i popullit*, February 2, 1965.

[57] *Neues Deutechland*, January 19, 1963: cited in Griffith, *The Sino-Soviet Rift* (Cambridge, Mass.: The MIT Press, 1964), p. 102.

[58] Although Staar has referred to a 5th meeting of the PCC (January 30–February 1, 1962) as voting to exclude Albania from the Warsaw Pact [Staar, "The East European Alliance"], there is no public record that such a meeting occurred. Soviet sources mentioned only a meeting of the defense ministers of states participating in the Warsaw Treaty. *Pravda*, February 2, 1962.

Rather the Warsaw Pact officially ignored Tirana's absence, while representatives of other member states countered the Albanian charge that Albania had not been invited, and hence WTO and CMEA were operating illegally, by simply stating that the Albanians had refused to attend. Second, the organization as such did not express bitter hostility toward Albania or Albanian leaders. Warsaw Pact meetings were not used to channel a barrage of public abuse against the offender, despite the reiteration of Soviet criticism by individual member states. Instead Soviet-Albanian differences made themselves felt, first in a gradual decline in the position held by Albanian representatives; then in Albanian absence. Chinese support for Albanian deviation, in turn, led to the end of China's role as the only official observer at Warsaw Treaty meetings.

Rather it appeared that the Warsaw Treaty Organization had withered politically. Speeches had ceased being published; meetings became briefer, and differences apparently were suppressed or handled through other noninstitutional channels. Simultaneously, the military aspects of the treaty predominated both in terms of activity and Soviet perception of the Warsaw Pact's importance. After 1961, joint maneuvers took place regularly each fall and often during the year as well. East European sources tend to confirm the Western assumption that these exercises served a practical military purpose.[59] In short at least temporarily the appearance of internal conflict had primarily resulted first in the disappearance of diversity, then in the exclusion of the bulk of political content from the Warsaw Treaty Organization.

The problem of Albania's relations to the Warsaw Pact soon subsided into more-of-the-same polemics on the appropriate anniversaries. It was not to take on real significance again until the multilateral invasion of Czechoslovakia precipitated Tirana's formal withdrawal from the Warsaw Treaty Organization—an unprecedented move that will be discussed in the context of the crisis between Prague and the other pact

[59] In the CPSU program coming out of the 22nd Congress, there is only one implied reference to the Joint Command, i.e., "the party works unremittingly . . . to educate soldiers in the spirit of courage, bravery, heroism, and comradeship with the armies of the socialist countries." (*The New Soviet Society: Final Text of the Program of the Communist Party of the Soviet Union,* annotations and introduction by Herbert Ritvo [*New Leader* paperback, 1962], p. 187.) Following the Congress, however, articles in the Soviet military journal *Kommunist vooruzhennykh sil* stressed the importance of its decisions relating to the defensive capacity of the socialist camp. See "XXII S'ezd KPSS ob ukreplenii," *Kommunist vooruzhennykh sil* 5 (March 1962): 70–79; I. Kalozi, "Pust' k serdtsam voinov," *Kommunist vooruzhennykh sil* 23 (December 1961): 89–91.

members. Rather, from 1963 until 1968 the Albanian question within the alliance was on ice, overshadowed by Bucharest's challenge to Soviet organizational control of the Warsaw Pact. Therefore interim Albanian developments will be discussed in the context of, to follow Oscar Wilde, "the importance of being Rumania."

4
RUMANIA:
A CASE FOR
CONTAINMENT

SIGNS OF STRAIN in the economic relations of Rumania and other members of the Council for Mutual Economic Aid (CMEA) have been documented as early as 1953,[1] with the Rumanians openly stating their case in bloc ideological literature in 1958.[2] The organizational consequences of this had only begun to be apparent by 1962. Indeed, the Rumanians had been so circumspect that while the Soviet-Albanian split and the Sino-Soviet rift were accepted as facts of international Communist life in 1962, Western analysts spoke somewhat gingerly of Soviet-Rumanian "differences." At that time it was far from clear what those differences entailed.

Subsequent Soviet-Rumanian maneuvering within the Warsaw Pact was, in part, a logical extension of Bucharest's rejection of supranational planning within CMEA. Political jockeying within both organizations closely interacted. Therefore, the chapter that follows is in part the story of CMEA, for it would be as vacuous to analyze Soviet-Rumanian conflict within the Warsaw Treaty Organization without reference to its economic counterpart as to ignore the options opened to East European members of the Warsaw Pact by the Sino-Soviet split—particularly since the tensions first appeared in the economic sphere.

As for the Warsaw Pact, in 1962 Soviet-Rumanian differences appeared nonexistent. Yet in retrospect, even Gheorghe Gheorghiu-Dej's statement to the 1955 Warsaw Conference was slightly off key. Whereas

---

[1] John Michael Montias, *Economic Developoment in Communist Rumania* (Cambridge, Mass.: The MIT Press, 1967), pp. 187 ff. See also Michael Kaser, *COMECON: Integration Problems of the Planned Economies* (London: Oxford University Press, 1965), pp. 91 and 105–107.

[2] Montias, *Economic Development in Communist Rumania*, pp. 194–195.

other East European leaders spoke only of Soviet liberation of their countries, Dej reserved part of the credit to the Rumanians emphasizing that:

> In August 1944, in conditions created by the victorious advance of the
> liberating Soviet Army, the *Rumanian people overthrew the fascist dic-
> tatorship*. The *Rumanian Army* turned its weapons against the Nazi in-
> vaders and *fought side by side* with the Soviet Army to crush the Nazi
> hordes.[3] [Italics mine.]

The Importance of Hungary in 1956

In 1956, Soviet and Rumanian forces again collaborated. By the beginning of October, the number of Soviet troops in Rumania had increased
well above the two divisions ostensibly stationed there since 1948. War-
time communication lines were reestablished and urgent measures taken
to stem internal unrest. Although there is no evidence that Rumanian
troops fought with the Soviets in Hungary, Bucharest certainly facilitated
passage of Soviet soldiers across the Hungarian border. Subsequently,
Rumania sent economic and medical aid to Kádár's government.[4]

Most important, the Soviet declaration of October 30 promising to
review the question of Soviet troops stationed in Warsaw Pact countries
was directly relevant to Rumania. To use a favorite Marxist phrase, it
was no accident that a joint Rumanian-Hungarian communiqué stressing
that the Hungarian government's decision to ask for assistance of Soviet
troops was "necessary and correct" appeared in the Rumanian Press
November 24,[5] one day before a high-level government delegation went
to Moscow.

Soviet-Rumanian negotiations lasted from November 26 to December
3. Despite Soviet concessions, the subsequent joint statement was un-

---

[3] "Statement by Gheorghe Gheorghiu-Dej," *New Times* 21 (May 21, 1956): 52. In 1955,
this was a minor difference in shading, one which Ceauşescu significantly reformulated in
1963: ". . . *our heroic party* on 23 August 1944 *initiated, organized*, and *led the armed
insurrection which resulted in the overthrow of the fascist dictatorship*, in Rumania's
leaving the war on the side of Nazi Germany, and in Rumania's joining the anti-Hitlerite
coalition. The entire Rumanian Army turned their weapons against the true enemy and
fought heroically side by side with the glorious Soviet Army in the war for liberation of
the national territory of the fatherland from the fascist invaders. . . . The common fight
of Rumanian and Soviet soldiers waged until final victory over fascism cemented the
fraternal friendship between the Rumanian people and the Soviet people." [Italics mine.]
Scînteia, August 23, 1963.

[4] Ghita Ionescu, *Communism in Rumania, 1944–1962* (London: Oxford University
Press, 1964). See also *UN Report Supplement*.

[5] *Scînteia*, November 25, 1956; reported in *Pravda*, November 26, 1956.

doubtedly lacking from the Rumanian point of view. Both parties pledged
to develop "perfect mutually beneficial" political, economic, and cultural
relations on the basis of "full equality, respect of each for the territorial
integrity, independence, and national sovereignty of the other, and noninterference in internal affairs." Both recognized the "joint armed struggle" for liberation of Rumania. The delegations "exchanged opinions" on
events in Hungary. The Rumanians considered that in going to the aid
of Kádár's government, "the Soviet Union was performing its international duty to the working people of Hungary and of the other socialist
countries." But Soviet troops stayed in Rumania, their presence mitigated
only by the promise that "dependent on the course of international developments" the Soviets, the Rumanians, and "other parties to the Warsaw Treaty" would take the matter up again.[6] Nor was the rearrange-
ment of Soviet-Rumanian economic relations as favorable to Rumania as
Soviet-Polish negotiations had been to the Poles.[7]

Rumanian dissatisfaction was evident. In reassessing the events in
Hungary at a Party Conference of the Hungarian Autonomous Province,
the lessons Dej drew from the "defeat of counterrevolution" in Hungary
were entirely domestic.[8] He did not mention Moscow's international
duty: a sharp contrast to Široký's report to the Czechoslovak National
Assembly that the aid given by Soviet army units to the Hungarian government was "not only justified but also absolutely necessary and inevitable." [9] Nor was Bucharest's response to the Sino-Soviet Declaration

[6] *Pravda*, December 4, 1956; quoted from English version in *New Times* 50 (December 6, 1956): 1–3. For analysis see Stephen Fischer-Galati, *The New Rumania: From a
People's Democracy to a Socialist Republic* (Cambridge, Mass.: The MIT Press, 1967), pp.
62–67.

[7] The joint Polish-Soviet statement had specified economic concessions. Polish debts
as of November 1, 1956 based on coal deliveries to the USSR from 1946 to 1953 were
cancelled. The Soviets agreed to deliver 1,400,000 tons of grain to Poland in 1957 on
credit, and to grant the Poles long-term credits amounting to 700,000,000 rubles to pay
for Russian goods. *Pravda*, November 19, 1956; *Current Digest of the Soviet Press* (*CDSP*)
8, no. 45 (December 19, 1956): 28. The Soviet-Rumanian statement referred only to a
"comprehensive examination" of economic cooperation between the Soviet Union and the
Rumanian People's Republic. According to Ionescu this amounted to postponing payment
on Soviet credits granted to Rumania between 1949–1955 for four years, a Soviet agreement "to lend" Rumania 450,000 tons of wheat and 60,000 tons of fodder, and Moscow's
promise to supply plant and installation for building of chemical industrial works on
credit (a value of 270 million rubles). Ionescu, *Communism in Rumania*, p. 274.

[8] *Pravda*, December 24, 1956. Two days later a delegation of the Chinese National People's Congress headed by P'eng Chen arrived in Bucharest for a visit lasting until January
3, 1957. See *Survey of China Mainland Press* 1441 (January 2, 1957), 1443 (January 4,
1957), and 1445 (January 8, 1957).

[9] *Pravda*, December 9, 1956.

of January 18 effusive. Its text appeared in the Rumanian press. However, the leading article of *România Libera* simply concluded that the Soviet-Chinese negotiations demonstrated the validity of a favorite Rumanian formula, i.e. friendship between socialist countries rests on the "Leninist principles of equality, mutual respect for national interests, brotherly mutual aid, non-interference in internal affairs; on the common deep devotion to proletarian internationalism." [10]

Maneuvering in the Late 1950s: The Issue of Soviet Troops

Indeed there is evidence suggesting that as early as 1957, Rumania had begun to play a cautious game of tit for tat. On January 25, the Rumanian foreign minister, M. Popescu, arrived to discuss the Soviet-Rumanian trade agreement for 1957. Although Dej's election speech of February 2 emphasized that the basic element of Rumanian foreign policy was "friendship with the Soviet Union, the People's Republic of China and other socialist countries," he reiterated the Leninist principles governing relations among socialist countries, the principles put forth in "the famous Soviet Declaration of 30 October 1956." He pledged continued support for the Warsaw Treaty but did not praise Soviet internationalism or mention the events in Hungary.[11]

Pravda reprinted Dej's speech, and there was some general coverage of Rumanian election activities. Yet the coolness in Soviet-Rumanian relations had affected more than the tone of Dej's references to the Soviet Union and the socialist camp. From February 8 to March 2, the Soviet press reported events in Albania, Bulgaria, Czechoslovakia, Hungary, Poland and Yugoslavia—but not Rumania.[12] On March 2, the communiqué of Soviet-Rumanian Scientific and Technical Cooperation appeared. The next day a *Scînteia* editorial entitled "Unity of the Socialist Camp Is a Prerequisite for Building Socialism" reevaluated the Hungarian situation in the form of an attack on Yugoslavia:

> The recent period, the period of attack by the most reactionary forces, put the unity of the socialist countries through a real test of fire. The might and resources of this unity were again demonstrated and reaction's hopes of seeing the socialist camp disintegrate turned out to be vain. Whoever

[10] *Pravda,* January 20, 1957.
[11] *Pravda,* February 3, 1957.
[12] Based on checking *CDSP* 9, no. 7 (March 27, 1957); 9, no. 8 (April 3, 1957); 9, no. 9 (April 10, 1957).

rejects the real and profound unity of the socialist countries rejects that which is obvious. . . .

It was this very unity of the countries of the socialist camp and their friendly ties with the Soviet Union, *the sons of which have again shed their blood in the struggle to defend the freedom of the Hungarian people,* that made it possible to oppose the formation of a reactionary fascist Hungarian state with chauvinist and revisionist tendencies directed against all its neighbors, including Yugoslavia.[13] [Italics mine.]

The Soviet-Rumanian trade agreement for 1957 was signed March 4.[14]

The agreement regulating the legal status of Soviet troops on Rumanian territory followed in April. Therefore the decision to withdraw Soviet forces must have been taken between April 1957 and its announcement at the May 1958 meeting of the Warsaw Pact political consultative committee. Why did Soviet troops leave Rumania?[15] This is crucial to Rumania's role in the Warsaw Pact. For not only did the absence of Soviet forces greatly facilitate later Rumanian maneuvering but the circumstances of Soviet withdrawal cast an interesting light on the Rumanian use of indirect political leverage within the socialist camp.

From April 1957 to May 1958, high-level Soviet-Rumanian leaders met only twice publicly: at the November celebrations of the October Revolution and then briefly when a Rumanian delegation returned from an extended tour of Asia in April 1958.

The Moscow 1957 Meeting

Although the Rumanian delegation to the Moscow 1957 meeting remained in the USSR from November 7 to November 21, there was no

[13] *Scînteia,* March 1, 1957; reprinted in *Pravda,* March 6, 1957; quoted from the *CDSP* 9, no. 12 (May 1, 1957): 3.

[14] *Pravda,* March 5, 1957.

[15] Undoubtedly the military consideration of Rumania belonging to what has been called "the second strategic echelon" within the Warsaw Pact is important. See Tykocinski, "Poland's Plan for the Northern Tier," *East Europe* 15, no. 11 (November 1966). But by that reasoning Soviet forces should also have left Hungary for fear of repercussions stemming from the Hungarian uprising of 1956, if not in 1958, certainly by 1970. Ionescu, *Communism in Rumania,* p. 289 considers the withdrawal to be motivated by Moscow's desire to strengthen the credibility of peaceful coexistence by improving the image of the "peace-loving" Soviet Union and making Rumania's peace offensive in the Balkans more convincing. Admittedly, these were fortuitous side effects. Yet the propaganda advantage could have been gained by a partial withdrawal (as in the case of Hungary) with complete withdrawal being made contingent on equivalent NATO concessions. Nor have the Soviets appeared to feel that Soviet soldiers in Poland negated the value of Rapacki's plan for an atom-free zone in Central Europe. Thus, Fischer-Galati's view that Chinese pressure was the determining factor appears to be more relevant. Fischer-Galati, *The New Rumania,* p. 70 ff.

evidence that an agreement was reached on withdrawing Soviet troops at that time. Certainly, the "course of international developments" as described in the Moscow declaration did not seem promising for such a move. Europe was threatened by the rivival of German militarism. The Dulles-Eisenhower doctrine created a threat to the peace in the Middle East. SEATO brought the danger of war to Southeast Asia. The Declaration admitted "a real possibility of averting war," but its examples were not reassuring:

> [This] was demonstrated graphically by the failure of the imperialists' aggressive designs in Egypt. Their plans to use counterrevolutionary forces for the overthrow of the people's democratic system in Hungary likewise failed.[16]

Moreover, had an agreement been reached one might have expected more enthusiastic Rumanian participation in the festivities; or, conversely, more Soviet enthusiasm for the Rumanians. In each case, the *Pravda* announcement of arriving East European delegations had included a speech by the leader of that delegation.[17] This was true even of Yugoslavia, but not Rumania. Whereas the lack of an arrival speech might be explained by the mysterious airplane crash in which Rumanian Politburo member Grigore Preoteasa died and other members of the Rumanian delegation were "slightly injured," that accident could hardly have prevented the appearance of a lengthy Rumanian article praising the significance of the October Revolution. For such an article would have been prepared well in advance in any case. The Soviet press printed major salutatory articles from leaders of the other seven East European countries.[18] Bucharest remained silent. The Rumanian delegation did not appear at receptions, banquets, memorials, or the theater. Rumanian comment was limited to Stoica's speech at the opening of the anniversary session of the USSR Supreme Soviet, Greetings to Khrushchev from Groza, Bodnaras, and Gheorghe Gheorghi-Dej, and Stoica's brief farewell.[19] Also, why had Dej not gone to Moscow? Tito's reasons for staying in

[16] The 1957 Moscow declaration in R. F. Hudson, Richard Lowenthal, and Roderick MacFarquhar, *The Sino-Soviet Dispute*. (New York: Praeger, 1961).

[17] *Pravda*, November 6–7, 1957.

[18] Kiss [Hungary], *Pravda*, October 30, 1956; Novotný [Czechoslovakia], November 4, 1957; Gomułka [Poland], November 5, 1957; Hoxha [Albania]; Ulbricht [GDR], November 6, 1957; Yugov [Bulgaria], *Izvestia*, November 6, 1957; Tito [Yugoslavia], *Pravda*, November 9, 1957.

[19] *Pravda*, November 7, 1957; November 11, 1957; and November 21, 1957.

Yugoslavia were obvious. There was nothing in public Soviet-Rumanian relations to explain Dej's absence. Unlike the Yugoslavs, the Rumanians signed the Moscow Declaration of Ruling Communist Parties. Yet Dej was the only First Secretary of an East European Communist Party not present.

Journey to Peking

Most important, the Rumanian delegation that did attend the Moscow Meeting returned to Bucharest with a heightened awareness of Sino-Soviet differences. For in March 1958, a Rumanian delegation including Premier Chivu Stoica, former Defense Minister Emil Bodnaras, and Minister of Foreign Affairs Avran Bunaciu began traveling through Asia. When this delegation reached China in early April, the question of troops stationed on foreign territory was obviously central to Rumanian thinking. At a rally in Peking, Stoica praised the withdrawal of Chinese troops from North Korea, adding "It is high time that the US and the other countries that have troops stationed in South Korea pull their forces out." [20] Such a remark could well have been aimed at "other countries" with troops located in places other than South Korea. Then in the Sino-Rumanian joint statement of April 8 both parties explicitly reaffirmed that

> the military blocs in Europe and Asia should be abolished and replaced by systems of collective security; military bases established on foreign territory should be eliminated; and armed forces stationed on foreign territory should be withdrawn.[21]

After this suggestion that made no distinction between "imperialist" and "peace-loving" armed forces, the two governments pledged themselves to "strive unswervingly" to strengthen the socialist camp headed by the Soviet Union.

Soviet public reaction to the Rumanians' Asian tour was minimal.[22] Neither Stoica's speech nor the joint statement appeared in the Soviet Press. However, the Rumanian delegation returned via Moscow and was met at the airport by Soviet leaders Brezhnev, Mikoyan, Suslov,

[20] "Peking Mass Rally Welcomes Rumanian Government Delegation," NCN, English, Peking, April 3, 1958; *SCMP* 1748 (April 10, 1958): p. 38.

[21] "Sino-Rumanian Joint Statement," *SCMP* 1750 (April 14, 1958): 44. For analysis, Fischer-Galati, *The New Rumania*, pp. 70–71.

[22] A brief notice that the Rumanians were in China appeared in *Pravda*, April 4, 1958; that Mao Tse-tung had received the Rumanian delegation, *Pravda*, April 7, 1958.

Khrushchev, Kosygin, Gromyko, and Kuznetsov. "Friendly, comradely, discussions" followed.[23]

Most likely, this was when Moscow agreed that Soviet troops would leave Rumania. If so, it indicates that Bucharest had begun manipulating the Soviet desire to minimize Chinese influence within the socialist camp to achieve Rumanian national goals well before the West began to speculate along those lines.[24]

Another rather unlikely possibility is that agreement to withdraw Soviet forces was reached during December 1957 "consultations" of Warsaw Treaty members referred to by Khrushchev,[25] i.e., before the Rumanians went to China. It is not clear what form these consultations took. The only public gathering was one of Soviet–East European "communications" ministers.[26] Nor did the Soviet press mention a series of bilateral meetings. The consultations may have been a series of written exchanges, but a matter of such importance would not usually be handled in that way. Moreover, the sparse Soviet coverage of the Rumanian delegation's Asian tour suggests that they were not traveling with Moscow's approval and that even if a secret Warsaw Treaty meeting did occur in December the issue of Soviet troops on Rumanian territory was not resolved to Rumanian satisfaction.

The May 1958 PCC Meeting: Soviet Troops Go Home

Dej went to Moscow for the May 1958 meeting of the Warsaw Pact Political Consultative Committee. A series of bilateral discussions took place between East European leaders and Khrushchev before the formal PCC meeting.[27] Then the Declaration of the Warsaw Treaty States announced:

> The conference participants heard and discussed a proposal by the Soviet government—agreed to by the government of the Rumanian People's Republic—that the Soviet troops stationed in Rumania under the Warsaw

[23] *Ibid.*, April 17, 1958.
[24] See J. F. Brown, "Rumanian Out of Line," *Survey* 49 (October 1963): 19–35 and the third article in Philippe Ben's series "La Roumanie entre Moscou et Pekin," titled "Le Comecon, Homme Malade de l'Europe de l'Est," *Le Monde*, December 3, 1963. Western analysts previously felt that Soviet-Rumanian economic disagreements had begun affecting Sino-Rumanian relations during 1963. This impression is largely corrected by Fischer-Galati, *The New Rumania.*
[25] Speech to Warsaw Pact meeting, *Pravda*, May 27, 1958.
[26] *Pravda*, December 4, 1957.
[27] *Pravda*, May 23, 24, 25, 1958.

Treaty be withdrawn. The conference participants approve this suggestion and express the conviction that it will be interpreted by all peoples as a new proof of the consistent peace-loving policy of the socialist countries.[28]

Seen in the context of Soviet-Rumanian negotiations in 1956, "the course of international developments" as described by the Warsaw Pact Declaration did not appear appreciably more favorable for Soviet withdrawal. NATO forces were increasing. The NATO council had decided on May 1, 1958 to supply atomic weapons to those member states not presently possessing them. Military preparations in Western Germany were becoming "particularly dangerous."[29]

In point of fact, Chinese support combined with apparent Rumanian economic concessions may have been the key to Soviet withdrawal. The Soviets had been pushing coordination within CMEA since 1956,[30] with small success. During his visit to Hungary in the spring of 1958, Khrushchev had summed up the situation:

> Everyone understands the necessity and desirability of cooperation, but when they go back home from the conference everything remains as before and matters make no progress.[31]

Immediately prior to the Warsaw Pact meeting, the first secretaries of the Communist and Workers' Parties of the countries participating in CMEA formally approved recommendations for further integration and coordination of long-range planning. On an organizational plane, the first secretaries explicitly agreed to enhance the role of the council in intrabloc

---

[28] *Pravda*, May 27, 1958; quoted from *CDSP* 10, no. 21 (July 2, 1958): 18.

[29] *Ibid.*

[30] The most published material of all Communist regional organizations is available on the Council for Mutual Economic Assistance (CMEA). See István Ágoston, *Le Marché Commun Communiste: Principles et pratique du COMECON* (Geneva: Librairie Droz, 1965); Brzezinski, *The Soviet Bloc,* Appendix 1; Grzybowski, *The Socialist Commonwealth of Nations: Organizations and Institutions* (New Haven, Conn.: Yale University, 1964), Chapters III and IV; Reinhard R. Hartmann, "The Impact of the Council for Mutual Economic Assistance on Foreign Trade in the Soviet Bloc," Master's Thesis, Southern Illinois University, July 20, 1962; Oleg Hoeffding, *Recent Efforts Toward Coordinated Economic Planning in the Soviet Bloc* (Santa Monica, Calif.: The RAND Corporation, August 7, 1959); Kaser, *COMECON,* Andrzej Korbonski, "COMECON," *International Conciliation* 549 (September 1964), R. S. Jaster, "CEMA's Influence on Soviet Policies in Eastern Europe," *World Politics* 14, no. 3 (April 1962); Frederic L. Pryor, "The Foreign Trade System of the European Communist Nations," Ph.D. Dissertation, Yale University, 1961, later expanded into his book, *The Communist Foreign Trade System* (Cambridge, Mass.: The MIT Press, 1963); Egon Neuberger, *Soviet Bloc Economic Integration: Some Suggested Explanations for Slow Progress* (Santa Monica, Calif.: RAND Memorandum, July 1963); and A. Zauberman, "Economic Integration: Problems and Prospects," *Problems of Communism* 8, no. 4 (July–August 1959).

[31] Quoted in *East Europe* 9, no. 11 (November 1960), p. 24.

planning.[32] If Montias' analysis is correct, even in 1958 such a decision could hardly have pleased the Rumanians. Nor was Bucharest likely to consider Khrushchev's subsequent opinion that the "question of borders between socialist countries will be a pointless one" [33] compatible with the Leninist principles of mutual respect for national interests and noninterference in internal affairs.

Certainly, if the December 1959 article by M. Horovitz in the Rumanian Party Central Committee journal *Cercetări Filozofice* is regarded as an indication, Rumanian concessions in May 1958 had been more apparent than real. Attacking the concept of Rumania as a predominantly agricultural country, Horovitz said pointedly:

> The advancement of the socialist countries toward Communism will not develop on the basis of the directives of any supranational organ but will be accomplished under the leadership of the Communist and Workers' Parties of every socialist country acting separately *without any meddling from afar* in the internal affairs of other countries.[34]

Expanding Economic Tensions

Subsequently, Rumania's position within the Warsaw Pact as well as Bucharest's progressively neutral line on the Sino-Soviet dispute directly reflected the tug of war within CMEA. The Rumanians watched Sino-Soviet relations worsen; first at the February 1960 Warsaw Pact meeting, then in the violent confrontation at the Rumanian Third Party Congress in June. Increased Soviet willingness to consider Rumanian demands during the extended economic negotiation that lasted from the spring of 1960 until November,[35] i.e., just before the November 1960 Moscow Statement, must have strengthened the Rumanian sense of potential advantages to be gained from the deepening Sino-Soviet split.

---

[32] *Pravda*, May 25, 1958.

[33] Specifically the Soviet leader said: "Speaking of the future, it seems to me that the further development of the socialist countries will in all probability proceed along the lines of consolidation of the single-world socialist system. The economic barriers which divide our countries will fall one after another. The common economic basis of world socialism will grow stronger, eventually making the quest of borders a pointless one." [Italics mine.] *Pravda*, March 27, 1959; quoted from Brzezinski, *The Soviet Bloc*, 2nd ed., p. 451 (not quoted in 3rd ed.).

[34] M. Horovitz, "The Simultaneous Transition of Socialist Countries to Communism," *Cercetari Filozofice*, December 1959, pp. 35–54, and *JPRS* 3173 (April 13, 1960): p. 7. Horovitz had also advanced a number of protectionist arguments prior to the May 1958 meeting. See Montias, *Economic Development in Communist Rumania*, pp. 194–195.

[35] *Pravda*, November 12, 1960.

Gheorghiu-Dej went to Moscow for the November 1960 meeting. He attacked the Chinese for factionalism and strongly supported Khrushchev. Whether or not Fischer-Galati is correct in implying that the Rumanians traded support for the Soviets against the Albanians and the Chinese in return for delayed economic integration at the Warsaw Pact meeting in August 1961,[36] two points are clear. First, no immediate steps were taken toward economic integration, although the draft program of the CPSU—first published in July 1961—strongly had implied the necessity for such steps.[37] Second, Bucharest did echo Soviet attacks against Albania at the Soviet 22nd Party congress.[38]

It was during this period that Soviet sources began emphasizing the military aspects of the Warsaw Pact. Increased military consolidation was apparent in the joint maneuvers of October 1961, and there is little reason to suppose that Rumania had perceptibly more enthusiasm for military integration than economic. No Rumanian troops took part in the first series of joint field exercises.[39]

Then in December, a month after the Soviet Party Congress, the 16th CMEA council plenum officially recommended the Principles of the International Socialist Division of Labor and a number of unspecified organizational changes.[40] These principles were then dramatically accepted by a meeting of the first secretaries of the Communist parties of member countries in June 1962. Between December 1961 and June 1962, there appeared more articles reiterating East European reluctance and Soviet reassurances. This time Rumania was not alone.[41] The Poles who, ironically, had proposed the June meeting, stressed that objective conditions were not yet mature for a single plan encompassing the entire socialist

---

[36] Fischer-Galati, *The New Rumania*, pp. 83–84.

[37] The draft program praised the socialist international division of labor. Communists everywhere were reminded that each socialist country could develop its productive potential to the fullest only through cooperation. A vigorous attack on nationalism followed, a clear sign that the Soviets expected less than unanimous support. "Program of the Communist Party of the Soviet Union," *Pravda*, July 30, 1961; *CDSP* 13, no. 28 (August 9, 1961): 7.

[38] Griffith, *Albania and the Sino-Soviet Rift*, p. 150.

[39] This may have been the result of logistic considerations, however. For these maneuvers were, in part, a response to the Berlin crisis of 1961 and primarily involved those countries vitally affected by the German question: the Soviet Union, Poland, East Germany, and Czechoslovakia. No Bulgarian forces participated, and Hungarian troops took part only in the second wave of maneuvers in November.

[40] *Pravda*, December 17, 1961.

[41] See I. P. Oleinik, "The Equalization of the Economic Development Level of the Socialist Countries," *Probleme Economice* 4 (April 1962) and RFE Rumanian Press Survey, no. 322, June 8, 1962. Oleinik is a pro-Rumanian Soviet economist frequently presenting

system.[42] A Hungarian article pointed to the difficulties of decision-making at the present time and underlined the unfairness of using economic effectiveness as the sole criterion for CMEA project allocation.[43] Meanwhile the Soviets alternated between soothing East European fears and attacking them as un-Communist.[44] Fadayev, the general secretary of CMEA, once again emphasized that the Council was not a supranational planning organ, that coordination did not, of necessity, mean a single plan, and that CMEA recommendations were subject to the approval of member governments.[45]

Although the June conference of Communist and Workers' Party representatives lasted only two days, its results completely dwarfed the brief session of the Warsaw Pact political consultative committee that followed.[46] CMEA's membership, organizational structure, and power expanded. Mongolia was accepted as a member, while the conference recognized the need to increase the council's powers and worked out "specific" but unspecified organizational measures to that end. The communiqué contained only one direct suggestion:

The participants in the conference decided that it would be advisable in the future to conduct regular consultations and exchanges of opinion among Party and state leaders on important economic questions.[47]

Bucharest's side of the question. Montias, *Economic Development in Communist Rumania*, p. 198.

[42] Henryk Rózański, "Budowa komunizmu w ZSRR a rozwó wspólnracy gospodarczej pánstw socjalistycnych," *Nowe drogi* 12, no. 151 (December 1961): 99. I am grateful to Natasha Cyker Lisman for checking this Polish source.

[43] Nor did Soviet reassurances appear to mitigate this worry, for the same point was made by Dr. S. Ausch, "A KGST orszàgok gazdàsàgi együttmüködés a felödès perspektivdi" (Economic Cooperation Between the Countries of CMEA and the Perspectives of Development), *Közgadasági Szemle* (Budapest 9 (September 1962): 1017–1030, 1026–1027; extensively quoted by Ágoston, *Le Marché Communiste*, pp. 143–144.

[44] See A. Alekseev, "Ukreplenie ekonomicheskoi moshchi mirovoi sistemy sotsializma," *Mirovaia ekonomika i mezhdunarodnye otnosheniia* 5 (1962); also Jiři Hendrych, "The XXII Congress of the CPSU and the Development of the Socialist World System," *World Marxist Review* 5, no. 1 (January 1962).

[45] Fadayev, N. "New Features in Socialist Economic Cooperation," *New Times* 4 (January 24, 1962): 3–6.

[46] The PCC terse declaration gave perfunctory support to the Soviet position in Soviet-American talks, "unanimously" expressed concern over the German situation and restated the willingness of Warsaw Treaty States to sign a separate peace treaty with East Germany if the West should continue to be recalcitrant. *Pravda*, June 10, 1962. The issue of when such a treaty would be signed was left hanging, a considerable weakening of the August 1961 declaration which had specified "by the end of the year."

[47] Communiqué, *Pravda*, June 9, 1962.

The Problems of Supranational Planning

Recommendations worked out at the party conference were passed on to CMEA for practical implementation. The 16th council plenum met on June 7. Mongolia was officially admitted, and the charter was changed to allow membership to non-European countries. Yet the change was not as far-reaching as its advertisement. Neither the communiqué of representatives of Communist and Workers' parties participating in CMEA or that of the council plenum mentioned the issue of supranational planning. The party representatives spoke of "further strengthening" economic co-operation between member countries with a view to the entry of the world socialist system into a new stage of development. They referred to "still greater rapprochement between the individual national economies," recognizing that the basic form of CMEA cooperation would continue to be the coordination of national economic plans. They did not suggest that such coordination take the form of a single plan. The brief communiqué of the 16th plenum was equally circumspect.[48] It cited the decision to strengthen the organization of CMEA, the creation of a new CMEA Executive Committee, and the new standing committees without comment.

A glance at the Soviet leaders' intrabloc travel immediately before and after the June meetings gives a clue to this silence. In May a Party delegation visited Bulgaria. Then in June Khrushchev headed another Soviet group touring Rumania and specifically explained the advantages of recent CMEA decisions. The Soviet leader emphasized two points: (1) that the international division of labor would not harm the industrial development of the socialist countries, and (2) that such cooperation would be advantageous to both big and small countries alike.[49] That these visits involved Bulgaria and Rumania, both agriculturally oriented countries with relatively low levels of industrialization and that Khrushchev felt it necessary to speak to the Rumanians in such a fashion underlined concrete fears. The Bulgarians and Rumanians alike had a legitimate worry lest the international division of labor keep them in a have-not category when it came to industrial development by overemphasizing their agricultural contributions to bloc production. Consequently, these countries stressed the mutual aid aspects of CMEA, heavy industry, and the need

[48] *Pravda*, June 10, 1962.
[49] *Izvestia*, June 26, 1962.

for raising the level of the less industrialized members so that all may enter the stage of Communist construction simultaneously. Even before the Rumanian statement officially delineating the Rumanian conception of relationships among CMEA member states in April 1964, these positions were stubbornly, if quietly, reiterated by Rumania in particular.[50]

East European reluctance notwithstanding, the Soviets moved ahead. In August, Khrushchev publicly speculated on "Vital Questions of Development of the World Socialist System" in an article that remains the most authoritative statement on the importance of the June 1962 meeting to date. The Soviet leader left no doubt that at least the Soviet concept of CMEA had reached a turning point.[51]

> The socialist countries are now at a stage when the conditions have ripened for raising their economic and political cooperation to a new and higher level. At this level special significance is acquired by coordinated national-economic plans, socialist international division of labor, and by coordination and specialization of production which will guarantee successful organic development of the socialist countries.
>
> The socialist world system is now at a stage when it is no longer possible correctly to chart its development by merely adding up the national economies. The task is to do everything to consolidate the national economy of each, broaden its relations and gradually advance towards that single worldwide organism embracing the system as a whole that Lenin's genius foresaw.
>
> With the emergence of socialism beyond the boundaries of a single country, its economic laws found much greater room for action and their operation became more and more complex.
>
> For example, the law of planned and proportional development operating on the scale of the system as a whole calls for planning and definite proportions both in each of the socialist countries taken separately and on the scale of the entire commonwealth.[52]

[50] John Michael Montias, *Economic Development in Communist Rumania*, 197–198. See also Kaser, *COMECON*, pp. 91 ff and 106–107.

[51] For a discussion of the role played by the Common Market in this changed Soviet perception see Marshall D. Shulman, "The Communist States and Western Integration," *International Organization* 17, no. 3 (Summer 1963): 649–662. Although it is undoubtedly correct that Moscow's reaction to the Common Market strongly influenced the Soviet attitude toward CMEA, Shulman's conclusion that "COMECON has become transformed into an instrument through which the states of Eastern Europe are being absorbed into the Soviet economic complex and are being moved in the direction of political merger. Integration in Western Europe is producing integration by induction in Eastern Europe. . . ." (p. 660) seems a bit sweeping.

[52] N. S. Khrushchev, "Nasushchnye voprosy razvitia mirovoi sotsialistichkeskoi systemy" (Vital Questions of Development of the World Socialist System), *Kommunist* 12 (August 1962). Quoted from *World Marxist Review* 5, no. 9 (September 1962).

Khrushchev reasoned that at the time of the organization of CMEA in 1949, conditions were not ripe for an extensive division of labor. Since some of the participating countries had little or no industry, multilateral cooperation among socialist states took place first in foreign trade and then in production. Now, however, all member countries possessed the necessary industrial base in order to move to a higher level of coordination. Previously, a lack of power hampered CMEA in taking advantage of the new situation. After admitting that according to the Council's charter CMEA did not have the right to revise the system of coordinating plans, Khrushchev referred to the decisions of the June meeting as enabling the work of the Council to "be organized in a new way." [53] He stated categorically:

> The socialist world system is not just a socio-political union of countries, it is a world economic system. It follows then that the coordination should be pursued not within the restricted limits of each socialist economy but on the scale of the socialist world economy, which means overcoming the exclusiveness inherited from the past. Our planned production will enable us to do this successfully. . . .
>
> We are now advancing towards a much higher level, a level from which it is possible to observe and to take account much more fully the interests of the entire socialist world economy.[54]

It is not surprising that when the East German leader, Walter Ulbricht, and the GDR planning chief, Bruno Leuschner, visited Rumania shortly after Khrushchev had made the Soviet position explicit and just before the September CMEA executive committee meeting, Leuschner's suggestion that the socialist division of labor must "pervade even more the bilateral relations between socialist states . . ." [55] was met with cold formality.

Interaction of Maneuvers within CMEA and the WTO, 1962–1963

The renewed Soviet drive toward economic integration was followed by an upgrading of Rumania within the Warsaw Pact. Rumanian, Soviet, and Bulgarian forces maneuvered in Southeastern Rumania in October. The Soviet press noted that these exercises "which were conducted under a plan of the joint armed forces" had been commanded by the Rumanian

[53] *Ibid.*, p. 7.
[54] *Ibid.*, pp. 6, 9.
[55] Quoted from *Neues Deutschland,* September 18, 1962, in J. F. Brown, "Rumania Steps Out of Line," *Survey* 49 (October 1963): 25.

defense minister, L. Salajan.[56] This was the first time that an East European had been publicly described as in charge of Warsaw Pact maneuvers. The only slight sign of strain appeared in differing analyses of the importance of the joint exercise. Bucharest publicized their military value.[57] Moscow, on the other hand, considered that the joint maneuvers demonstrated much more than mere combat readiness. Rather,

> Their most important role has been that they promoted the further deepening of cooperation between the fraternal armies and strengthened the comradeship in arms and cohesion of the soldiers of the socialist countries.[58]

From the Soviet view anything lacking along these lines most likely was in Rumania.

One month after the military maneuvers, Khrushchev renewed the Soviet initiative for a single planning organ. Speaking to a CPSU Central Committee Plenum, he said:

> In all probability representatives of CMEA member countries will in the near future have to meet at a top-level conference to make another step forward on the road of development of economic cooperation. We should take bolder steps toward the establishment of a *single planning body* for all countries.[59] [My italics.]

The 17th CMEA Session and the third meeting of the executive committee took place in Bucharest, December 14–20. Before leaving for Rumania, the head of the Polish delegation Jaroszewicz announced that the coming meeting would modify the statutes of the council so as to permit the creation of a central planning organ for the entire bloc.[60] Despite its unofficial source, his announcement certainly reflected Soviet and to some extent Polish hopes. However, although a lengthy CMEA session followed, these hopes went unfulfilled. There was no mention of a single planning organ either in the communiqué of the plenum or the executive committee.[61] Since CMEA decisions must be unanimous, the omission meant concrete resistance on the part of at least one of the smaller member states. Contrary to Fadeev's ritualistic assurance of the full unanimity of

[56] *Pravda,* October 19, 1962.
[57] Bucharest Domestic Service in Rumanian, 2100 GMT, October 18, 1962.
[58] *Krasnaya zvezda,* October 13, 1962.
[59] *Pravda,* November 20, 1962.
[60] *Le Monde,* December 15, 1962.
[61] *Ekonomicheskya gazeta,* December 29, 1962; p. 30; *CDSP* 14, no. 52 (January 1963): 36–37.

the countries participating in the Seventeenth Council Plenum and the Third Executive Committee meeting,[62] the CMEA charter was not changed formally to incorporate the executive committee into the council's organizational structure nor were the powers of the executive committee defined.

Thus, by the end of 1962, the issue of CMEA as a unified planning organ had been publicly endorsed by the Soviets and quietly sidetracked presumably in large part by Rumanian resistance. The consequences of this for CMEA and for the Warsaw Pact were diametrically opposite. Throughout 1963–1964 CMEA meetings increased in length and number, if not results. Warsaw Pact political activity continued at a minimal level in 1963 and became practically nonexistent in 1964.

The July 1963 Conference

Yet the terse *Pravda* announcement that a conference of the first secretaries and heads of government of Warsaw Treaty states[63] had supported Soviet-American test-ban negotiations signaled an important change both in Rumania's position within the Warsaw Pact and the price the Soviets were willing to pay for the appearance of unanimity. The brief Warsaw Pact decision not only supported the test-ban but claimed that the possibility of such an agreement was the result of "the peace-loving foreign policy course of the Soviet Union and *all* socialist countries." All socialist countries had to include China and Albania. It was a Rumanian formula that the Soviets had otherwise avoided.[64]

In short, by the summer of 1963 the Rumanians had continually opposed Soviet schemes for economic integration within CMEA, taken a decidedly neutral stance in the Sino-Soviet dispute,[65] and, indeed, persisted until a

[62] Radio Moscow, January 2, 1963.

[63] *Pravda*, July 27, 1963.

[64] Neither Khrushchev's interview (*Pravda*, July 27, 1963) nor the subsequent editorial (*ibid.*, July 29, 1963) praising the test-ban treaty referred to "all" socialist countries; whereas the Rumanian editorial celebrating the test ban (*Scînteia*, July 27, 1963; quoted in *Pravda*, July 29, 1963) did so—with a wording identical to that of the joint Warsaw Pact document. Simultaneously, other Rumanian announcements emphasized the unity of the "whole" international Communist movement (*Pravda*, August 1, 1963). For a good analysis, see C. Duevel, "Rumania's Position After the Moscow 'Summit' Meeting," Radio Liberty Daily Information Bulletin, 1568 (August 7, 1963) and Griffith, *The Sino-Soviet Rift*, p. 186.

[65] Although the Soviet and other East European press did not publish the Chinese "Proposal Concerning the General Line of the International Communist Movement," a three-column summary of it appeared in *Scînteia*. See also *The Times* (London), June 24, 1963.

formula expressing its neutrality was endorsed by an official Warsaw Pact document. These moves were carefully balanced with ostentatious support for Soviet East-West objectives (i.e., the test ban), emphasis on the importance of the decisions of the CPSU 20th, 21st, and 22nd congresses, and personal praise for Khrushchev.[66] Despite such conciliatory gestures, Albania had been almost buried in abuse for less public refusal to follow Moscow's line.

This time there was no overtly hostile Soviet reaction. Rather the Soviets went out of their way to demonstrate good feelings for the Rumanians. Not only did *Pravda* reprint Rumanian references to "the peace-loving foreign policy of all socialist countries" but two Rumanian messages appeared on the 60th anniversary of the second RSDRP Congress.[67] *Izvestia* featured Rumanian support of the test ban on page one with a red headline.[68] Equally important, from subsequent CMEA activity it appeared that Moscow had given in to the Rumanian insistence that bilateral agreement precede multilateral economic coordination.[69]

Sino-Soviet-Rumanian Polemics

By 1964, however, Soviet control in Eastern Europe had slipped enough so that the Russians could not be sure of even well-rewarded unanimity. There was no Warsaw Pact meeting in 1964. Since Khrushchev had called for "improving" the organizations of CMEA, of the Warsaw Pact in April, this probably was not the result of declining Soviet interest. Rather the leadership struggle going on in Moscow probably inhibited Soviet initiatives toward East Europe. Also by 1964, Rumanian ambition extended far beyond defensive parrying within CMEA or minor influence in the Warsaw Pact. The level of Rumanian maneuvering had shifted. Thus when Moscow wanted Rumanian support for a world Communist conference to condemn the Chinese, Bucharest stalled.

It is doubtful if the Soviet leaders were pleased to have Rumania assume the role of mediator in the Sino-Soviet dispute. But accept it they

---

[66] Rumanian Central Committee message, *Pravda*, August 1, 1963.

[67] *Pravda*, July 30 and August 1, 1963.

[68] *Izvestia*, August 4, 1963.

[69] A summary of an unpublished speech by Ulbricht to the 3rd SED CC Plenum issued by the West Berlin news agency *Informationsbureau West* (IWE), August 20, 1963, strongly indicates that the Soviets conceded this point at the CMEA summit meeting in July 1963; cited by Griffith, *The Sino-Soviet Rift*, p. 185. The timing is further confirmed by the interview with the Rumanian representative to CMEA, Alexandru Bîrladeanu, in *Pravda*, October 25, 1963.

did, at least temporarily. These events have been analyzed in detail else-where.[70] Briefly, on February 12, 1964, the Soviets sent a letter to all but pro-Chinese Communist parties strongly condemning Chinese polemics and factionalism and calling for an international conference. It told the recipients that a forthcoming CPSU central committee plenum would discuss the situation and publish its proceedings. Two days later, the Suslov Report violently attacked the Chinese and renewed Soviet pressure toward an international Communist conference. However, the Suslov Report was not published for two months, a delay largely due to the Rumanians. Bucharest had protested, appealing to both the Soviets and Chinese.[71] The Soviets waited. The Chinese agreed to a bilateral Sino-Rumanian meeting.

These talks came to nothing. Yet in Moscow on the way back from Peking the Rumanians persuaded the Soviets to continue to suspend pub-lic polemics if Bucharest could get a similar concession from the Chinese. The Rumanians then drafted an appeal to be sent to all parties by the Soviets, Chinese, and Rumanians. The Soviets agreed in general terms; the only Chinese reply seems to have been the eighth comment on the Soviet Open Letter, published March 31.

On April 4, Suslov's report and Khrushchev's speech advocating im-proving the organizational forms of both CMEA and the Warsaw Pact were published simultaneously. For the Rumanians this was a sinister juxtaposition. The Soviets wanted more than expelling the Chinese from the world Communist movement. They wanted to regain lost control through already existing institutions. Isolating the Chinese was only the first step. The remarkable "Statement on the Stand of the Rumanian Workers' Party Concerning the Problems of the International Communist and Working Class Movement" followed.

The Rumanian party statement contained only one direct reference to the Warsaw Pact:

We stand for the abolition of all military blocs, and as a transitional meas-ure in this direction, we declare ourselves in favor of the conclusion of a

[70] Griffith, *Sino-Soviet Relations 1964–1965* (Cambridge, Mass.; The MIT Press, 1967), and Fischer-Galati, *The New Rumania*.

[71] This is the Rumanian version in "Statement on the Stand of the Rumanian Workers' Party Concerning the Problems of the International Communist Movement," complete text in Griffith, *ibid.*, pp. 269–296.

non-aggression pact between the Warsaw Treaty Organization and the North Atlantic Treaty Organization.[72]

It was a standard, joint formulation in Warsaw Pact documents. However, repeated at the time, it could hardly be interpreted as support for Khrushchev's suggestion to "improve" the organizational form of the alliance. Nor did Bucharest hesitate to draw pointed historical analogies on the danger of misusing Communist organizations.

> As far back as the last stage of existence of the Comintern, it had become obvious that the solution of the problems of the working class movement, in one country or another, by an international center was no longer adequate at that stage of development of the world Communist and working class movement. Wrong methods, interference in the domestic affairs of Communist parties went as far as the removal and replacement of leading party cadres and even of entire Central Committees, as far as the imposing from without of leaders, the suppression of distinguished leading cadres of various parties, as far as the censure and even dissolving of Communist parties. . . .
>
> The practices engendered by the cult of the individual within the Comintern also found a reflection in the Information Bureau. After the emergence of the world socialist system those practices were also extended to interstate relations, which further aggravated their consequencs. In 1948 the Communist Party of Yugoslavia was condemned and excluded from the Information Bureau, and Yugoslavia—a country that builds socialism was expelled from the community of socialist states. . . .[73]

Only the parallel of Albania's exclusion from the Warsaw Pact and CMEA remained unstated. The one public Soviet response was a 50-word announcement that a plenum of the Rumanian Central Committee had discussed recent Rumanian negotiations in China, Korea, and the USSR.[74] Then silence. In early May *Pravda* reprinted pro-Soviet statements and resolutions of the French, Indian, Portuguese, Finnish, and Canadian parties, but not the Rumanian Statement. Nor was there any general reporting of Rumanian activities in the Soviet press until May 28

[72] *Ibid.*, p. 11. By implication the principles that Rumania insisted governed socialist cooperation within CMEA extended to the Warsaw Treaty Organization as well: full equality, sovereignty, mutual advantage, comradely assistance, and noninterference in internal affairs. Simultaneously the statement flatly rejected the idea of a single planning body for CMEA members and proposed that ways should be found for *all* (implying China and Albania) socialist countries to participate in the Council.

[73] *Ibid.*, pp. 292–293.

[74] *Pravda*, April 28, 1964.

when a terse announcement appeared of discussions between Khrushchev and a Rumanian delegation headed by Stoica.

Actually intensifying Soviet polemics with Peking appeared to be aimed at the Rumanians as well. *Kommunist* accused the Chinese of deliberately curtailing economic ties with CMEA countries, attempting to block economic cooperation, undermining the international socialist division of labor, and preaching the "subversive" theory of "relying upon one's own efforts.[75] These charges could easily apply to Bucharest. As for the Comintern, Moscow approvingly referred to that organization "with its statutes that were binding on all parties" as able to unite Communists of all countries by relying on ideological unity.[76]

1964: Lack of Progress in "Perfecting" the WTO

With the Rumanian delegation's visit to Moscow in late May, Soviet-Rumanian relations visibly improved. After discussions with Khrushchev, the Rumanians toured numerous industrial enterprises and the Soviet text even featured stories on Rumanian industrialization.[77] During their stay the *Izvestia* editorial series on relations among socialist countries put forth a modified Soviet position:

> What matters is that it is necessary to defend in a complex and contradictory situation the principles worked out by the joint efforts of the fraternal parties on the mutual relations of the socialist countries, and to find ways and means for overcoming the divergencies and contradictions which are emerging. What matters here is the reestablishment of the unity and cohesion of the fraternal parties and countries.[78]

The esoteric nature of this critique was a direct reflection of the seriousness of the innerparty struggle going on in Moscow. Had the Rumanian statement appeared at any other time, Soviet displeasure might well have been sudden and direct. Yet even if the timing had been less propitious, Khrushchev's lack of success in containing Tirana could have had a marginally inhibiting effect. Open polemics with the Albanians, even with the support of large portions of the international movement, had

---

[75] *Pravda*, May 6–7, 1964. "Proletarian Internationalism is the Banner of the Working People of All Countries and Continents," *Kommunist* 7 (May 1964), translated *JPRS: 25,043* (June 11, 1964): 22–23.

[76] "Marxism-Leninism is the International Doctrine of Communists of all Countries," *Pravda*, May 10, 1964; *CDSP* 16, no. 19 (June 3, 1964), p. 3.

[77] *Izvestia*, June 8, 1964.

[78] *Ibid.*, May 31, 1964.

neither brought down the Hoxha regime nor mitigated the Soviet-Albanian dispute. Even if Moscow had been referring only to the Chinese, this was a far cry from the "resolute" rebuff called for by Suslov.

Consultations among Warsaw Pact countries were praised (the only such consultations in process were the Soviet-Rumanian talks). The mutual advantage aspects of CMEA cooperation were stressed:

> The economic links among the socialist countries actively contribute to the process of expanding socialist production in each country, and they further the industrialization of economically underdeveloped socialist countries by raising them to the level of the industrial advanced states. Participation in the work of CMEA is voluntary.

This was the Rumanian interpretation, a retreat from Soviet emphasis on specialization and integration. Most important in terms of this study, the goal of improving the organizational forms of CMEA and the Warsaw Pact had been scaled down.

> The practice of the world socialist system has already worked out quite adequate forms for relations and coordinating actions among the socialist countries. These forms consist in bilateral and multilateral negotiations and consultations, in permanently functioning organs such as CMEA and the Warsaw Pact. Yet life does not stand still. As each socialist country becomes stronger the relations among them become richer and more complex. Obviously, the question of intensifying mutual coordination and bringing the policy of the socialist countries into agreement, providing more efficient and more regular forms of jointly solving common problems, is topical. A *periodic conference of the ministers of the socialist countries should,* perhaps, be set up, and coordination meetings of specialists on this or that question should be held more often. . . .
>
> However, whatever the forms of coordinating the policy and exchanging opinions among socialist countries, one thing is clear. The main role in this matter is played not so much by the form as by the nature, tone, and method of exchanging opinions.[79] [Italics mine.]

In short, pressure to tighten existing military and economic organizations so as to eliminate diversity among Soviet supporters was off. So was the second Soviet attempt to use a world Communist conference to expel the Chinese.

From the point of view of Soviet domestic developments, the difference in tone between the *Izvestia* editorials and Khrushchev's statement of April 4 was reminiscent of the sudden switches in early Soviet interpreta-

[79] *Izvestia,* June 6, 1964.

tions of the Warsaw Pact, and one might suspect also a sign of the new leadership struggle. For at the same time, Suslov had effusively praised Khrushchev, warning the Chinese that the Soviet Central Committee was united and monolithic as never before.

> Comrade N. S. Khrushchev, with his inexhaustible energy, his truly Bolshevist ardor and adherence to principle, is the recognized leader of our party and people. He expresses the most cherished thoughts and aspirations of the Soviet people. The Leninist line pursued by our party cannot be divorced from the Central Committee, from Nikita Sergeyevich Krushchev.[80]

Yet Khrushchev was headed on a collision course with China in the international Communist movement. He was completely committed to organizationally isolating Peking, to a world Communist conference. Twice now he had tried and failed. Even before retreat from the conference plan in the summer of 1964, there must have been factions within the Soviet leadership strongly opposed to his method of trying to bring the Chinese into line as well as to the list of incompetent domestic policies used to justify his fall. Moreover, expelling the Yugoslavs had not gotten rid of them. Isolating the Albanians had not made them less recalcitrant.

The New Collective Leadership: Brezhnev and Kosygin

Khrushchev fell on October 16, 1964. On the same day, Moscow signed an economic agreement promising to provide Rumania with full sets of power equipment and technical assistance for the construction of thermal power plants with a total capacity of 1,000,000 kw during 1965–1967.[81] Indeed, the new government headed by Brezhnev and Kosygin rapidly began to mend fences in Bucharest. Khrushchev was accused of contributing to deterioration of Soviet-Rumanian relations by opposing Rumanian industrialization, applying economic pressure, and attempting to force his agricultural theories on Gheorghiu-Dej.[82] On October 25, *Pravda* printed an article by the Rumanian Defense Minister, Salajan, that amounted to a detailed account of the contributions of the Rumanian Communist Party and the Rumanian army to liberation of Rumania.

---

[80] Suslov's Report, in Griffith, *Sino-Soviet Relations,* p. 265. Ironically, the official announcement of his fall said that he resigned for reasons of age and ill health. *Pravda,* October 16, 1964.

[81] *Pravda,* October 18, 1964.

[82] See analysis of Rumanian reaction from Bucharest, *The Times* (London), November 2, 1964.

As he put it, "inspired by enthusiastic patriotism, the Rumanian army bravely struggled, together with the glorious Soviet army. . . ." [83] Despite token references to fraternal socialist armies and the Warsaw Pact, throughout the Soviet contribution came second.

Although by blaming Khrushchev, the new Soviet leaders would seem to have removed all obstacles to close relations with the Rumanians, Bucharest's reserve did not perceptibly lessen. Other than publishing the Soviet official version, there was no Rumanian response to the fall of Khrushchev; a matter which Rumania treated as a strictly Soviet affair. Gheorghiu-Dej did not go to Moscow for the October revolution celebrations,[84] and the communiqué on Soviet discussions with the Rumanian delegation that did attend said only that the talks were held in a "friendly and cordial atmosphere." [85] There was no sign that Rumania agreed with Brezhnev that "the need for a new international conference of fraternal parties has obviously matured." [86]

Nonetheless, Soviet concessions continued in the period before the January 1965 meeting of the Warsaw Pact political consultative committee. In December, a long article elaborated the "profound dialectical interrelationship" between bilateral and multilateral cooperation within CMEA.[87] Then in early January a Soviet-Rumanian protocol on mutual deliveries of goods for 1965 was signed.[88]

The first public sign that the new Soviet leaders intended to revive the political aspect of the Warsaw Pact had come in Kosygin's December speech to the Supreme Soviet. At that time, the Soviet leader tied the need for Warsaw Pact consultations directly to a common socialist response to military threat in Europe:

> The Soviet Union, like the other socialist countries, is waging and will continue to wage a resolute struggle against the creation of the NATO multilateral nuclear force. Taking into account the situation that has

---

[83] *Pravda*, October 25, 1964.

[84] Ion Gheorghe Maurer headed the Rumanian delegation, *Pravda*, November 7, 1964.

[85] *Ibid.*, November 13, 1964; the "complete identity of views" present in recent Soviet meetings with the Poles (*Pravda*, October 26, 1964) and the East Germans (*Pravda*, November 11, 1964) was lacking.

[86] Brezhnev's speech on the anniversary of the revolution, *Pravda*, November 7, 1964.

[87] N. Piichkin, "Important Factor in Development of Cooperation," *Vneshnyaya torgovlya* 12 (December 1964); *CDSP* 16, no. 52 (January 20, 1965): 14–15.

[88] *Pravda*, January 9, 1964. Unlike the Soviet-Polish protocol, the Rumanians did not claim that the preceding negotiations contributed to "a further developing and deepening of the international socialist division of labor."

evolved, the Soviet government shares the opinion that it would be expedient to hold consultations among the Warsaw-Treaty member-states, which have a vital interest in ensuring security in Europe.[89]

With whom the Soviet Union shared that opinion was not clear. Although the joint Soviet-Czechoslovak communiqué had sharply condemned West German participation in a multilateral nuclear force and agreed to take steps "in the spirit of the December 12, 1943 treaty and the Warsaw Treaty of May 14, 1955" to protect European security, it did not call for Warsaw Pact consultations.[90] Nor was there any reference to such consultations in connection with the earlier Soviet-East German and Soviet-Rumanian discussions.

January 1965 PCC Meeting

The subsequent political consultative committee meeting showed a marked change in Moscow's perception of the role of the Warsaw Pact in Soviet-East European relations. Albania was invited,[91] and from the extensive Soviet press coverage, it appeared that the Warsaw Pact had jumped several rungs on Moscow's hierarchy of importance. Roughly 18 column-inches were needed to simply list the articles and editorials devoted to the PCC meeting in the *Current Digest of the Soviet Press;* a sharp contrast to the lack of attention paid the July 1963 session.

As for the Rumanians, despite somewhat slighting comments about the Warsaw Pact coming from Bucharest,[92] Dej attended the Warsaw

[89] *Pravda,* December 10, 1964; quoted from *CDSP* 16, no. 49 (December 30, 1964): 12.

[90] *Pravda,* December 5, 1964.

[91] Tirana violently rejected the invitation. "Letter from Albanian Government to the Participants of the 19 January Warsaw Pact Meeting," *Zëri i popullit,* February 2, 1965. In addition to insisting that the Warsaw Treaty Organization publicly condemn the Soviets for mistreating Albania, this letter maintained that according to Warsaw Pact rules and regulations the Albanians could not simply be informed of such a meeting. Rather the current Warsaw Pact chairman should have consulted Tirana beforehand regarding the agenda, date, place, and rank of representatives to attend. There was no public response either from the Soviets or the PCC. Also according to the Albanian press, the committee simply noted that Albania refused to participate in Warsaw Pact proceedings with the observation that "in these circumstances the matter of Albania's further participation in Warsaw Pact proceedings depends on the decision of the Albanian government." *Zëri i popullit,* February 2, 1965.

[92] In interviews with Western correspondents in November and December 1964 Rumanian officials again said bluntly "our policy is directed against military pacts" (David Binder, *The New York Times,* November 20, 1964) and spoke of "the need for new ways" of reaching decisions inside the Warsaw Pact. Max Frankel, *The New York Times,* December 19, 1964. In 1964 Soviet-Rumanian differences had begun to affect Rumania's military participation in the Warsaw Pact. Although Rumanian troops did take part in the

meeting. That the "complete unity of views" the Soviets claimed for the meeting existed is doubtful.[93] Its concluding communiqué referred only to "complete unity and solidarity in the face of the imperialist threat," a much more issue-oriented formula.[94]

The increased importance of the Warsaw Pact from the Soviet point of view was not limited to its defensive role in Europe. Moscow was equally, if not more concerned with its implications for relations among socialist countries. Although the joint communiqué made only one (and certainly not a Soviet inspired) reference to other socialist countries, this time Soviet commentary focused heavily on the socialist nature of the Warsaw Pact.

> . . . but the meetings in Warsaw and Prague (19th Session of CMEA) will serve a single end—to ensure the successful building of a new society in the socialist countries and to implement by every means the socialist precept: Everything for man, everything in the name of man.
>
> Both these meetings show the great and complicated tasks the socialist countries must solve. But they demonstrate something else: Firm, indestructible unity, fraternal solidarity, and extensive cooperation and mutual aid are multiplying the forces of the socialist countries. . . . The work of the committee, which proceeded in an atmosphere of complete mutual understanding and fraternal friendship, demonstrated the complete emptiness of the imperialists' hopes of disuniting the socialist countries. There was a complete unity of views on all questions discussed in Warsaw.[95]

Subsequently, the presidium of the CPSU central committee and the USSR council of ministers fully approved the activities of the Soviet delegation to the Warsaw meeting.[96] This decidedly un-Soviet-like move both added to the stature of the Warsaw Pact and reflected the current Soviet emphasis on strictly collective leadership.

---

fall maneuvers of the Joint Command, *Pravda*, September 21, 1964, Bucharest was the only pact member to reduce compulsory military service from 24 to 16 months. David Binder, *The New York Times*, June 5, 1965.

[93] *Izvestia*, January 22, 1965. This is particularly likely in that neither of the two major Soviet editorials in *Izvestia*, January 23 and 31, 1965 included the joint communiqué's reference to "all" socialist countries resolutely condemning US aggression in Cuba and Vietnam. Since it was included in the Rumanian editorial in *Scînteia*, January 22, 1965, this was probably a compromise to satisfy Dej.

[94] *Pravda*, January 22, 1965. For a general account of the meeting and its implications see Eugene Hinterhoff, "Die Potentiale des Warschauer Paktes," *Aussenpolitik* 8 (August 1965): 535–547.

[95] *Izvestia*, January 31, 1965, quoted from *CDSP* 17, no. 5 (February 24, 1965): 3.

[96] *Pravda*, February 6, 1965.

Rising Soviet Pressure

Part of Soviet enthusiastic accounts of the Warsaw Pact gathering as a reflection of socialist unity may have been wish projections for the "consultative" Communist party meeting scheduled for March 1965 in Moscow. Despite a favorable Soviet-Rumanian economic agreement for 1966–1970,[97] the Rumanians refused to come to the March meeting.[98] Almost immediately, Soviet references to the Warsaw Pact shifted back to its defensive nature.

Moscow's concern with the military aspects of the Warsaw Pact became particularly marked during the May celebrations of the Warsaw Treaty's 10th anniversary. There was a meeting of the joint command, and *Pravda* printed a long article by the Commander-in-Chief of the Joint Armed Forces, Soviet Marshal Grechko, detailing military cooperation among the member states.[99] Grechko and Kosygin,[100] speaking at a military parade in East Germany, returned to emphasizing the socialist nature of Warsaw Pact states. The joint Soviet-Hungarian communiqué recommended "strengthening the defensive capacity of the socialist countries and development of cooperation within the Warsaw Treaty Organization."[101] As yet there was no suggestion from the new Soviet leaders for "improving the organizational form" of the Warsaw Pact. That was still to come.

Meanwhile although Gheorghiu-Dej's death made no substantial change in Rumanian policies, the Soviets were particularly conciliatory toward the new Rumanian leaders throughout the spring and summer of 1965. Grechko conferred first with Maurer and then Ceauşescu, probably on the issue of Rumania's role in Soviet plans to increase the defense capacity of the Warsaw Pact joint command. Brezhnev, speaking to the Rumanian Party Congress in July, praised Rumanian industrialization, refrained from polemicizing with the Chinese (who were also present)

---

[97] *Pravda*, February 18, 1965; for analysis see Fischer-Galati, *The New Rumania*, pp. 111–112.

[98] See Griffith, *Sino-Soviet Relations 1964–1965*, p. 83.

[99] *Pravda*, May 19, 1965 and May 13, 1965; a similar article by the Chief of Staff of the Joint Armed Forces, Batov, appeared in *Izvestia*, May 14, 1965.

[100] *Pravda*, May 8, 1965. At this time, Grechko referred only to "the European socialist states" as having signed the Warsaw Treaty. Albania had totally disappeared from the Soviet version of Warsaw Pact history. The Rumanians however continued to pointedly list the signatories. *Scînteia*, May 14, 1965.

[101] *Ibid.*, May 30, 1965.

and pledged that the Soviets would "spare no effort to strengthen and develop fraternal relations with all the countries of socialism." [102]

The result was the first top-level Rumanian Party government delegation visit to Moscow since 1961. Brezhnev did not refer publicly to the Warsaw Pact during the Rumanians' stay. But that the question had come up was evident, for the concluding Soviet-Rumanian communiqué recommended "continued strengthening of the might and defense potential of the Warsaw Pact member states and of all socialist countries." [103]

Within a matter of days, however, Brezhnev made clear that the Soviets had much more in mind than simply streamlining the joint command. He returned to Khrushchev's phrase of April 1964.

> The problem of defense, of shielding the vital political and economic interests of the countries of socialism from the intrigues of the imperialist aggressors, demands the further strengthening of their unity. Present conditions place on the agenda the task of further perfecting the Warsaw Treaty Organization, that mighty instrument for defense of the socialist world. . . .[104]

East European Reaction

Brezhnev made his suggestion at a Soviet-Czechoslovak rally celebrating consultations with a Czechoslovak Party government delegation in Moscow. Even Novotný was less than enthusiastic. His response—". . . we fully realize the significance of strengthening our defense potential and our armed forces, in accordance with our obligations as a member of the Warsaw Treaty Organization." [105]—was really not the same thing. Nor was the Soviet preference included in the joint communiqué that only noted the contribution of the Warsaw Pact to the stability of Czechoslovak borders.[106]

Other members of the Warsaw Pact simply ignored Brezhnev's statement. The subsequent joint Rumanian-Bulgarian communiqué[107] avoided

---

[102] *Pravda*, July 21, 1965.

[103] *Pravda*, September 11, 1965. This formulation was similar to Ceauşescu's statement that the Rumanians "along with the Warsaw Pact signatories and all socialist countries" were strengthening their country's defense potential.

[104] Brezhnev's speech to the Soviet-Czechoslovak Friendship Rally, *Pravda*, September 16, 1965.

[105] Novotný's speech, *Pravda*, September 16, 1965.

[106] Joint Soviet-Czechoslovak Communiqué, *ibid.*

[107] Joint Rumanian-Bulgarian Communiqué, Bucharest Domestic Service in Rumanian, 0500 GMT (September 19, 1965).

any mention of the Warsaw Pact. The East Germans, usually hard-line Soviet supporters, agreed only that should NATO give the West Germans nuclear weapons, the Warsaw Pact states would "be forced to introduce the necessary protective measures to secure their security." [108]

Temporarily the Soviets retreated. Then at the CPSU 23rd Congress in March 1966 Brezhnev said categorically:

> In the field of military cooperation, in the face of the intensified aggressive actions of the imperialist forces headed by the United States of America, the process of further strengthening our connections with the socialist countries and the process of further strengthening and *improving the mechanism of the Warsaw Pact* have continued. The Warsaw Pact is a dependable shield of the achievements of the peoples of the countries of socialism. The armies of the member countries participating in this pact are armed with the most modern weapons. On the military training field, in the air, and on the sea, joint action of the armies and other services of the allied states is elaborated and the power of the modern military equipment is tested. The militant fraternity of the armed forces is strengthening the Warsaw Pact member countries. If it becomes necessary, *the whole closely knit family of members of this pact will put forward a formidable force in defense of the socialist system* and for the defense of the free life of our peoples, and will strike a shattering blow at any aggressor.[109] [Italics mine.]

Not one of the East European members of the Warsaw Pact speaking at the Congress echoed Brezhnev's view.[110]

May 1966: The Rumanian Red-Herring

This time the Rumanians struck back. In his speech on the 45th anniversary of the Rumanian Communist Party, Ceaușescu said:

> . . . military blocs and the existence of military bases and of troops on the territory of other states is one of the barriers in the path of collaboration among the peoples. The existence of blocs, as well as the sending of troops to other countries is an anachronism inconsistent with the independence and national sovereignty of peoples and normal relations among states. Increasingly wide circles of public opinion and an increasing num-

---

[108] GDR-USSR communiqué, *Neues Deutschland,* September 28, 1965.

[109] *Pravda,* March 29, 1966.

[110] Ceaușescu, Gomułka, Zhivkov, and Ulbricht did not mention the Warsaw Pact. Kádár supported "enhancing the effectiveness" of international organizations such as CMEA and the Warsaw Pact. Budapest MTI Domestic Service in Hungarian 1430 GMT, March 31, 1966.

ber of states show the tendency—which is recently gaining more and more ground—to liquidate military blocks. . . .[111]

Bucharest had called for liquidating military blocs before,[112] but never in such a blatantly anti-Soviet context as Ceauşescu's speech. The Secretary-General went into great detail on the negative aspects of the Comintern during 1938–1940, a period when it was well-known that the Communist International was simply the shadow of Soviet policy. He attacked "a number of theoreticians" for trying to foster the belief that nations are an outdated social category. Perhaps most uncomfortable from Moscow's point of view, he bluntly raised the issue of Rumanian territory under foreign control.

> As is known, the Dictate of Vienna was imposed on Rumania in August 1940; under this, the northern part of Transylvania was stolen and delivered to Fascist Hungary. . . .
> The Rumanian land—Moldavia, Transylvania—has been under foreign domination for many centuries. This entire period is characterized by the plunder of the country's riches, by the ruin of the economy, and the destruction of innumerable goods, material and spiritual. Nonetheless, foreign domination did not succeed in smothering the people's desire for freedom and in changing its strong wish for unity.[113]

A flurry of Western speculation (apparently heightened by contradictory news leaks from Rumanian diplomats) began on the issue of Rumanian alienation within the Warsaw Pact.[114]

There was no public Soviet response. Moscow proceeded to join in celebrating the Rumanian Communist Party's 45th anniversary as if nothing had happened.[115] *Pravda* printed a carefully cut version of Ceauşescu's

---

[111] *Scînteia*, May 8, 1966.

[112] For example, see *The Rumanian Party Statement of April 1964;* Gheorghiu-Dej's speech on the 20th anniversary of Rumanian liberation, *Scînteia*, August 23, 1964; Gheorghiu-Dej's election speech, *Scînteia*, March 6, 1965; and Ceauşescu's report to the ninth Rumanian Communist Party Congress, *Scînteia*, July 21, 1965.

[113] Ceauşescu's speech, quoted from excerpts in *The New York Times*, May 14, 1966.

[114] See particularly the reporting of Henry Kamm from Bucharest and Peter Grose's dispatches from Moscow, *The New York Times*, May 15, 17, 18, and 22, 1966. Bucharest was supposed to have circulated a note to other Warsaw Pact forces insisting on a larger voice for individual members in planning the Pact's strategy, i.e., that command of the joint armed forces rotate among member states.

[115] In addition to official congratulations from the CPSU Central Committee to its Rumanian counterpart, the Soviet press featured a long article by Maurer *Izvestia*, May 8, 1966; talks between a Rumanian delegation and the USSR Minister of Petroleum *Pravda*,

speech praising Rumanian industrialization and Soviet-Rumanian friendship. It did not include the Rumanian leader's criticism of the Comintern, the question of Rumanian territory under foreign domination, or any reference to the life span of the nation in the period of building socialism.[116] However immediately Brezhnev flew to Bucharest on an unofficial visit. The Soviet leader stayed three days exchanging opinions with Ceauşescu on "the further development" of Soviet-Rumanian cooperation and "other questions of mutual interest." [117]

Undoubtedly, Rumania's role in the Warsaw Pact was one of those questions. On May 14, *Pravda* had repeated the Soviet claim that "the mechanism of the Warsaw Pact organization is constantly improving and growing stronger." As for liquidation of military blocs:

> As long as the threat posed by the imperialist aggressors continues to exist, the fraternal armies of the states participating in the Warsaw Pact will join ranks still more closely and the cooperation of the socialist countries in the military sphere will continue to strengthen.[118]

Ceauşescu retorted that while the danger of imperialism existed socialist countries must work to strengthen the defensive capacity of our countries and also the unity of the working class and all anti-imperialist forces.[119] He ignored the question of perfecting the mechanism of the Warsaw Pact. Yet tacitly Soviet-Rumanian differences within the alliance were set aside. The Rumanian foreign ministry officially denied Western reports that Rumania had sent notes to other pact members favoring drastic revision of the Warsaw Treaty Organization,[120] and preparations began for the July political consultative committee meeting in Bucharest.

May 11, 1966; a party held in honor of the Rumanian anniversary in a Moscow plant, *Pravda*, May 12, 1966; and miscellaneous articles on socialist construction in Rumania.

[116] *Pravda*, May 8, 1966. Ceauşescu had specified: "History shows, however, that the appearance of the nation as a form of human community and the development of the national life of the peoples is a social process governed by law, a necessary and obligatory stage in the evolution of all peoples. . .

There is no doubt that the nation will continue for a long time to come to be the basis for our society's development throughout the entire period of building Socialism and Communism." Quoted from *The New York Times*, May 14, 1966.

[117] *Pravda*, May 14, 1966.

[118] *Pravda*, May 14, 1966; quoted from *CDSP* 18, no. 19 (June 1, 1966): 25. At the same time a Soviet spokesman, Novikov, spoke of "strengthening and perfecting the mechanism of the Warsaw Pact." *Izvestia*, May 15, 1966.

[119] *Pravda*, May 22, 1966.

[120] *The Times* (London), May 19, 1966.

July 1966: The Bucharest Meeting

There is good reason to think that these preparations were stormy. What was expected to be a three-day June meeting of Warsaw Pact Foreign Ministers in Moscow dragged on for 12 days. The Foreign Ministers meeting ended on June 18, two days after Chou En-lai arrived in Bucharest. Chou was met with a 21-gun salute and Maurer's welcoming speech praised "unshakable Sino-Rumanian friendship." [121] Despite the signs of strain evident during the Chinese leader's visit, its timing underlined Bucharest's independent foreign policy on the eve of joint Warsaw Pact discussions.

At the July meeting, Rumanian determination to influence the nature of the Warsaw Pact was more open than ever before. What began as a joint session turned into a four-hour exchange between Brezhnev, Kosygin, and Ceauşescu.[122] Then on the second day of the conference, Radio Moscow warned against endangering the interests of the socialist community by nationalism and chauvinism,[123] a scarcely concealed slap at Rumanian territorial complaints. The meeting ended without any mention of Soviet plans for "perfecting" the Warsaw Pact. At least temporarily, Bucharest had won. However, the Rumanians paid a price for their refusal to accept greater centralization of the pact's command structure. After the joint declaration's somewhat polemical support for the "inviolability" of the existing East German, Polish, and Czechoslovak borders came one crucial sentence: "The Warsaw Treaty member-states declare that for their part they have no territorial claims with respect to any state in Europe." [124]

Ceauşescu had traded his territorial irridenta (at least temporarily) for organizational influence within the coalition, and there is at least an interesting possibility that the Rumanian leader had raised the issue as a throw-away card in the first place.

Most important, the May 1966 maneuvering showed a distinct change

[121] *Scinteia*, June 17, 1966. *Pravda* tersely announced the Chinese delegations' departure. *Pravda*, June 25, 1966.

[122] See Joseph Lelyveld's dispatch from Bucharest, *The New York Times*, July 4, 1966.

[123] For an excellent analysis see Christian Duevel, "Radio Moscow Issues Warning to Rumania," *RL Daily Information Bulletin* 2280 (July 8, 1966).

[124] "Declaration on Strengthening Peace and Security in Europe," *Pravda*, July 9, 1966, and Document 3, p. 209.

in Moscow's method of dealing with a direct challenge to Soviet authority from one of the smaller members of the Warsaw Pact. An extended meeting of the Foreign Ministers of Warsaw Treaty states followed bilateral Soviet-Rumanian consultations. Genuine discussion and compromise seem to have taken place at the July Bucharest political consultative committee meeting, which the Soviets hailed as demonstrating the possibilities for "deepening and reinforcing" unity and collaboration among socialist countries.[125] The Soviets did not insist on formal strengthening of the WTO; Bucharest obviously retreated from the territorial demands implicit in Ceaușescu's May 7 speech.

Even after Bucharest had effectively blocked any political "perfecting" of the Warsaw Treaty Organization, Soviet leaders continued to cite foreign policy coordination among Warsaw Pact member states to demonstrate "that the unity and cohesion of the socialist countries is not an abstract idea." [126]

Recognition of West Germany

Moreover, Soviet reaction to Rumanian recognition of West Germany in February 1967 was to contain the issue within the Warsaw Treaty Organization. Moscow did not attack Rumania directly. Rather Soviet commentary limited itself to implying that conditions were not ready for such recognition; that the joint conclusions "regarding the policy of West German ruling circles contained in Warsaw Pact documents of January 1965 and July 1966 retained their significance." [127]

Developments surrounding the February 1967 meeting of the WTO foreign ministers indicate that participation in the Warsaw Pact was, indeed, more "vital" than Moscow might have wished. That meeting's communiqué was as brief as it was uninformative. The participants had exchanged opinions relating to questions of European security. In fact they appeared to have argued bitterly over Rumanian diplomatic recognition of West Germany. Rumania was the only member state represented by a deputy foreign minister, a sure sign of Bucharest's displeasure. Seen

[125] V. Smolyansky, "Bucharest Conference of the Political Consultative Committee of States Participating in the Warsaw Pact," *Sovetskaya Rossiya* September 1, 1966; *JPRS* 37:755. For a detailed non-Communist analysis, see Gerhard Wettig, "Die europaische Sicherheit in der Politik des Ostblocks 1966," *Osteuropa* 17, nos. 2–3 (February–March 1967): 94–114.
[126] Kosygin October 13 speech in Sverdlovsk, *Pravda,* October 14, 1966.
[127] *Pravda,* February 8, 1967.

in the light of Ulbricht's statement that the Warsaw Pact had supported GDR proposals of which the crucial issue was "recognition of the GDR frontier and all existing European frontiers" [128] and Gomułka's blunt evaluation that "establishment of diplomatic relations between the German Federal Republic and the socialist states will not influence the improvement of the climate in Europe even the slightest unless the West German Government radically revises its stand toward fundamental problems concerning the vital interests of socialist states," [129] it is doubtful if "friendly" was an accurate description.

Prior to the meeting, the East German newspaper *Neues Deutschland* criticized both Bucharest's policy and the Rumanian foreign minister Corneliu Manescu's conduct in Bonn as "regrettable." [130] The Rumanians responded with news leaks to the effect that they would not go to Berlin.[131] The meeting place was quickly shifted to Warsaw. Subsequent Soviet comment on the meeting, on the one hand, insisted that the Warsaw conference exemplified the desire of socialist countries for concerted foreign policy action, while on the other, warned that only through solidarity and unity of action could there be any hope of exerting influence on the situation in Europe.[132]

Spring and Summer 1967

The desired unity of action appeared highly unlikely if it required integrating Rumanian foreign policy with that of other Warsaw Pact members. The Rumanians did not attend the Karlový Vary Conference of European Communist Parties in April.[133] At the time of the mid-East crisis Ceaușescu headed a delegation to the Moscow Conference of Socialist Countries only to leave without signing the joint statement.[134] There

[128] Speech to Berlin SED party aktiv, East Berlin ADN Domestic Service in German, 1452 GMT, February 15, 1967.

[129] Warsaw Domestic Service in Polish, 1910 GMT, February 8, 1967.

[130] *Neues Deutschland,* February 3, 1967.

[131] According to David Binder, a Rumanian diplomat in Berlin had "indicated" that his government refused to go to Berlin in view of GDR personal criticism of Manescu. *The New York Times,* February 7, 1967.

[132] *Pravda,* February 24, 1967.

[133] See *Pravda,* April 25, 27, 1967; *CDSP* 19, no. 17 (May 17, 1967): 5–13.

[134] *Pravda,* June 10, 1967. Moscow Radio announced Rumanian attendance on June 9 (Moscow Domestic Service in Russian 2130 GMT 9 June 1967) but in all press reports it was as if Rumania did not exist. Bucharest Domestic Service announced the return of the Rumanian delegation from Moscow, noting that they had been seen off by Brezhnev, Kosygin, and other Soviet dignitaries (Bucharest Domestic Service in Rumanian 1100 GMT 10 June 1967).

is speculation that the Rumanians were not invited to participate in the July Budapest meeting on implementation of aid to Arab countries;[135] and from June 8 to July 27 a total of 200 words on events in Rumania appeared in the Soviet Press. (The July 22 item was a report of results in research on life expectancy pointedly entitled "Who Lives Longer?".)

A *Pravda* editorial succinctly articulated the subsequent Soviet position:

> The cooperation of the socialist countries has been embodied in concrete organizational forms whose effectiveness has been tested by life itself. Of these forms, the most important are the Warsaw Pact and CMEA. By setting up these international organizations, the socialist countries have strengthened their relations of alliance and have assumed certain definite obligations the aim of which is to defend their common interests on the international arena, to unite their efforts in the interest of more rapid economic development, and to strengthen their defensive capacity. . . .
>
> The fraternal countries of socialism consider their participation in the Warsaw Pact not a formalist membership in this organization but a vital and creative workers' cooperation in military and political questions.[136]

Strained Soviet-Rumanian relations were once again directly tied to organizational issues within the Warsaw Pact. At the Karlovy Vary Conference, Brezhnev again called for strengthening the Warsaw Pact.[137] East Germany hastened to use this as the rationale for negotiating a series of bilateral friendship, cooperation, and mutual assistance treaties with other member states. These treaties, generally considered as an extension of the Warsaw Pact, reiterated the inviolability of European frontiers and specifically pledged the signatories to defend the border between the GDR and West Germany. Moscow greeted the bilateral pacts with enthusiasm.

> The socialist countries consider it their duty to render all possible support to the GDR, which is in the front lines of the struggle against the forces of militarism, and to further the strengthening of its positions and prestige. It was not without reason that the militarist circles on the Rhine let out a heartrending wail after reading the texts of the documents signed in Warsaw and Prague. The plans of those who cherish hopes of driving wedges between the countries of socialism will not be realized.[138]

The treaties were described as in full accord with the Warsaw Pact and

---

[135] See analysis by Richard Eder, *The New York Times,* July 13, 1967.

[136] *Pravda,* July 23, 1967.

[137] *Pravda,* April 25, 1967.

[138] *Pravda,* March 28, 1967; quoted from *CDSP* 19, no. 13 (April 19, 1967): 29.

the July 1966 Bucharest declaration. Somewhat less officially, they were credited with "improving and developing the defensive mechanism" of the Warsaw Pact.[139] This was a scaled-down version of Brezhnev's formula of perfecting the organizational mechanism. Since the formula had been dropped after Soviet-Rumanian maneuvering in May 1966, its revival reminded Bucharest that Moscow had retreated but not abandoned the concept.

Nevertheless, at this time there was no bilateral treaty of mutual assistance signed between Rumania and East Germany. Even more significant, the Soviet-Rumanian mutual assistance pact was not renewed at that time, although it had been signed before the Soviet-Bulgarian and Soviet-Hungarian alliances renegotiated May 12 and September 7 respectively.[140]

The New WTO Commander-in-Chief

Concurrently, Bucharest appears to have balked at accepting the Soviet choice of a commander-in-chief of the joint command to replace Soviet Marshal A. A. Grechko. Grechko had been appointed Minister of Defense of the USSR following Malinovsky's death at the end of March. At the same time, it was announced that I. I. Yakubovsky had become a marshal and a first deputy minister of defense, Grechko's former rank.[141] A series of consultations with East European defense ministers began in Moscow. The Rumanian Minister of Armed Forces, Ion Ionita, was conspicuously missing.[142]

First the Soviets delayed; then shortly after the Rumanians left Moscow without signing the statement on the mid-East crisis, Yakubovsky commanded Warsaw Pact maneuvers in Hungary and Czechoslovakia.[143] While he conducted the joint exercises, Ceauşescu spoke to the Party

---

[139] Moscow in Rumanian to Rumania, 1800 GMT, May 19, 1967.

[140] The original Soviet-Rumanian pact was signed February 4, 1948, and renewed July 7, 1970, Document 14, p. 242.

[141] Pravda, April 13, 1967. Grechko had become commander-in-chief of the joint command when Konev resigned for reasons of health in 1960. His appointment underlined the close relationship of the Warsaw Pact to Soviet East German policy, for Grechko had been the Soviet Army Commander who put down the East Germany uprising in 1953 [Institute for the Study of the USSR, Biographic Directory of the USSR (Munich: 1958), p. 194] Yakubovsky also served as commander of Soviet forces in the GDR from 1960–1965. This pattern has continued at a lower level for General Pavel I. Batov, who replaced Antonov as chief-of-staff of the joint forces, served in Germany after the war. Ibid., p. 67.

[142] Lomský (Czechoslovakia) went to Moscow April 14; Czinege (Hungary), April 17; Dzhurov (Bulgaria) April 22–25; Hoffmann (GDR) May 19, 1967.

[143] Pravda, June 20, 1967.

Active of Brasov on the virtues of abolishing both NATO and the Warsaw Pact, although he qualified his assertion that so long as the Warsaw
Pact existed Rumania would continue to develop joint training of the
member states' armed forces with the limitation that such training proceed: ". . . of course, from the principles which govern relations between
the socialist countries, from the fact that each country, each army, must
be well organized, powerful from all points of view, and have its own
command able to answer any call." [144]

Formal announcement of Yakubovsky as commander-in-chief of Warsaw Pact forces did not follow immediately. Rather, on July 3 the East
German Defense Minister H. Hoffmann sent the new commander a
congratulatory telegram.[145] The communiqué on Yakubovsky's appointment "by agreement among the governments of Warsaw Pact member
states" appeared July 8.[146] A glance at his East European travels strongly
suggests that Bucharest had tabled but not dropped its objection. The
new post commander conferred with Ulbricht on June 26, called on
Gomułka and Spychalski July 24, and consulted with Novotný and Czech
Minister of Defense Lonský on September 9. There was as yet no meeting in Bucharest despite Rumanian participation in August Warsaw Pact
maneuvers.

A Temporary Balance

That the Rumanians took part in the joint exercises for the first time in
three years seems to have been an initiative from Bucharest designed to
thaw the chill that marked Soviet-Rumanian relations during the spring
and summer of 1967. Speaking to the Rumanian National Assembly,
Ceauşescu praised the "many-sided' relations between Rumania and the
Soviet Union. He reiterated Rumanian support for the inviolability of
European borders, recalled the political consultative committee's Bucharest
declaration, and emphasized the importance of attempting to improve
relations among European countries on the basis of "mutual trust." [147]

The Soviets were not slow to take the hint. Polyansky met with the

[144] *Scînteia,* June 19, 1967.

[145] There is at least the possibility that the East Germans deliberately leaked Yakubovsky's appointment without Moscow's prior consent so as to isolate the Rumanians. See Fritz
Ermarth, "The Warsaw Pact and Its New Commander," RFE Research Report, July 3, 1967.

[146] *Pravda,* July 8, 1967.

[147] *Scînteia,* July 26, 1967.

Rumanian ambassador on August 1. *Pravda*'s coverage of news from fraternal countries again included Rumania.[148] A Rumanian friendship delegation appeared in Moscow, greeted by extensive laudatory reporting of the anniversary of Rumanian liberation. [149] Then on August 27 the Soviets announced that Rumanian forces had participated in a week of Warsaw Pact joint exercises—a maneuver that undoubtedly reinforced Soviet perception of the value of the Warsaw Pact as a channel for containing if not resolving conflicts with dissident East European allies.

Indeed, in 1967 there were even minor signs that Moscow was not unaware of the possibility that the Warsaw Pact could contribute to normalizing Soviet-Albanian relations as well. According to a Moscow radio broadcast:

> Albania's strengthening and extension of close cooperation with other socialist countries is of special significance; these socialist countries are continuously strengthening and perfecting their defenses and are in a position to guarantee the borders of their states. Now the armies of the fraternal countries belonging to the Warsaw Pact have the most modern weapons. The military might of the land armies is being continuously perfected, and this also applies to the air and naval forces.[150]

It was an overture that came to nothing. Yet this did not diminish the importance of containing Soviet-Rumanian tensions within the organizational framework. Bucharest had become a past master at the art of flexible responses—Moscow seemed to have accepted a pattern of compromise rather than insisting on Soviet fiat. Could a similar adjustment be worked out with other members of the pact, or was the Rumanian model unique to Rumania? The first test was not long in coming, for the Prague spring was just around the corner.

[148] See *Pravda,* August 6, 8, 1967.
[149] *Pravda,* August 23, 24, 25, 26, 1967.
[150] Moscow in Albanian to Albania, 1500 GMT, April 7, 1967.

5

CZECHOSLOVAKIA:
MULTILATERAL
INTERVENTION[1]

IN AUGUST 1968, five members of the Warsaw Treaty Organization (WTO) invaded Czechoslovakia, also a member of the Warsaw Pact. Moscow justified that invasion as an obligation under the Warsaw Treaty. Prague denounced it as a violation, as it was, given any reading of the text. Yet the Warsaw Pact's relationship to the occupation of Czechoslovakia went much deeper than that of a convenient legal cover for the Soviet representative to the United Nations. The invasion marked a sudden break in what had appeared to be the rules of the game within the coalition itself. For throughout 1965–1967, Rumania had achieved an increasingly independent foreign policy within the framework of the Warsaw Pact. Allegiance to the Pact provided formal underpinning for a coalition more and more openly subject to the conflicts of interest common to such groupings throughout history. Such allegiance served as the minimum common denominator of coordination for East European Communist states. It was ritualistically essential, and was recognized as such by Rumania and, more recently, by Czechoslovakia.[2]

Sofia and Dresden

Even before Alexander Dubček's visit to Moscow at the end of January 1968,[3] the new Czechoslovak leadership stressed the importance of im-

---

[1] The substance of this chapter first appeared as an article "Czechoslovakia and the Warsaw Pact," in the *East European Quarterly* 3, no. 3 (September 1969). I am grateful to that journal for permission to reuse it in this book.

[2] See Václav Kotyk, "Some Aspects of the History of Relations Among Socialist Countries," *Československý časopis historický* 4 (1967): in *Czechoslovak Press Survey*, No. 1973, RFE/233 (October 30, 1967), p. 14.

[3] *Pravda*, January 30, 31, 1968; *Izvestia*, February 1, 1968.

proving military cooperation under the Warsaw Pact and the primacy of Soviet military doctrine within the coalition.[4] On his return, the new first secretary carefully committed Czechoslovakia to the common task of strengthening the Warsaw Treaty.[5] *Pravda* summarized the speech, quoting Dubček's reference to the Warsaw Pact in the context of his pledge that Prague—"in unity" with the Soviet Union and other socialist states—continued to stand shoulder to shoulder with the East Germans in their struggle against the rebirth of Nazism in West Germany.[6] There was a strong implication that in foreign policy Dubček had promised more of the same. Soviet reporting assiduously avoided his domestic program of party and social reform.

Indeed, at first the Soviet leadership responded to Czechoslovak developments with an almost patterned version of noninterference in the affairs of fraternal countries. After a quick trip to Prague in December 1967, Brezhnev opted for neutrality on the KSČ internal struggle.[7] There was no public regret at Novotný's passing in Moscow.[8] Nor was there any overt sign that the Prague spring was even a topic for discussion at the March 1968 political consultative committee meeting. Yet the isolation of Rumania that began in Sofia could easily work to the disadvantage of Czechoslovakia as well. When Moscow and the other East European countries agreed to a declaration endorsing the nonproliferation treaty, Bucharest refused to sign.[9] For the first time a document not unanimously accepted was issued at a Warsaw Pact meeting,[10] while Soviet editorials took pains to give the PCC communiqué and the Statement on Nonproliferation equal weight.[11] It was a move clearly limiting Rumanian and potentially Czechoslovak room for maneuver within the Warsaw Pact. Moreover, according to Polish sources, the structure of the Warsaw

[4] Article by Lt. General Václav Prchlík, Head of the Main Political Administration of the Czechoslovak People's Army, *Krasnaya zvezda*, January 27, 1968.

[5] *Rudé Právo*, February 2, 1968.

[6] *Pravda*, February 3, 1968.

[7] See V. Mencl and F. Ouředník, "What Happened in January," *Život strany* 16, 17, 18 (August–September 1968) and Document 4 in Robin Alison Remington, ed., *Winter in Prague: Documents on Czechoslovak Communism in Crisis* (Cambridge, Mass.: The MIT Press, 1969).

[8] For a detailed chronology of Soviet and East European reaction to the events following the KSČ CC January Plenum see William F. Robinson, "Czechoslovakia and Its Allies," *Studies in Comparative Communism* 1, nos. 1–2 (July–October, 1968): 141–170.

[9] *Pravda*, March 9, 1968; *CDSP* 20, no. 10 (March 27, 1968): 5–6.

[10] See Michel Tatu, *Le Monde*, March 7, 1968.

[11] *Pravda*, March 11, 1968; *Izvestia*, March 12, 1968.

Pact command had been considered at Sofia,[12] a fact later confirmed by Ceauşescu,[13] in his speech protesting that such problems were improperly discussed at Dresden without Rumanian participation.

By the end of March, Soviet anxiety at the possible consequences of liberalization in Prague had ended all but the flimsiest pretense of non-interference in Czechoslovakia's affairs. Not only were there signs that Dubček might be under pressure to stand less closely to Ulbricht with respect to West Germany[14] but how were orthodox Communist regimes to interpret the unheard-of call of censors for an end to censorship?[15]

At Dresden Dubček explained post-January developments in Czecho-slovakia. The meeting attempted to define limits of permissible diversity. It was a warning by Moscow and the increasingly jittery East German regime that "special attention" must be paid to West German activity "directed against the interests of East Germany and other socialist countries."[16] The Rumanians, who have consistently opposed meetings devoted to the internal affairs of any socialist country, were not invited—thereby ending Bucharest's veto power apparently exercised at Sofia to prevent any agreement on reorganizing the Warsaw Pact. The Dresden summit unanimously agreed to concrete, if unspecified, measures to strengthen the Warsaw Treaty "in the near future." Although Dresden was not formally a WTO meeting, Moscow treated the East German gathering as a parallel to Sofia.[17] Rumanian absence was ignored. Thus Bucharest's isolation implied at the earlier political consultative committee session became fact. Seemingly, the Soviets had decided to cut their losses within the alliance, to control Czechoslovakia by eliminating Rumania.[18]

The coincidence of Czechoslovak, Rumanian, and Yugoslav interests apparent at the Budapest consultative conference of Communist parties in late February–early March may well have contributed to such a decision. Despite formal condemnation of Bucharest's walkout, Prague's representative, Vladimír Koucký, both substantively supported some of

---

[12] Zenon Kliszko, Secretary of the Polish Central Committee, on Polish Television; RFE Polish Press Survey, no. 2129, April 17, 1968.

[13] Scînteia, April 28, 1968.

[14] Rudé Právo, March 16, 1968.

[15] Remington, Winter in Prague, Document 8, p. 54.

[16] Communiqué of the Dresden Meeting, Pravda, March 25, 1968; CDSP 20, no. 12 (April 10, 1968): 16–17.

[17] Pravda, March 25, 1968; Izvestia, March 26, 1968.

[18] For analysis of the Czechoslovak position in Budapest, see Michel Tatu in Le Monde, March 3, 1968.

the Rumanian views and reserved the right to return to the issue at a "more suitable" occasion. Moreover, he openly criticized documents of former international Communist meetings as out of date on the issue of Yugoslavia. Although Rumanian deviation had been marginally acceptable, Moscow had no intention of allowing a revived little entente directed against Soviet interests in Eastern Europe.

If Prague had doubts about what Dresden meant, the Soviet military newspaper *Krasnaya zvezda*'s statement, attributed to Dubček, that Czechoslovakia was protected from "all upheavals" by its alliance with the Soviet Union and other Warsaw Pact states could have done little to quiet them.[19]

Indeed, Dresden had created uneasy speculation in Czechoslovakia. Dubček felt called upon to explain the "natural" anxiety among Soviet and East European Communist leaders that "anti-socialist" elements should not take advantage of the process of democratization in Prague.[20] Subsequently the youth daily *Mlada fronta* seconded Rumania's objection that Warsaw Pact problems had been discussed at a meeting to which Bucharest had been uninvited.[21] The matter was the more serious because Czechosolvak politicians who had returned from Dresden had given a different interpretation—i.e., that the Rumanians had stayed away because the discussion had concerned setting up a really effective joint command. The implications for Czechoslovakia if Rumania had simply decided not to go to Dresden were one thing, if Bucharest had been excluded quite another.

Throughout April the conflict of interest widened. Although the KSČ Action Program[22] assured its allies that the Warsaw Pact was fundamental to the Czechoslovak road to socialism, Moscow and certainly Ulbricht must have found the theory of the necessity for giving support to "realistic" forces within West Germany unpalatable, particularly given the marked drop in Czechoslovak anti-West German propaganda and an increasing exchange of high-level visitors with Bonn. Further, the ČSSR Government declaration of April 24 went beyond the Action Program to

---

[19] Commentary by Col. V. Alexeyev and Lt. Col. O. Ivanov, *Krasnaya zvezda*, March 30, 1968.

[20] Dubček interview with ČTK, *Pravda*, March 28, 1968; *CDSP* 20, no. 13 (April 17, 1968): 20–21.

[21] Miroslav Pavel, commentary in *Mlada fronta*, April 27, 1968.

[22] Text of the KSČ Action Program is included in Remington, *Winter in Prague*, Document 16, pp. 87–141.

recognize "democratic" (instead of merely "realistic") trends in the German Federal Republic and favored normalization of relations.[23] The issue of Germany was crucial. Neither the Soviets nor the East Germans could afford to have Czechoslovakia recognize West Germany on other but their terms. Dresden had been called partially to emphasize how seriously Moscow viewed Prague potentially contributing to further isolating Pankow. And by April, Moscow must have wondered whether or not Dubček had gotten the message.

Prague's attitude toward Bonn was not the only problem. By early spring there were pressures for change in Czechoslovak policy toward Israel as well. In Bratislava the attitude toward Israel had become an index of whether one was for or against liberalization. Demands could be heard that the Slovak writer Ladislav Mňačko, who had left Czechoslovakia in protest at the government's anti-Israeli policy following the June 1967 war, be allowed to return home.[24] The Czechoslovak press and radio openly condemned the Polish anti-Zionist campaign following the March student protests at Warsaw University. Not only were letters of protest presented by members of the Czechoslovak Academy of Science to the Polish Embassy but following their dismissal Professors Leszek Kołakowski and Bronisław Baczko were invited to lecture at Charles University in Prague.[25] On May 6 the Polish Ambassador to Czechoslovakia formally protested against this "anti-Polish" campaign. Tension was building up.

The May–June Maneuvers

May was a month of intensive political and military maneuvering. At the end of April, Commander-in-Chief of the Warsaw Pact Armed Forces, Soviet Marshal Ivan I. Yakubovsky, traveled to East European capitals to work out what appeared to be the first of the "concrete measures" agreed upon at Dresden. In Prague he brought up the issue of Warsaw Pact exercises on Czechoslovak territory,[26] a suggestion for which the Czechs

---

[23] *Rudé Právo*, April 25, 1968.

[24] Gustav Husák referred to a press, radio, and television campaign for the return of Mňačko as early as mid-March, pointing out with apparent annoyance that nothing could be done because at that time the writer had not, in fact, applied to return. Bratislava Domestic Television Service in Slovak, March 20, 1968. Mňačko did return to Czechoslovakia on May 17, 1968.

[25] Robinson, "Czechoslovakia and Its Allies," pp. 144–147.

[26] *Krasnaya zvezda*, May 9, 1968.

had little enthusiasm. Dubček flew unexpectedly to Moscow on May 4. He returned, reportedly having reassured Moscow that democratization would not be allowed to turn against socialism in Czechoslovakia, to announce that joint military exercises in individual countries were a part of practical military cooperation under the Warsaw Pact.[27] Prague had agreed, but so far only in principle.

Despite Dubček's assurances, a meeting of Soviet and other East European leaders (once again minus Rumania) convened in Moscow May 8. Simultaneously, Soviet and Polish troops maneuvered on Czechoslovak borders. The maneuvers, particularly in the context of General Yepishev's rumored remarks about the willingness of the Red Army to do its duty should it be necessary to save socialism in Czechoslovakia,[28] caused serious speculation that invasion was imminent.[29] Prague dismissed such reports as provocation and insisted that the proper Czechoslovak bodies had been informed in advance about routine Warsaw Pact exercises in Southern Poland.

True or not, the fact of these maneuvers did not improve the atmosphere created by Soviet, Polish, and East German press attacks throughout May. Unlike earlier pact maneuvers in Hungary, they were certainly not handled so as to minimize pressure on the Dubček regime[30] but rather appeared part of a concerted campaign against Prague. On May 8, the former Warsaw Pact Commander I. S. Konev arrived to celebrate Czechoslovakia's liberation day, May 17, Kosygin appeared on May 17 for a ten-day "rest cure" at Karlovy Vary. Simultaneously but separately an eight-man military delegation led by Soviet Defense Minister Grechko and including General Yepishev came for a week's visit. Before this barrage of guests departed, it was agreed that Warsaw Pact staff maneuvers would be held on Czechoslovak territory in June.[31] The question of such maneuvers had become a measure of Prague's good faith, conceivably representing a compromise between Moscow's desire for Warsaw Pact troops

[27] *Rudé Právo*, May 7, 1968; reprinted in *Pravda*, May 8, 1968.

[28] *Le Monde*, May 5, 1968. As Yepishev is head of the main political administration of the Soviet armed forces, such comments from him would hardly be taken lightly. The report caused consternation in Czechoslovakia, *Rudé Právo*, May 9, 1968. Yepishev did issue a denial but only two weeks later at the airport in Prague.

[29] See *The New York Times*, May 10, 1968.

[30] *Nepszabadság*, March 23, 1968 announced that the plans for maneuvers had been approved in 1967, thereby lessening if not eliminating the suspicion that they were timed to coincide with the Dresden meeting. See also *Le Monde*, March 26, 1968.

[31] ČTK, May 24, 1968; *The New York Times*, May 25, 1968.

on the Czechoslovak–West German border and Prague's distaste for any joint military activity in the country until the political situation was more stable.

Preparations for the June maneuvers coincided with continued political upheaval in Prague. Czechoslovak Defense Minister Martin Dzur announced that small Soviet units had begun entering the country just one day after former President Antonín Novotný had been ousted from the KSČ Central Committee and suspended from party membership.[32] Both Dzur[33] and subsequently Warsaw Pact commander-in-chief Yakubovsky[34] took pains to minimize the number of forces involved. Ostensibly only position-marking and logistic troops would take part. Yet rumors of Soviet demand for tank squads continued, while the press spokesman for the allied command staff exercise, Major-General Josef Čepický, felt called upon to deny reports that Warsaw Pact troops would be permanently stationed in Czechoslovakia.[35]

The tone of Soviet articles explaining the necessity for such joint maneuvers can only have heightened the tension. Emphasis went far beyond combat efficiency. Rather Moscow focused on the uniformity of social and state systems, the common nature of "their Marxist-Leninist world outlook" as the political-ideological foundation for cooperation within the Warsaw Pact. There was consistent and ominous juxtaposition of the issue of strengthening the Warsaw Pact with the CPSU CC April plenum pledge that Soviet Communists remained ready to "do everything necessary" for political, economic, and defensive consolidation of the socialist community.[36] It was undoubtedly no accident that the April plenum resolution, published one day after the Czechoslovak Action Program, warned that "ideological saboteurs" working on "revisionist, nationalist, and politically immature elements" would not be permitted to subvert socialist society from within.[37] The plenum showed a hardening of Soviet policy

[32] The most detailed and helpful chronology on events within Czechoslovakia is *ČSSR: The Road to Democratic Socialism* (*Facts on Events From January to May 1968*) (Prague: Praguepress, 1968).

[33] Dzur interview with *Zemědelské noviny*, May 31, 1968.

[34] Yakubovsky interview with *Rudé Právo* correspondent in Moscow, Radio Moscow in Czech to Czechoslovakia, June 17, 1968.

[35] Prague Domestic Service in Czech, June 6, 1968.

[36] The bulk of these commentaries appear in the Soviet military newspaper. See particularly Lt. Col. O. Ivanov, *Krasnaya zvezda*, June 12, 1968 and Col. K. Sprov, *Krasnaya zvezda*, June 14, 1968.

[37] *Pravda*, April 11, 1968; *CDSP* 20, no. 15 (May 1, 1968): 3–4.

across the board. Its implications for foreign policy coordination within the Warsaw Pact potentially meant a good deal of backtracking along the Czechoslovak road to democratic socialism.[38]

Nor was Prague's nervousness at the ambiguous circumstances surrounding the planned maneuvers unfounded. For once on Czechoslovak territory Soviet forces were in no hurry to leave. Begun on June 20, the joint exercises officially ended July 1.[39] However, TASS almost immediately rescinded that announcement, and throughout July there was, in fact, no clear indication that Moscow intended Soviet troops to depart.

Prchlík and the Warsaw Letter

Lieutenant General Václav Prchlík's press interview suggesting basic revisions in the Warsaw Pact along the lines of more rather than less control for East European member states added still another dimension.[40] Head of the KSČ CC military department, the Lt. General said flatly that Soviet representation on the joint command was out of proportion. On a more political level, he attacked "fractionist activities" within the Warsaw Pact that lead to violating principles of sovereignty and noninterference in internal affairs. Prchlík clearly was alluding to the meeting of five pact members in session in Warsaw. For following Ludvík Vaculík's "Two Thousand Word Statement"[41] favoring demonstrations, strikes, and boycotts to force out the remaining Czechoslovak conservatives who misused their power, Prague's dispute with Moscow and the more orthodox East European Communist regimes had escalated into a formal confrontation.

Not only had Vaculík's statement opened the pandora's box of questions surrounding a proper interpretation of "the leading role of the Communist party" but the sensitive issue of an "independent" Czechoslovak military doctrine cropped up almost simultaneously. On July 2, a "memorandum" prepared by members of the Klement Gottwald Military-Political Academy in Prague was published under the title "How Czechoslovak State Interests in the Military Sphere Are to Be Formulated."[42] Although the recommendations were a far cry from advocating withdrawal from

---

[38] See, for example, Sh. Sanakoyev's article in *Izvestia*, June 16, 1968.

[39] *Pravda*, July 1, 1968. Dzur's interview indicated that the Czechoslovak command was busy creating optimum conditions so that the main-command time objective could be met, *Izvestia*, June 22, 1968.

[40] Remington, ed., *Winter in Prague*, Document 32.

[41] *Mlada fronta*, June 27, 1968.

[42] *Lidova armada* 3 (July 2, 1968).

the Warsaw Pact or neutralization of Czechoslovakia as later charged,[43] the document was bluntly critical of earlier pact policies and did demand a more genuinely multilateral decision-making mechanism.

Between July 4 and 6 the leaderships of the Soviet Union, Bulgaria, East Germany, Hungary, and Poland sent letters to the KSČ calling for a multilateral conference to discuss antisocialist activity in Czechoslovakia.[44] The Dubček regime parried by agreeing to bilateral meetings. His suggestion was ignored. Soviet and other East European leaders met in Warsaw as planned. The outcome of that meeting was the famed five-party "Warsaw Letter"—in effect an ultimatum outlining the rationale for invasion. Although not claiming to be an official Warsaw Pact document, the letter justified its interference in Czechoslovak internal affairs, in part, as a common obligation under the Warsaw Pact. The Dubček leadership was accused not only of weakening before demands to abandon "the common coordinated policy" toward West Germany but of tolerating a campaign against Warsaw Pact staff maneuvers on Czechoslovak territory.

Prague's reply answered the charges point by point, citing the Warsaw Treaty staff exercises as "concrete proof" of Czechoslovak faithful fulfillment of commitments. Questions had arisen among the population only after repeated changes of the departure time of allied armies following the end of maneuvers.[45] Moscow's retort did not specifically raise the issue of the Warsaw Pact[46] and had much the general tone of Stalin's reply to Tito in 1948—"We regard your answer incorrect and therefore completely unsatisfactory." [47]

---

[43] See "The So-Called 'Memorandum'—What It Was and the Purpose It Served," *Život strany* no. 42 (October 15, 1969) and RFE Czechoslovak Press Survey, no. 2273 (November 18, 1969). The memorandum certainly does express discontent with the past state of affairs, while the very stress on an "independent" Czechoslovak military doctrine more in line with the nation's interests implies a distaste for coalition policies as formed in early years. However, the level of retroactive attack is somewhat suspicious in that had Moscow found the memorandum so heretical there likely would have been some mention of this offense in the "Warsaw Letter" along with the criticism of Vaculík's statement.

[44] The letters were not published. However, they were alluded to in the subsequent Five-Party Warsaw Letter, *Pravda*, July 18, 1968; *CDSP* 20, no. 29 (August 7, 1968): 4–6, and described in Dubček's July 19 speech, *Rudé Právo*, July 20, 1968.

[45] *The New York Times,* July 19, 1968.

[46] "Concerning the Point of View of the CCP Central Committee," *Pravda*, July 22, 1968; *CDSP* 20, no. 29 (August 7, 1968): 10–11.

[47] Robert Bass and Elizabeth Marbury, eds., *The Soviet-Yugoslav Controversy, 1948–1958: A Documentary Record* (New York: Prospect Books, 1959), pp. 6–12. Prague was well aware of the similarities to 1948, openly ranking the Warsaw Letter with the Comin-

Moreover, the Prchlík interview had been temporarily ignored, not forgotten. On July 21 Moscow formally protested his press conference in a diplomatic note to the Prague leadership. Two days later the Soviet military press, *Krasnaya zvezda,* attacked the Czech General for "antisocialist, counterrevolutionary distortion of the Warsaw Pact." [48] Prague responded somewhat indirectly by reorganizing the KSČ Presidium so that Prchlík's party post was eliminated ostensibly because it overlapped with other government agencies and he returned to army duties. He was not immediately repudiated. [49] The incident created strong feeling in Czechoslovakia, and Prague party organizations even nominated the Lt. General as a candidate to the KSČ Central Committee in early August. [50] Prchlík personally expressed amazement at the "irresponsible Soviet reaction" to his views. [51]

Confrontation: Čierná-Bratislava

In short circumstances were hardly favorable for the bilateral Soviet-Czechoslovak negotiations to which Dubček had reluctantly agreed. [52] Large-scale Soviet maneuvers along the Czechoslovak-Soviet border coincided with the Čierná talks, while Soviet troops in East Germany were reportedly moving toward Czechoslovakia. [53] After four days of reportedly heated discussion, the other signers of the Warsaw letter were invited to Bratislava where the confrontation continued.

---

form resolution against Yugoslavia as "one of the darkest aspects of the history of the working class movement," L. Svoboda, "The ČSSR is Not Going to Commit Suicide," *Obrana lidu,* July 27, 1968; Remington, ed., *Winter in Prague,* Document 39.

[48] *Krasnaya zvezda* editorial, July 23, 1968. Subsequently the Soviets verified Prchlík's account in a backhanded way by accusing him of revealing to the enemy "secret" information about the Warsaw Pact; Soviet White Book, *On Events in Czechoslovakia* (Moscow, 1968), p. 7.

[49] ČTK, The Czechoslovak Press Agency, released a statement on July 27, 1968, to the effect that Prchlík did not "express the official viewpoint"; quoted in *The New York Times,* July 28, 1968. Two weeks later the Military Council of the Defense Ministry agreed with the ČTK statement in substance, but denied any knowledge of its origin. Prague, ČTK, International Service in English, August 15, 1968.

[50] *Práce,* August 8, 1968.

[51] Prchlík interview with *Práce,* July 25, 1968. In the course of postinvasion normalization in Czechoslovakia General Prchlík has been sentenced to three years in prison for "frustrating and jeopardizing the activity of state agencies." *International Herald Tribune,* March 27, 1971.

[52] Originally the Soviets proposed meeting in Moscow, Kiev, or Lviv (*Pravda,* July 20, 1968). However, when the Dubček regime apparently refused to leave Czechoslovakia, practically the entire Soviet Politburo went to the border town of Čierná-nad-Tisu.

[53] *Pravda,* July 31, 1968 and *The New York Times,* August 1, 1968.

Substantively, the Bratislava statement was a collection of orthodox platitudes that did not so much as refer to what the participants had gone to thrash out—the limits of Czechoslovak domestic reform and foreign policy deviation acceptable to Moscow and other increasingly threatened East European Communist regimes. Rather, the statement committed Prague to a general platform of strengthening the leading role of the Communist party and creating an ever-closer policy coordination within CMEA and the Warsaw Pact. It reiterated the hard line of the CPSU April plenum resolution on West Germany and Israel, pledging the signers to consistently follow "a concerted policy that meets the common interests of the socialist countries" in matters of European affairs. On the nature of the Warsaw Pact, however, the statement was most explicit:

> . . . It serves as an invincible barrier to all who would like to revise the results of the second world war. It reliably defends the gains of socialism and the sovereignty and independence of the fraternal states. . . .
>
> The present situation requires our unremitting efforts to raise the defense capability of every socialist state and the whole socialist commonwealth and to strengthen political and military cooperation in the Warsaw Treaty Organization.[54]

Such a formulation was just one step away from the demand that Warsaw Pact troops be permanently stationed in Czechoslovakia along the border with West Germany.

Rumania, as in the case of Dresden, protested that problems of the Warsaw Pact should not be discussed at meetings to which some member states were uninvited.[55] *Scînteia* condemned the Bratislava meeting as a violation of socialist norms for relations between fraternal parties. Not unexpectedly, Bucharest was ignored. Both Moscow and Prague officially hailed the Čierná and Bratislava meetings as a victory for socialist unity.[56]

Yet Prague's diplomatic activity following Bratislava indicates that the Dubček regime had few illusions about the extent of such unity. For a few days overt hostility ceased. During this brief lull, Czechoslovakia worked furiously to consolidate support. Tito arrived in Prague on August 9; a Rumanian delegation headed by President Ceauşescu, August

---

[54] Bratislava Statement, *Pravda*, August 4, 1968; *CDSP* 20, no. 31 (August 21, 1968): 4–5.

[55] Editorial, *Scînteia*, August 8, 1968.

[56] See Černík interview in *Rudé Právo*, August 2, 1968; Dubček, *Rudé Právo*, August 4, 1968; Zhukov in *Pravda*, August 5 editorial, August 8, 1968 and *Krasnaya zvezda* editorials August 6 and 8, 1968.

15. Both leaders were warmly welcomed, in marked contrast to the reception for Ulbricht, who came for talks in Karlovy Vary. Perhaps more important, the East German visit ended inconclusively with only vague agreement that both sides would continue to oppose the rise of Nazi forces in West Germany.[57] In contrast Tito and the new Czechoslovak-Rumanian Treaty of Friendship, Cooperation, and Mutual Assistance signed during Ceauşescu's visit focused on the principle of noninterference in each other's affairs—a guarantee conspicuously absent from the Bratislava Statement.

Moscow again may have had visions—and with some reason—of a "Communist Little Entente" directed against Soviet hegemony in Eastern Europe. Soviet polemics resumed while Ceauşescu was still in Prague.[58]

Simultaneously final arrangements for the military attack must have been under way when Soviet Defense Minister Grechko, Head of the Warsaw Pact Joint Forces Yakubovsky, and Director of the Political Administration Yepishev conferred with the East German Defense Minister H. Hoffman August 16. They then went to "Southwest Poland" where they were joined by the new Warsaw Pact Chief of Staff S. M. Shtemenko for talks with Polish Deputy Minister of National Defense B. Chocha that included "Division General Tadeusz Tuczapski, Deputy Minister of National Defense and Chief Inspector for Combat Readiness of Polish Troops." [59]

Pravda described Czechoslovakia as slipping over the edge of counterrevolution. Hooligans had attacked the Central Committee building; honest, pro-Soviet workers were faced with "frenzied" persecution.[60] The stage was set. Now it was only a matter of time and last-minute political jockeying.[61]

---

[57] Later candidate member of the SED Politburo and Secretary of the Central Committee, Hermann Axen, later accused the Dubček regime of consciously sabotaging the Čierná and Bratislava accords by "fiercely" opposing any formulation relating to the struggle against bourgeois ideology at Karlovy Vary. Hermann Axen, "Proletarischer Internationalismus in unserer Zeit," *Einheit* 10 (September 18, 1968): 1207. *Neues Deutschland*, August 14, 1968; summarized in *Pravda*, August 14, 1968.

[58] Zhukov in *Pravda*, August 16, 1968.

[59] *Pravda*, August 17 and 18, 1968. Also on August 17 *Pravda* reprinted a long article from the Hungarian *Népszabadság* detailing the horrors of the Hungarian counterrevolution in 1956.

[60] I. Alexandrov, *Pravda*, August 18, 1968; *CDSP* 20, no. 33 (September 4, 1968): 9–10.

[61] Kádár, perhaps still attempting to negotiate a compromise, met with Dubček August 17. See Richard Lowenthal, "The Sparrow in the Cage," *Problems of Communism* 17, no. 6

Invasion

The TASS announcement of the occupation of Czechoslovakia avoided any direct mention of the Warsaw Pact, although it maintained that the decision to come to the aid of unidentified party and government leaders in Prague was in "complete accord" with "allied treaties among the fraternal socialist countries." [62] Nor was the alleged appeal for aid addressed to the Warsaw Pact. Rather attacks against Warsaw Pact staff maneuvers in Czechoslovakia were seen as part of a filthy" systematic campaign to weaken friendship with the socialist countries." [63] In sum, Prague's bad attitude toward Warsaw Pact obligations was one reason to intervene; but the WTO was not considered an institutional instrument of intervention. The Soviet editorial entitled "Defense of Socialism is the Highest International Duty" made quite clear, however, that from Moscow's point of view this was a matter of dual responsibility. The defense of socialism in Czechoslovakia was anything but Prague's internal affair. It was the common affair of the socialist commonwealth. It was the CPSU's international duty as Communists, added to obligations under the Warsaw Pact, that had brought Soviet and "allied socialist" troops into Czechoslovakia. Warsaw Pact countries had "a solemn commitment— to stand up in defense of the gains of socialism." [64]

As for the pact as an index of Prague's good faith, the editorial reiterated charges concerning the June maneuvers. Prchlík was attacked. Such attempts to impair the pact became a question for all participants of the Warsaw Treaty Organization, for: "It is impossible to tolerate a breach in this organization. Such a line contradicts the vital interests of all the member countries of the Warsaw Treaty Organization, including the vital interests of the USSR." [65]

Moscow had laid it on the line. The Warsaw Pact was an institutional arrangement for protecting the interests of the socialist commonwealth as defined by the Soviet Union. It was an interpretation that left Rumania no place to go. And one to which Prague could hardly agree.

(November–December 1968): 20–21. On August 19, in a gesture designed to ensure mixed response from Washington to the imminent invasion, Kosygin informed President Johnson that he was ready for the summit meeting the President had desired and suggested August 21. *The New York Times*, August 23, 1968.

[62] *Pravda*, August 21, 1968.

[63] *Pravda*, August 22, 1968; *CDSP* 20, no. 34 (September 11, 1968): 3–5.

[64] *Pravda*, August 22, 1968; *CDSP, ibid.*, p. 11.

[65] *Ibid.*

The Czechoslovak government quickly declared the invasion illegal, demanding immediate withdrawal of all foreign troops and "correct adherence" to the Warsaw Treaty.[66] Rumania, despite Bucharest's exposed position, condemned the use of troops as a "flagrant violation of the sovereignty of a fraternal socialist country."[67] Ceauşescu further warned that Rumania would not permit any violation of its territory, and reactivated the People's Militia.[68]

Moscow's angry response reiterated and refined the August 22 editorial interpretation of the function of the Warsaw Pact. According to Kudryavtsev:

When the imperialists call the fulfillment of the socialist countries' internationalist duty "intervention," it shows why they are imperialists. But it is strange, to say the least, to hear exactly the same phrases from the mouths of the Rumanian and Yugoslav leaders. Don't they know that the Warsaw Pact was concluded not only to defend the signatory states' national borders and territories? It was concluded in order to defend socialism in response to the creation of the aggressive NATO military bloc, which is openly aimed against the socialist states for the purpose of counteracting communism. And those who now attempt to interpret the Warsaw Pact in narrowly nationalistic terms ('it's none of my business') contribute to the imperialists' frenzied anti-socialist campaign. The defense of socialism in Czechoslovakia is not only the internal affair of that country's people but also a problem of defending the positions of world socialism. . . .[69]

Rumors that Soviet troops had moved to Rumanian borders persisted as did reports that the Soviet Ambassador to Bucharest Alexander V. Basov was demanding Warsaw Pact maneuvers on Rumanian territory.[70]

---

[66] "Declaration of the Czechoslovak Government" *Studies in Comparative Communism* I, nos. 1/2 (July/October 1968): 297.

[67] *Scînteia*, August 22, 1968.

[68] *Ibid.*, August 21, 1968.

[69] V. Kudryavtsev, *Izvestia*, August 25, 1968; *CDSP* 20, no. 35 (September 18, 1968): 7–8.

[70] *Washington Post*, August 26, 1968; Paul Hoffman, *The New York Times*, August 27, 1968. In response to intelligence reports apparently confirming such rumors, Washington publicly stated that it would view any Soviet military intervention in Yugoslavia or Rumania with the utmost seriousness, *The New York Times*, August 31, 1968 providing a marked contrast to American response to intensive Soviet pressure on Prague at the time of the Čierná meeting, see Tom Wicker in *The New York Times*, August 1, 1968. For an increasingly sharp denunciation of the Rumanian position ridiculing such speculation as Western fabrications, see N. Gribachev, *Pravda*, September 4, 1968.

Ceauşescu's criticism softened but he did not back down.[71] There is little doubt that the Rumanian leader continued to hold his opinion, expressed during the July Warsaw Meeting to which Rumania was not invited, "When the Warsaw Pact was set up, it was conceived as an instrument for collective defense . . . not a reason for justifying interference in the internal affairs of other states." [72]

In fact, notwithstanding Kudryavtsev's vehemence, Czechoslovakia was floundering in a political vacuum. Soviet and East European troops could not find the comrades they had come to assist. The Kádár solution Moscow desired had collapsed when 72-year-old President Svoboda flatly refused to appoint the puppet regime proposed to him by KSČ secretary Alois Indra, who was to have been Prime Minister.[73] Although the Soviet military plan had gone flawlessly, politically the "allied socialist" rescue operation was a fiasco.

Svoboda had flown to Moscow, where progress toward replacing the Dubček regime with pro-Soviet collaborators seemed no greater than in Prague. Soon Dubček (who had been attacked by the August 22 editorial for leading a "right-wing, opportunist, minority" in the KSČ Presidium) and the other arrested leaders joined the negotiations. Thus, since Moscow was unwilling to adopt the Hungarian solution of simply arresting the negotiators,[74] the Soviet leadership ended by restoring to office the Czechoslovak leadership that Soviet troops had invaded Czechoslovakia to replace.

The Soviet-Czechoslovak Communiqué of August 28 euphemistically dismissed the invasion as a "temporary entry of troops" to be withdrawn

[71] Speeches by Ceauşescu August 26 and September 9 emphasized that Rumania would never betray socialist friends. For analysis of Bucharest's maneuvering, see Philippe Ben in *Le Monde*, September 10, 11, 12, and 14, 1968

[72] *Agerpress*, July 15, 1968.

[73] *Frankfurter Allgemeine Zeitung*, September 23, 1968, and *Der Spiegel*, October 21, 1968, p. 147. According to the current rewriting of history by the KSČ, "thousands of Communists, individual citizens, and whole collectives of working people" [including members of the Central Committee and the CSSR government] had turned to the "fraternal parties" to prevent a civil war by halting "the frontal onslaught of counterrevolution." "Lesson Drawn from the Crisis the Party and Society after the 13th Congress of the Communist Party of Czechoslovakia," *Rudé Právo*, January 14, 1971. Although he spoke approvingly of this "lesson" in his speech to the CPSU 24th Congress, Brezhnev more modestly referred to an invitation by unidentified party and state leaders. *Pravda*, March 30, 1971.

[74] Paul E. Zinner, *Revolution in Hungary* (New York: Columbia University Press, 1962) p. 317. For a description of the negotiations with the Czechoslovak delegation, see Robert Littell, ed., *The Czech Black Book* (New York: Praeger, 1969).

when the situation "normalized." It reaffirmed the Bratislava commitment to shore up the effectiveness of the Warsaw Pact, one aspect of the strengthening of the defensive might of the socialist commonwealth.[75]

The Brezhnev Doctrine

Interestingly enough, the subsequent Soviet theoretical justification known as the Brezhnev Doctrine did not mention the Warsaw Pact. First formulated by S. Kovalev in *Pravda,* it put forth a concept of limited sovereignty within the socialist community.[76] In Kovalev's view, sovereignty among socialist states must not be understood abstractly. Rather, within the socialist commonwealth international law must be subordinated to the laws of class struggle. In short, Moscow reserved the right to intervene militarily or otherwise if developments in any socialist country inflicted damage upon either socialism in that country or the basic interests of other socialist countries. Obviously incompatible with Warsaw Treaty guarantees of independence and noninterference in internal affairs, the logic of this interpretation would restrict the Warsaw Pact to an instrument for political and military coordination among European Communist states.

Emphasis was on consolidation in a world situation threatening the survival of socialism. The idea was hardly new. It echoed the "two-camp theory" outlined by Zhdanov at the founding of the Cominform in 1947, and it implied reimposition of the Soviet hegemony that had reduced East European policy to a gray imitation of Moscow's initiatives until Stalin's death and well into the 1950s. For the invasion of Czechoslovakia left the crux of the matter unambiguous. Moscow, not Prague, had decided that the danger existed. Prior consultation had been limited to those members of the Warsaw Pact that agreed. The threat to Rumania was clear.

Yet, 1968 was not 1947, and the "allied socialist" invasion of Czechoslovakia had left the fading myth of monolithic international Communist unity in shambles.[77] Bucharest side-stepped. Rumania became less publicly critical of the occupation and shifted to a more cooperative stance on

---

[75] *Pravda,* August 28, 1968.

[76] *Pravda,* September 26, 1968; *CDSP* 20 no. 39 (October 16, 1968): 10–12. For analysis see Christian Duevel, "Ideological Acrobatics on Sovereignty," Radio Liberty Research, CRD 361/68 (October 7, 1968).

[77] Kevin Devlin, "The New Crisis in European Communism," *Problems of Communism* 18, no. 6 (November–December 1968): 57.

the issue of a world Communist conference. A Rumanian delegation attended the September working group in Budapest that agreed to postpone the November 25 Conference date in favor of another preliminary meeting on November 17. Rumania's Defense Minister Ionita took part in a meeting of Warsaw Pact ministers in Moscow in late October,[78] seemingly to give assurance of Bucharest's willingness to fulfill its military obligations under the Treaty. Despite such tactical retreats, however, Ceauşescu adamantly rejected the Brezhnev Doctrine. In his view, it was incompatible both with socialist principles governing relations among fraternal states and with the Warsaw Pact.[79] He attacked the thesis of limited sovereignty within the socialist commonwealth as a return to old methods going against the interests of individual parties and the international movement as a whole. Meanwhile, within the Warsaw Pact itself Bucharest had, at least temporarily, sidetracked demands for joint maneuvers on Rumanian territory. The communiqué of the meeting of the chiefs-of-staff referred only to strengthening defensive capacity,[80] while Ceauşescu's December 9 interview indicated that the matter had not come up.[81]

October Treaty

As for Czechoslovakia, the treaty "temporarily stationing Soviet troops on ČSSR territory "for the purpose of safeguarding the security of the countries of the socialist commonwealth against the mounting revanchist ambitions of West German militarist forces" was a logical extension of the Brezhnev Doctrine. Despite the treaty's contention that the presence of such Soviet troops did not violate the sovereignty of Czechoslovakia and would not interfere in the host country's internal affairs,[82] Moscow

[78] *Pravda*, October 31, 1968.

[79] *Scînteia*, November 30, 1968; for analysis, *Neue Zürcher Zeitung*, December 7, 1968.

[80] *Izvestia*, December 1, 1968; that Ceauşescu's attack on the Brezhnev Doctrine should have appeared on the same day as the communiqué of this Pact meeting should be considered no accident.

[81] *The Times* (London), December 9, 1968.

[82] The incident of the philosophy student Jan Palach who set fire to himself January 16, 1969 partially as a protest at the continued distribution of *Zpravy*, a Soviet occupation news sheet featuring bitter attacks on Czechoslovak reformers provided a tragic index of how meaningless that pledge was in practice. Not only did circulation of *Zpravy* violate Czechoslovak publishing laws but no such publication appeared in other East European countries where Soviet troops are stationed. See Eric Bourne, *The Christian Science Monitor*, January 23, 1968.

was at least as concerned to contain reformers in Prague as militarists in Bonn.

The treaty was harsh. In return for the gradual withdrawal of the majority of Soviet and East European troops occupying the country, the Dubček regime legalized the stationing of an unspecified number of Soviet troops on Czechoslovak territory for an indefinite period of time.[83] It went beyond the similar treaty with Hungary in 1957, for that treaty (as had the one with Poland in 1956) required agreement of the host government for Soviet troop movement outside the area of their stationing. There was no such provision in the Soviet-Czechoslovak Treaty of 1968. Nor was Prague granted any compensation for damages inflicted during the invasion. The Treaty claimed to be in accordance with the Bratislava Statement and the "understanding" reached during bilateral Soviet-Czechoslovak negotiations August 23–26 and October 3–4, 1968. It did not officially derive its authority from the Warsaw Treaty.

Since the October Treaty formally ended "allied socialist" occupation of Czechoslovakia, it provides a convenient cut-off for the present chapter. The crisis had been resolved by a bilateral treaty between Prague and Moscow. However, conflict continued, and the relationship of the Warsaw Pact to "normalization" in Czechoslovakia is an ongoing problem qualitatively different from the role of that alliance at the time of confrontation.

> Politics as a game for and with power is always a struggle in which one side tries to force the other to accept its view of reality and its interpretation of events.
>
> Karel Kosík, "Illusion versus
> Realism," *Listy*, November 7, 1968

Normalization for Czechoslovakia meant going back, rewriting the history of 1968 to fit the contemporary Soviet view of reality.[84] For once the October Treaty had legitimated Soviet troops remaining in Czechoslovakia, Prague had lost. As Kosík predicted, Moscow prescribed the formulas of capitulation and it was only a matter of time before those

[83] *Pravda*, October 19, 1968; *CDSP* 20, no. 42 (November 6, 1968): 3–4.

[84] For example, a circular distributed to all career officers of the Czechoslovak Army in 1970 asked them to state their reactions to the attempt to proclaim the neutrality of Czechoslovakia and withdraw from the Warsaw Pact, when in fact there had been no such attempt. For an English translation of the circular see *Le Monde* weekly edition, July 15, 1970.

Czech and Slovaks who wanted to remain within the political elite began to play the game, redefine the situation in Soviet terms, judge the Prague Spring through Soviet eyes, and use the search for "counterrevolutionaries" to secure their own positions. That sad process has its own impetus which may have pushed the KSČ further into corruption and decline than Moscow would desire. But that is another story, for another time, because in terms of the Warsaw Pact, "normalization" entailed much more than the return to an acceptable model of Communist society in Prague.

6
POSTINVASION
NORMALIZATION:
1969

ONCE THE PRESSURE of intense intra-Communist conflict over Czechoslovakia had subsided, 1969 seemed to open possibilities for "normalization" in many dimensions. Now that internal developments in Czechoslovakia had been contained at an acceptable anxiety level for the more orthodox member states, the Warsaw Pact began to function again and turned away from exclusively intraalliance concerns. When Willy Brandt's government came to power in West Germany, the desire for improved relations among European states gained a substantial political basis. Simultaneously the SALT talks gave hopes for an ongoing US–Soviet détente. Undoubtedly these signs of relaxation in the international sphere encouraged the Warsaw Pact drive toward a European Security conference, and gave additional reason for the focus on Germany. Yet, in fact, the outlines of these policies had begun to form before the favorable international setting appeared. That was the message of the Budapest Appeal.

The Budapest Appeal

Although the invasion of Czechoslovakia split the international Communist movement, the main divisive impact was outside the East European core. Among WTO member states only Rumania neither participated in nor condoned the "allied socialist entry of troops." Moreover, organizationally the scars healed faster than in 1956. Thus, in a touch of procedural irony, Alexander Dubček served as chairman of the first postinvasion meeting of the Warsaw Pact political consultative committee when "all seven" member states[1] convened in Budapest March 17, 1969

---

[1] This subtle emphasis on the nonexclusory nature of the meeting strongly indicated East European member state priorities. See K. Malcuzynski in *Trybuna ludu*, March 19, 1969; also referred to by the Czechoslovak Minister of Foreign Affairs in his television broadcast of March 20, 1969. Soviet press coverage simply listed the participating states.

—just short of one year after the Dresden meeting that had excluded Rumania. August 1968 had made possible March 1969.

It was a meeting more important for form than content, with an agenda most significant for its omissions. Despite the recent Sino-Soviet border clash, neither the appeal nor the communiqué referred to China. The invasion of Czechoslovakia was not mentioned. Nor was there any public discussion of the Brezhnev doctrine.

Indeed, on the surface it almost appeared that there was no discussion at all. The formal meeting lasted only an hour and a half. It is frequently a mistake, however, to assume that brief meeting means pro forma acceptance. Delegations had begun arriving in Budapest two days before the PCC session. According to the Czechoslovak Minister of Foreign Affairs Jan Marko's television speech March 20, 1969, the session included "informal and direct exchanges of views on topical problems of mutual relations in the socialist community." [2] Its brevity had been made possible by "intense work" on the part of the delegations of member countries— led by the deputy ministers of foreign affairs—which (he added in a rare insight) edited the appeal on the basis "of suggestions prepared by the Hungarian comrades."

Addressed to all European states, the text of the appeal was low-keyed and largely free of propagandistic overtones. The usual violent attack on revanchist forces in West Germany was conspicuously absent. Nor was the appeal directed against American imperialists. Rather emphasis was on peace, détente, and coexistence. Recognizing that Europe consisted of states with different social systems and differing interests, these were not judged irreconcilable. Although some "aggressive forces" still strove to annul the results of World War II, a social and political milieu opposed to warlike conflict continued to develop. Consequently the Warsaw Pact member states repeated their call for an all-European security conference, reaffirmed their belief in peaceful settlement, and reiterated their distaste for a world divided into military blocs. They did not repeat the long-standing offer to dissolve the Warsaw Pact in exchange for abolition of NATO.[3]

There was no suggestion that the United States would participate in the

---

[2] In general, Czechoslovak reporting of the Budapest meeting was quite open about both hopes and fears in Prague. See particularly the outspoken youth newspaper *Mlada fronta,* March 20, 1969; also Dubček interview in *Rudé Právo,* March 19, 1969.

[3] *Pravda,* March 18, 1969; Document 7, p. 225.

projected security conference,[4] but given the normal bargaining process surrounding East-West meetings that was to be expected. If the Warsaw Pact states wanted the conference to materialize they would accept American presence—as they did in June 1970—which does not mean they would welcome it or make the first move at this time however. The appeal somewhat pointedly left both agenda and participants on an open issue. Yet it was more specific than usual on direction. A European security conference was step one toward the wider goal of a "security system." Based on the favorite Rumanian principles of respect for equality, independence, and sovereignty, such a system would make possible joint projects to contribute to the well-being of the European continent in the sphere of power generation, transport, and health.

The Budapest Appeal reactivated and subtly modified a long-standing Soviet/Warsaw Pact initiative toward Europe, underlining that the Soviet invasion of Czechoslovakia interrupted but did not break the pattern of Moscow's European policy. Institutionally the appeal itself was less significant than the manner in which it was written. Rather than acting out the current stereotype of Soviet-East European dialogue where a Soviet-preferred draft is whittled down to what Rumania will sign, it appears to have been a genuine collective effort. Marko's speech pointed to a major Hungarian input. The Poles have claimed that their delegation contributed substantially to the document,[5] subsequent Rumanian commentary stressed that "the opinions of each country" were considered,[6] and its terminology leaves no doubt of Rumanian influence. Moreover, although the final version was accepted unanimously, there was no attempt to hide the fact that different perspectives existed among the member states.[7]

That the final product did not conform strictly to a Moscow-dictated line is evident in even a quick survey of Soviet commentaries. Despite overt enthusiasm for the Appeal, Soviet press on the Budapest meeting struck a more militant note than the joint document. Although crediting "realistic" circles in Western Europe with an understanding that complex

---

[4] See A. Ross Johnson, *The Warsaw Pact "European Security" Campaign*, RAND RM-565-PR, Santa Monica, California, November 1970. For background, see Charles Andras, "The Evolution of the Warsaw Pact's Approach to European Security," RFE, August 1968.

[5] Polish Politburo member Jaszczuk in *Trybuna ludu*, May 5, 1969.

[6] *Scînteia*, March 20, 1969.

[7] See Malcuzynski in *Trybuna ludu*, March 19, 1969, and reference to differences on issues of principle by Hungarian Party Secretary Z. Komocsin, *Népszabadság*, September 25, 1969, quoted by Johnson, *The Warsaw Pact "European Security" Campaign*.

problems are better solved by peaceful negotiation than by the use of force or the threat of it, *Pravda* and *Izvestia* editorials repeated the ritual warnings against imperialist reaction;[8] *Izvestia* specifically quoting Brezhnev's Karlovy Vary demand that "aggression by German imperialism be ruled out forever." These attacks were mild, however, when compared to the *Krasnaya zvezda* polemic against NATO bosses, Bonn revanchists, and Peking adventurists.[9]

Reminiscent of its dire forecasts in January 1956, the military newspaper put forward an unyielding cold war interpretation of the European political situation in which the Budapest Appeal seemed almost irrelevant, a convenient peg from which to hand the outburst. The article stressed fraternal, socialist solidarity in the face of imperialist attempts to undermine the socialist community. It emphasized the importance of military reorganization within the Pact, accused West Germany of implicitly allying itself with the Chinese, and warned that any attempt to take advantage of Moscow's troubles to the East would be "suicide" for Bonn—"The Warsaw Pact countries have stated this repeatedly and resolutely." It was a clever twist obviously stretching a point to bring the East European members of the Pact into the fray against Chinese provocateurs if only indirectly and on the Western front.

This was the only mention of China in Soviet news coverage of the Budapest meeting.[10] It added fuel to rumors that Moscow wanted to expand the Warsaw Pact's military commitments eastward. Nor was this tack irrelevant to Soviet goals for the proposed world Communist conference. It was in all probability not a coincidence that the first meeting of the preparatory committee for such a conference ended in Moscow on March 19. For while it is undoubtedly a mistake to divide Soviet leaders into the favorite U.S. aviary of hawks and doves, there continue to be longstanding differences of opinion in Moscow not only on such fundamental issues as national security versus international unity but on what it takes to be secure and from whom.

In this sense *Krasnaya zvezda*'s harsh words about West Germany were out of key with both the tone of the Budapest Appeal and the general trend of Soviet policy toward Bonn at that time. During the latest crisis over Berlin in January and February Soviet diplomacy had been concilia-

---

[8] *Pravda*, March 20, 1969; *Izvestia*, March 20, 1969.

[9] *Krasnaya zvezda*, March 19, 1969.

[10] The *Trud* editorial of March 19, 1969, which was also heavy on cold war language, did not mention China.

tory. Moscow adopted the role of mediator and, indeed, appeared less than pleased at East German obstinacy.[11] Despite severe GDR attacks on Bonn's decision to hold the presidential election in Berlin, the Soviets proceeded to brief Kiesinger on the Sino-Soviet border clashes in early March. Although Gromyko's visit could have been intended to "warn" Bonn not to take advantage of the trouble on the USSR's Eastern border, it had more the appearance of a fence-mending tour to the West.

Westpolitik: A Problem of Strategy

A joint position on the threat to peace inherent in Sino-Soviet border clashes may or may not have been rejected at Budapest, but European border problems undeniably had high priority. In this context, the appeal dealt directly with the question of Germany—reiterating long-standing demands for West German recognition of the Oder-Neisse border and the frontier between East and West Germany, it also specified that the Federal Republic should (1) renounce its claim to represent all Germany; (2) sign the nonproliferation treaty, thereby reassuring the rest of Europe that it had no intention of acquiring nuclear weapons; and (3) recognize a "special status" for Berlin. Yet these long term objectives were not in any way held up as prerequisites for the desired conference. Moreover, it remained unclear as to what extent the signers of the Appeal actually wanted Germany discussed. For although the problem of Germany is central to the issue of European security, there are no easy or generally acceptable solutions at this time; a fact recognized by both East and West European policymakers.

In the past the states participating in the Budapest meeting had come closer to agreeing on a preferred solution than on the concrete steps in that direction. Certainly the Ceausescu's earlier justification of Rumanian recognition of West Germany as "an act [that] contributes to developing European interstate cooperation and to the effort being made to consolidate peace and security on the European continent"[12] did not square with Walter Ulbricht's interpretation of Bucharest's initiative.[13] Rather

---

[11] For an excellent analysis of increasing tensions between Moscow and the Ulbricht leadership vis-à-vis Soviet policy toward Bonn, see Lawrence L. Whetten "The Role of East Germany in West German-Soviet Relations," *The World Today* 25, no. 12 (December 1969): 507–520.

[12] *Scînteia*, February 4, 1967.

[13] For detailed discussion of the East German reaction, see *Neues Deutschland* February 3, 1967.

the East Germans have tried consistently to control the policies of the other Warsaw Pact members toward the Federal Republic by virtue of the GDR's special interests in the German question.[14] There is some evidence that Bucharest had resisted such an interpretation of its internal obligations as early as 1965,[15] while in 1967 the Rumanian press characterized *Neues Deutschland's* criticisms as an attempt to interfere in Rumania's internal affairs, by "setting itself up as the foreign policy advisor of another state." [16] *Scînteia* categorically rejected such attempts as harmful to relations among socialist countries. It was an opinion undoubtedly agreed with in Prague by 1968,[17] and possibly in Budapest as well.

Ironically, for the Poles have long been hardline supporters of Ulbricht on this issue, the most recent challenge to the GDR's preference for multilateral dealings with Bonn came from Warsaw. Just two months after the Budapest PCC meeting, Gomułka made a major foreign policy speech in which he noted that the West German Social Democratic Party formula on the Oder-Neisse border constituted a step forward and proposed a treaty with the Federal Republic recognizing Poland's western border.[18] Although the Polish leader referred to the Budapest position that West Germany should also renounce its claim to be the sole representative of the German people and recognize the GDR, he in no way indicated that a border agreement with Poland could be reached only as a package deal. On the contrary, Gomułka emphasized that Warsaw was ready to conclude such an agreement "at any time." He paid token respect to East Germany's special interests, but was clearly not going to let them inhibit solving the Polish border problem on a bilateral basis if Bonn was now ready to do so. Poland's national interests came first. It was a major shift

[14] Such attempts have not excluded Moscow by any means. The East Germans strongly pushed their interpretation of the dangers in increasing contacts between Prague and Bonn in 1968, and Ulbricht certainly contributed to the Soviet decision to invade Czechoslovakia. As for Berlin, I would agree with Mr. Whetten's analysis that "A display of disunity on this scale was not due to misunderstanding or lack of coordination, but was most likely part of a deliberate attempt by East Germany to exploit the present disarray in the Kremlin and establish new dimensions and prerogatives in foreign policy." Whetten, "The Role of East Germany in West German-Soviet Relations," p. 516.

[15] "Suveranitatea de stat in optica unor ideologi burghezi," *Lupta de Classa*, September 1965; for analysis Victor Zorza, *The Guardian*, May 19, 1966.

[16] *Scînteia*, February 21, 1967.

[17] *Rudé Právo*, March 27, 1968, for example, suggested that the Czechoslovak policy toward West Germany could make a more active contribution than simply echoing the GDR.

[18] *Trybuna ludu*, May 18, 1969.

from Warsaw's long-standing willingness to simply second GDR initiatives.

Within the Pact, Poland was in good company, for Moscow had taken the occasion of the 50th anniversary of the Comintern to historically rehabilitate "social democracy" and to imply that Comintern extremism had been the main cause of the failure of the united front policy.[19] Such an interpretation opened the way for favorable collaboration with the Social Democrats in West Germany. Not surprisingly, Ulbricht disagreed, reminding the meeting that even after German fascism had come to power in 1933, the Social Democrats had opposed the Communist-sponsored general strike—i.e., not the Comintern but the SPD leadership had been to blame.[20] By implication new attempts to find common ground with the Social Democrats would be equally fruitless.

Indeed Polish national assertiveness vis-à-vis Bonn could at best only be marginally less distasteful to the East German leadership than the earlier independent Rumanian recognition of the Federal Republic. Somewhat precipitously the deputy foreign ministers of all Warsaw Pact states met in East Berlin May 20. Although this session might have been scheduled to discuss the May 5 Finnish offer to sponsor a European security conference,[21] it also could have been called at Ulbricht's request to remind Warsaw of East German sensitivity with respect to bilateral contacts between other East European states and Bonn.[22] The meeting was chaired by the GDR representative, O. Fischer. Both its timing and the brief, rather uninformative communiqué to the effect that participants had "exchanged information on questions connected with the Budapest Appeal"[23] lend weight to the latter interpretation; as noted in Communist terminology, "to exchange opinions" had classically meant to disagree. Had the focus of the meeting been on Finnish sponsorship of an already prominently supported East bloc project, there would have been no cause for differences and the communiqué would most likely have been effusive.

[19] Suslov's keynote speech in *Pravda*, March 26, 1969.
[20] *Neues Deutschland*, March 27, 1969. For analysis, RFE Research "Comintern Commemorated—II," April 1, 1969.
[21] The Finnish government sent a note to all European states, the US, Canada, and the UN Secretary General proposing that the conference be held in Helsinki. UPI, May 5 and 7, 1969.
[22] For an excellent analysis of changing Polish policy toward West Germany in the post-Czech invasion period, see Johnson, *The Warsaw Pact "European Security" Campaign.*
[23] *Pravda*, May 22, 1969.

The simultaneous presence of a high-level Rumanian delegation in Poland May 19 and 20 was not a particularly esoteric signal by the Polish leadership that it intended to do as it pleased in such matters. Gomułka and Ceausescu toasted each other. The two sides stressed the importance of the Budapest Appeal and the importance of recognizing the inviolabiity of interstate frontiers, "including the Oder-Neisse." There was no specific reference to East Germany,[24] an omission undoubtedly noted by the East Germans.

The GDR's sense of threat at this drift toward bilateralism in dealing with Bonn compounded by hints of possible cooperation with Brandt's Social Democrats should they come to power was clearly revealed in Ulbricht's speech to the June World Communist Conference in Moscow. He flatly attacked the SPD *Ostpolitik* as a "trojan-horse tactic" designed to open the doors for "ideological diversion, economic dependence, and counterrevolution." West Germany was described as the main danger in Europe. Even the East German leader's criticism of Chinese provocation on the Sino-Soviet border was couched in terms of the support such tactics gave to West German imperialism. And there was a scarcely concealed irritation in his justification of Pankow's position:

> The GDR's foreign policy aims at working untiringly *with the Soviet Union and the other Warsaw Pact states* to support the Budapest Appeal for bringing European security to the people and governments of Europe. The GDR does not demand *any* precondition for the preparation and conduct of a conference on European security, in which all European states would take part with equal rights. The GDR is working to safeguard European security in order to bring about a reduction of tensions in a way which would facilitate normalization of relations between the German Democratic Republic and the Federal Republic of Germany.[25] [Italics mine.]

These warnings had found no echo in Moscow or Warsaw. On July 10, Gromyko spoke favorably of opening discussions with the West on the status of Berlin. Shortly thereafter Gomułka repeated his offer to negotiate a border treaty with West Germany, and simultaneously called for an

---

[24] Communiqué published in *Scînteia*, May 21, 1969. The summary of Gomułka's speech which appeared in *Scînteia*, May 19, 1969 bore little resemblance to the excerpts selected by *Neues Deutschland*, May 20, 1969. Clearly the Rumanians approved; the East Germans did not.

[25] *Neues Deutschland*, June 10, 1969.

international conference on Berlin,[26] setting off a violent East German attack on the Social Democrats' leaders that implicated Poland indirectly. Harsh criticism of the SDP leadership continued throughout the West German election campaign during which the GDR went so far as to accord full voting rights to the East Berlin deputies to the Volksrat. It was a move that did nothing to aid Moscow's attempt to get talks going on Berlin. Previously Berlin deputies had not voted in either Parliament, so this ploy increased East Berlin's ties to the GDR; thereby presenting the allies with a *fait accompli* in which they could either grant West Berlin deputies similar rights and thus complicate a potential future settlement (incidentally giving Brandt 13 additional votes in the Bundestag) or refuse to do so at the expense of subtly weakening West Berlin's future bargaining power. It was not an easy choice.[27]

When the Brandt government won the election, East German nervousness must have jumped several notches. Despite their desire to take the lead in dealing with the German question, the Ulbricht government had shown little enthusiasm for even the Grand Coalition's low-level initiatives toward East Europe. The Social Democrats' *Ostpolitik* might hold more opportunities but it could also be more dangerous. Brezhnev's speech at East Germany's 20th anniversary celebration did not help matters. The Russian leader spoke in much softer terms than his host, avoiding any demand for de jure recognition of East Germany by the new Bonn government.[28] This on top of the other signs of thaw in Soviet policy toward the Federal Republic could only increase the GDR's fears of isolation—notwithstanding Brezhnev's pledge that "the entire might of the armed forces of the Soviet Union and of the whole socialist community" stood ready to protect the inviolability of borders.

Moreover, the new West German government rapidly met two of the Budapest Appeal's criteria. In his October 28 inaugural address Brandt offered the formula of "two states in one German nation." [29] It stopped short of recognition of the GDR regime, but tacitly abandoned Bonn's claim to be the sole representative of the German people. He also pledged to sign the Nuclear Nonproliferation Treaty as soon as Washington and

[26] *Trybuna ludu*, July 22, 1969.

[27] See Whetten, "The Role of East Germany in West German-Soviet Relations," p. 517.

[28] *Pravda*, October 7, 1969. The version appearing in *Neues Deutschland* was drastically cut, a sure sign of East German displeasure. *Neues Deutschland*, October 7, 1969.

[29] *Frankfurter Allgemeine Zeitung*, October 29, 1969.

Moscow clarified the problem of West German access to nuclear information and research for peaceful purposes.[30] Only the question of borders remained to be negotiated.

Never had the objective possibilities for a European settlement appeared so good. It was an unparalleled situation in terms of East bloc coalition politics. Should the Warsaw Pact pick up the options or pretend that they did not exist? Foreign ministers of the member states met in Prague October 30. At first glance the depth of differences seemed to have paralyzed the meeting. Although they undoubtedly were discussed,[31] the resulting statement did not directly refer to the changes in West Germany. However the explicit approval of bilateral consultations[32] in preparing for a European Security Conference had direct implications in terms of the member states' contacts with the Brandt government. That this was not the preferred East German strategy was evident.

Shortly after his return, GDR Foreign Minister Otto Winzer tried to set limits. Couched in the form of an attack on Bonn's liking for bilateralism, his remarks had an obvious relevance for the GDR's socialist allies as well.

> The Bonn government has declared that it considers the successful conclusion of bilateral agreements on the renunciation of force "an important step on the road to a security conference for Europe." This view of Bonn gives rise to some doubts. It is true that an all European agreement on the renunciation of force would not exclude a bilateral renunciation of force, but it would in any case be wrong to regard such bilateral agreements as necessary preliminary steps on the road to a security conference and to an all European agreement on the renunciation of force to be concluded at such a conference.[33]

[30] Despite strong parliamentary opposition, the Bonn government actually signed the treaty one month later, November 28, 1969.

[31] Czechoslovak sources stressed that it had "above all" been necessary to analyze the "new aspects of Bonn's policy" (Prague Domestic Television Service in Czech 1800 GMT November 4, 1969). That the opinions of the member states differed on the issue of the Brandt government's intentions (*Mlada fronta*, November 4, 1969) was not surprising. The GDR leadership could not be expected to welcome Poland's cautious enthusiasm at Brandt's stated intention to respond to Gomułka's suggestion of May 17 by submitting a proposal to Warsaw for talks. See Karol Malcuzynski's commentary in *Trybuna ludu*, October 30, 1969. Such discussions would concern "not only Poland or her relations with the German Federal Republic" but were described as a question of stabilization and security in Europe.

[32] Statement of the Conference of Foreign Ministers of the Warsaw Pact Member States, *Pravda*, November 1, 1969. See also Ion Finenarus' commentary in *Scînteia*, November 4, 1969.

[33] *Neues Deutschland*, November 4, 1969.

In his interview with a Bulgarian newspaper, Winzer subsequently made quite clear that the GDR itself had no intention of participating in bilateral discussions with the Federal Republic on issues of European security or anything else. When asked his opinion on prospects for the desired conference, he emphasized the opposition in West Germany and dismissed the request by the West German Minister of Foreign Affairs for prior "intra-German talks" with the suggestion that Mr. Scheel read the proposals of the Prague Conference. The GDR government had "contributed" to the joint Warsaw Pact position. That was enough. The Brandt-Scheel government would do better to concentrate on overcoming "the aggressive and revanchist past of the Grand Coalition era in West Germany." [34]

The Moscow Summit: A Compromise Solution

East German reluctance aside, other pact members stressed the importance of bilateral initiatives. The Czechs pointed out that Moscow had already handed concrete proposals to Bonn. The Bucharest council of ministers emphasized Rumania's consistent support for bilateral and multilateral discussions and approved the activity of the Rumanian delegation in Prague.[35] Even the Bulgarians juxtaposed favorable bilateral progress toward European security to opportunities stemming from the change of government in West Germany.[36]

Bonn's signing of the Nuclear Nonproliferation Treaty in late November was followed almost immediately by a summit meeting of Warsaw Pact party and government leaders in Moscow. Ulbricht reportedly went to Moscow 48 hours ahead of the other delegations to seek Soviet support.[37] His early arrival signaled the depth of the East German leadership's anxiety at its differences with other member states on the question of how best to protect the GDR's interests vis-à-vis the Federal Republic.

If Ulbricht urged the case of exclusively multilateral contacts with West Germany (as he most likely did), he had limited success. The vague wording of the joint statement could be construed to cover both options. Bilateral contacts with Bonn were not explicitly sanctioned as in October; nor were they in any way forbidden. As is frequently the case with sensi-

[34] *Rabotnichesko delo*, November 28, 1969.
[35] *Scînteia*, November 15, 1969.
[36] See article by D. Bratanov in *Otechestven front*, November 14, 1969.
[37] *Le Monde*, December 3, 1969.

tive issues in Warsaw Pact documents, the advantages of bilateralism versus multilateralism simply were not mentioned. The statement itself referred to an "exchange of opinions" on the results of the elections in the Federal Republic and expressed "unanimous" viewpoints only twice; first on the need for vigilance against revanchist forces, second in favor of ending the arms race by means of universal and complete disarmament.[38]

The final document of the meeting included the first public Warsaw Pact assessment of Brandt's Social Democrat coalition. That it appeared at all was a step forward in intra-alliance negotiation. Obviously the product of compromise, the statement evaluated the changes in West Germany, praised the Federal Republic's signing of the Nuclear Nonproliferation Treaty, and identified growing West German social forces favoring cooperation among states. It balanced this positive picture with a warning against manifestations of revanchism and neofascism. These dangers must be kept in mind. Most important from Ulbricht's view, this statement (unlike Brezhnev's October speech) repeated the demand that existing European borders be recognized as final and unchangeable and called on all states to establish equal relations with East Germany on the basis of international law. It was the first Warsaw Pact document to put forth the East German leader's formula, i.e., de jure recognition for the GDR. Earlier statements had only demanded that Bonn accept the existence of the two German states, meaning de facto recognition at best.[39]

However, although the Ulbricht position was formally accepted as joint policy in this regard, it was not made a precondition for anything. The signers of the statement limited themselves "to reaffirming their opinion" on the issue of recognition. To state one's opinion is not to make a demand. Such a formulation implied that other opinions were at least open

[38] *Pravda,* December 5, 1969.

[39] For an interesting, if in my view somewhat too pessimistic, opinion of the extent to which Pankow continues to limit Warsaw Pact initiatives in Europe, see R. Waring Herrick, "Soviet Foreign Policy and the German Question," Radio Liberty Research, January 12, 1970. I can agree much more with his earlier analysis, "Moscow Summit Sanctions Controlled Steps Toward Bilateral Détente with Bonn," Radio Liberty Research, December 15, 1969. One of the pitfalls of intensive day-by-day analysis of events within the Warsaw Pact is that there is a tendency not to allow patterns enough time to emerge before judging their success or failure. By January 12, Ulbricht was still waiting for a reply to his draft treaty. It would have been strange indeed if the other member states had not suspended their own contacts with Bonn at least until Brandt's speech on January 14, and supportive statements during that time should not be taken as a willingness to allow a subsequent GDR veto over Soviet or even Polish policy.

for discussion, and it would come as a surprise to none of the European socialist countries that Bonn did not agree. The conclusion that the December session "confirmed the unity of view" among its participants was somewhat optimistic unless it is interpreted to mean that they agree to disagree.[40] Moscow almost immediately began talks with Bonn on the possibilities for a renunciation-of-force agreement. Although the East Germans seemed to have resigned themselves with respect to bilateralism, Winzer's statement after the Prague meeting had shown little enthusiasm for such discussions and the GDR Minister of Foreign Affairs did not seem to have changed his mind.[41] Despite these differences, preparations for Polish-West German border talks began in late December and other pact members continued to openly support bilateral consultation on the European Security Conference.[42]

In general, East European commentary indicated that the gathering was marked by Soviet willingness to allow genuine consultation within the coalition. Even the Rumanians were optimistic about its results;[43] stressing that now each socialist country could "make a contribution of major importance." Bucharest had not been noted for enthusiasm in regard to measures raising the level of pact policy coordination.[44] Thus, the price the Soviets paid for Rumanian support of continued political collaboration may well be an increased opportunity for East European influence on pact decision-making.

[40] Joint statement, *Pravda*, December 5, 1969, emphasized in a Soviet editorial, *Pravda*, December 6, 1969.

[41] In a harsh attack on Bonn, Winzer strongly implied that the Federal Republic had no right to conclude a treaty with the Soviet Union until it recognized East Germany—the criticism indirectly applied to Moscow as well. *Neues Deutschland*, December 17, 1969. Ulbricht had "welcomed the negotiations" just three days earlier (*Neues Deutschland*, December 14, 1969) leading to the conclusion that either the GDR leadership was divided (a possibility in any government Communist or not) or at best had extremely mixed feelings in the matter.

[42] For an authoritative Polish statement strongly endorsing bilateral relations among states, see Premier Jozef Cyrankiewicz's December 22 speech to the Sejm, *Trybuna ludu*, December 31, 1969. The Polish Premier made quite clear that in Warsaw's view recognition of the Oder-Neisse border was the starting point for more normal relations with Bonn. Re Czech and Hungarian articles to this effect, see Ross Johnson, *The Warsaw Pact "European Security" Campaign.*

[43] *Scînteia*, December 7, 1969.

[44] Radio broadcasts emphasized that similar meetings would follow, a sign that any substantive progress along bilateral lines might well require prior multilateral ratification. Radio Prague, December 7, 1969; Radio Budapest December 6, 1969; for a good analysis, see R. Waring Herrick, "Moscow Summit Sanctions, "Controlled Steps Toward Bilateral Détente with Bonn," *Radio Liberty Research Bulletin*, December 15, 1969.

The GDR Draft Treaty

As for the East Germans, the SED Central Committee Plenum, in a Rumanian-like gesture, approved the activities of the GDR delegation to the Moscow meeting. (It was a pattern begun by Bucharest some years before and in circumstances when its delegation clearly had been defending a minority position within the alliance.) Then, in part so as not to be isolated in the coming flurry of bilateral consultations, the GDR tentatively retreated from its hostile rejection of "intra-German talks" after the October pact meeting. Ulbricht spoke favorably of increased chances for cooperation with West Germany. A letter to the President of the Federal Republic proposing negotiations on an East German draft treaty for equal relations between the two German states soon followed his change in tone.[45] The proposed treaty hardly could be considered a concession. It listed familiar GDR demands: (1) normal, equal relations based on international law; (2) the inviolability of borders; (3) establishment of diplomatic relations and an exchange of embassies; (4) recognition of West Berlin as an independent political unit.[46] The only sign of softening came in the Ulbricht regime's willingness to start discussions without first being recognized as a sovereign, equal state. The earlier Kiesinger-Stoph exchanges had floundered over a GDR demand for recognition prior to negotiation.

Such a program was patently unacceptable to Bonn. On the other hand, Ulbricht probably did not expect it to be accepted. The GDR and the Federal Republic have had long experiences with each other's bargaining positions. Neither actually expects concessions of vital points prior to negotiations. Rather, as introduced at this time the draft served other purposes. It brought the GDR into East bloc dialogues with West Germany as a major actor, thereby avoiding the unpleasant position of disgruntled spectator. Further, and perhaps most important to the Ulbricht leadership, this move served as a temporary brake on Soviet and Polish bilateral discussions, which the East Germans could hope would be fraternally suspended until Bonn responded to Pankow's offer. Certainly East German commentary on the draft treaty was not the kind to raise hopes about the GDR's intentions. A major editorial article published in

[45] Unofficial translations in *The New York Times*, December 22, 1969.
[46] *Neues Deutschland*, December 21, 1969.

all GDR newspapers on December 23 flatly attacked the idea of intra-German relations as ideological subversion.

> The idle talk of so-called intra-German relations and allegedly still exist-ing "unity of the nation" is intended to fan nationalism and to serve the ideological political preparation of plans for subduing the GDR. *The experiences of the years 1953, 1956, 1961, and 1968* make it clear that all plans for wrenching a single member from the community of socialist states are completely hopeless. The governing circles of the Federal Re-public would be well advised to finally abandon, *after all these defeats,* this bankrupt policy of "all or nothing," that is to say, the attempts first to blackmail and patronize the GDR by nationalist methods in some form or other and then to subdue it.[47] [Italics mine.]

This interpretation of past upheavals within the bloc was a pointed re-minder to Soviet as well as West German governing circles.

In these circumstances, Bonn's response might be predictable but Mos-cow's was not. That the Soviet press waited a week before commenting on Ulbricht's offer indicated mixed feelings. On December 27 both *Pravda* and *Izvestia* warned that to reject the GDR's proposals might hurt Bonn's chances of improving relations with other Communist states in Europe. Yet the articles in no way explicitly tied acceptance of the East German draft with Soviet-West German talks on renunciation of the use of force, begun December 8, and their tone was much softer than that of the East German media's criticism of the Federal Republic's delayed response.

Still Ulbricht's press conference on January 19 did not move the two Germanies closer to one another.[48] He attacked Brandt's January 14 speech to the Bundestag, repeated the demands of the draft treaty, and in Bonn's view upped the ante by suggesting that revision of the West Ger-man constitution and amendment of the Paris treaties of 1955 might be necessary.

The Brandt government countered by suggesting negotiations to be conducted on the basis of "equality of rights and nondiscrimination." It ignored the proposed treaty but did not reject it. Instead the letter pro-posed talks on all open questions between the two governments. This gesture did not bring much warmth from the GDR. To the Ulbricht

[47] *Neues Deutschland,* December 23, 1969.
[48] *Neues Deutschland,* January 20, 1970.

regime, "equality of rights" was a weak substitute for equal relations based on the principles of international law. If the East German leadership had its way, there would be no discussions on those terms.

Yet despite Soviet general support of the East German draft treaty, Brandt is probably right that the road to "intra-German" talks (if not agreement) lies through Moscow rather than Pankow; and Soviet-West German relations improved radically within a matter of days. The West German Secretary of State Egon Bahr arrived in Moscow January 28. On February 3, Moscow and Bonn concluded a commercial agreement whereby the USSR would supply West Germany with natural gas, and West German banks extended credit of 1.2 billion deutsche marks to pay for "pipes" and other equipment.[49]

Serious rapprochement between Bonn and Moscow could mean significant changes in both East European policies toward West Germany and in Warsaw Pact politics in Europe. But before going into these political repercussions, there remains the military component of normalization. Therefore it is necessary to look at the progress on the institutional changes attempted by the Budapest March 1969 PCC meeting, i.e., the issue of stepped up military integration.

Reorganization of the Joint Armed Forces

Despite the politically divisive effects of the invasion of Czechoslovakia by five members of the Warsaw Pact in August 1968, military activity of the pact was intensified, if anything, as a result of that invasion. The defense ministers met in Moscow October 28–30. A session of the chiefs-of-staff followed in Bucharest roughly a month later.[50] Although the Moscow meeting had agreed in principle "to strengthen the Warsaw Pact" militarily,[51] this long-standing objective made no visible progress until

---

[49] *Pravda*, February 3, 1970. Polish-West German talks opened on February 5. The next day Gomułka received the order of Lenin award on his 65th birthday for "his outstanding services to the development of fraternal friendship and cooperation between the peoples of the Soviet Union and the Polish People's Republic." *Pravda*, February 6, 1970.

[50] That the Rumanians hosted the meeting was obviously a conciliatory gesture at a time when Bucharest was under heavy attack for condemning the Czech invasion. Ceauşescu's almost simultaneous restatement of his rejection of the Brezhnev doctrine of limited sovereignty within the socialist commonwealth defined the limits of such conciliation.

[51] Statement of the March 1968 PCC Meeting, Document 6, p. 224. In attack on March 1968 Dresden meeting to which Rumania had not been invited, Ceauşescu had revealed that the earlier Sofia session had decided that the ministers of the armed forces should draw up draft proposals for improving the activity of the joint command. *Scînteia*,

the March 1969 political consultative committee meeting in Budapest. The Budapest meeting approved both a standing committee of defense ministers and a new statute on the Joint Armed Forces. Based on drafts prepared by the member countries during the time that had elapsed since the PCC March 1968 meeting in Sofia, this reform was the first formal change in military aspects of the coalition since the communiqué on the establishment of the Joint Armed Forces in 1955. The documents were not published, so it is hard to say whether or not they represented a significant jump in actual integration of forces. But indirect evidence from Czechoslovakian and Rumanian sources make reasonably clear what the reorganization did not do.[52] Czechoslovak Foreign Minister Jan Marko denied rumors that increased economic commitment was involved, or that there had been any suggestion of using the armed forces of any country outside its own territories (a suspicion most likely tied to the speculation that Warsaw Pact forces would be asked to support the Soviets against the Chinese).[53] Alexander Dubček also reassured the Czechs that the military reforms were designed to improve the efficiency of existing defense expenditures rather than to increase them.[54] His carefully worded denial that relations with China were discussed at the PCC meeting left open the possibility that the question of China had figured prominently in the two days of discussion prior to the brief formal session.

As for Bucharest, Ceauşescu flatly told the joint meeting of the State Council and Council of Ministers asked to endorse the Warsaw Pact documents that

---

April 28, 1969. The process was interrupted by the invasion of Czechoslovakia, but according to the Czechoslovak representative at Budapest, Jan Marko, it was this work that made the reforms possible. Czechoslovak Foreign Minister Jan Marko's television speech of March 20, 1969.

[52] Marko's speech, *ibid.;* also Radio Prague in German to West Germany, 2000 GMT, March 20, 1969. Subsequently there have been a number of signs that Czechoslovak worries about defense strains on the economy are shared by both East Germany and Poland. See the article by Siegfried Schonherr, "Über den Zusammenhang zwischen Wirtschaft und Landesverteidigung beim Aufbau des entwickelten gesellschaftlichen Systems des Sozialismus in der DDR," *Wirtschaftswissenschaft* 8 (August 1969): 1161–1175. Similar economic concerns may also have contributed to Rumanian discontent within the pact as early as 1966. See Wettig, "Die europaische Sicherheit in der Politik des Ostblocks 1966," p. 98.

[53] Yugoslav commentators considered the Sino-Soviet border clashes high on the Warsaw Pact informal if not formal agenda, TANYUG, March 16, 1969, and went so far as to suggest that a last minute Soviet proposal to bring Mongolia into the organization had been turned down, *The Guardian,* April 16, 1969. See also Anatole Shub report of the account of an anonymous participant, *International Herald Tribune,* March 19, 1969.

[54] Dubček interview, *Rudé Právo,* March 19, 1969.

. . . in accordance with the constitution and the laws of our country, our army cannot be engaged in any action except by the constitutional organs. Furthermore, only these organs can approve the presence on our territory, in any situation, of foreign troops. We appreciate that the manner in which these problems are expressed in the military documents signed in Budapest correspond with this spirit and, therefore, we deem it necessary to adopt them.[55]

In short, only the Rumanian party and government would decide where Rumanian armed forces would fight, against whom, and under what conditions "foreign troops" would be present in Rumania. *Scînteia* went on to remind its readers that the Warsaw Treaty Organization had been created solely as an instrument to defend its members against outside aggression in Europe; that "this is the only plausible reason for the existence of this organization"[56] (an indirect restatement of earlier Rumanian criticism of the "allied socialist" invasion of Czechoslovakia). This unambiguous commentary once again put forth Bucharest's preferred version of reality within the Warsaw Pact—coalition politics hewing to the principles of equality, mutual advantage, independence, territorial integrity, sovereignty, and noninterference in internal affairs.

Generally East European reactions indicate that the Budapest reorganization does not violate these principles. In fact, if Hungarian Defense Minister Lajos Czinege's account is accurate, the influence of the smaller member states on joint military planning has been increased rather than weakened.[57] The new committee of defense ministers is in no way a supranational command. As Czinege put it: "This is actually a new body only in an organizational sense because these ministers have also conferred among each other regularly in the past."[58] The committee met for the first time in Moscow, December 22–23, less than two weeks after a

---

[55] *Scînteia*, April 11, 1969.

[56] *Scînteia*, April 12, 1969.

[57] *Népszabadság*, May 10, 1969. The Hungarian Defense Minister described another somewhat ambiguously constituted "organ to coordinate military technology" that is to work on rationalizing Pact resources in research and development as well as "perfecting" military equipment and weapons systems. This would most likely mean greater East European participation in what has previously been an area of primarily Soviet control. Indeed such articles as Schonherr's discussion of the relations of defense needs to the economy may be preparing the East German population for greater responsibility (and perhaps expense) in this respect. Czinege's opinion along these lines was subsequently restated by Czechoslovakia Minister of Defense Martin Dzur, *Rudé Právo*, May 13, 1970.

[58] Quoted by R. Waring Herrick, "Warsaw Pact Restructuring Strengthens Principle of National Control," Radio Liberty Research (Munich), March 6, 1970.

meeting of the Warsaw Pact "Military Council,"[59] which in turn followed the summit meeting of WTO party and government leaders during the first week of December. Its brief communiqué stressed "unanimous agreement," and atmosphere of "complete understanding," and "unity of views."[60] There were no contrary signals coming from Bucharest (at this point in time still the acid test for agreement within the pact), and, in fact, East European sources had expressed considerable satisfaction at results of the earlier summit session.[61]

All of which makes most unlikely the theory that the reorganization actually meant a Soviet-controlled, unified NATO-style command designed to enforce the Brezhnev Doctrine.[62] This speculation stemmed largely from Pact Chief-of-Staff General Shtemenko's contribution to the Lenin centenary series.[63] Although his wording may have been confusing, Shtemenko explicitly emphasized national control by each pact member of its own forces. Indeed his article is most interesting for what it does *not* say about the role of Soviet internationalism in Eastern Europe.

"As genuine internationalists, Soviet soldiers fought in the thirties in Spain, China, and Mongolia." Shtemenko does not mention the "saving" of Hungarian communism in 1956 (a point about which Khrushchev had been adamant at the May 1958 PCC meeting) or the Red Army's contribution to fighting counterrevolution in Czechoslovakia in 1968. Since the Soviet view of its role in these two cases is well known, not to mention them was a concession to East European sensitivities which would have been quite irrelevant if the chief-of-staff had been announcing the formation of elite Warsaw Pact contingents specifically to enforce the Brezhnev Doctrine's interpretation of military responsibility within

[59] *Pravda*, December 11, 1969. It is not quite so obvious what the "Military Council" is. (The name was most likely chosen to imply symmetry to the NATO Council.) Also created in Budapest, it has met three times, twice prior to the sessions of the Committee of Defense Ministers. The participants are not listed (although the Hungarian MTI Domestic service indicated that the Hungarian Defense Minister took part in the April 27–28, 1970 meeting held in Budapest). According to Yakubovsky, "The leadership and coordination of the joint armed forces activities is undertaken by the joint command, the military council, headquarters and other organs" (*Pravda*, May 14, 1970), indicating that the council is an implementing rather than a policy-making body.

[60] Communiqué in *Pravda*, December 24, 1969.

[61] Moreover the Soviet press took this occasion to quote in detail glowing East European statements on the earlier meeting, a sure sign that Moscow was not insensitive to a possible connection. *Pravda*, December 28, 1969.

[62] Tanjug, January 24, 1970, *Neue Zürcher Zeitung*, January 29, 1970, and *The Economist*, February 21, 1970.

[63] *Krasnaya zvezda*, January 24, 1970. Document 11.

the socialist community. Nor in that case is it probable that the next issue of the military newspaper would have published a long article by the Rumanian Defense Minister Ionita restating the principle that the Rumanian armed forces are directed by the Rumanian Party and Government.[64]

Rumanian response was delayed, and certainly the level of touchiness in Bucharest is high enough so that Ceauşescu would have shown major concern before February 5 if he had detected any such implications. When he did react, however, the Rumanian leader was straight forward. Speaking to a conference of the Rumanian armed forces, he reiterated that the Warsaw Treaty had been concluded to defend the member states against an attack in Europe by "imperialist powers." In this context he once again explained the pact's 1969 military reforms:

> The point of departure for these decisions was the necessity of strengthening the combat capacity of *each national army* to enable it to be ready to fight *side by side* with the other fraternal armies in case of aggression unleashing in *Europe* by the *imperialist forces* against a member state of this treaty. [Italics mine.]

Ceauşescu went on to stress that military cooperation, as understood by the Rumanians, rested on (1) principles underlying relations socialist states and (2) treaties currently in force.

> [Such cooperation] . . . rules out any interference in the internal affairs of a country or an army collaborating within these treaties.
>
> The only leader of our armed forces is the party, the government and the supreme national command. Only they can give orders and only these orders can be carried out. . . .
>
> The idea of yielding a part of the right of command and leadership of the army, however small, by the party and government is inconceivable.[65]

There was no doubt that Rumania would have walked out of any Warsaw Pact meeting that agreed to the rumored supranational military integration. Nor was Bucharest buying Shtemenko's ever-so-veiled suggestion that "internationalist" duty might cause socialist forces (hopefully from the Moscow's view East European as well as Soviet) to fight again in

---

[64] *Krasnaya zvezda*, January 25, 1970.

[65] *Scînteia*, February 6, 1970. Given the nature of intraparty esoteric communication, the fact that Ceauşescu's speech occurred the day after the anniversary of the at-that-time unrenewed Soviet-Rumanian Treaty of Friendship, Cooperation, and Mutual Assistance indicates what Bucharest considered an acceptable treaty as well.

China. Rumanian obligations were in Europe, in instances of "imperialist" attack on one of the members of the Warsaw Pact. Should such an attack occur, Rumanian armed forces taking orders only from the Rumanian National command would fight "side by side" with the other socialist armies. The language could not have been more blunt.

Perhaps most important, the flurry surrounding the Shtemenko incident brought sharply into focus the complicated interaction of intraalliance organizational issues, problems of policy, and external pressures within the Warsaw Pact. And it was primarily a Sino-Soviet-German equation that held the key to coalition developments throughout 1970.

7
EAST GERMANY:
THE POLITICS
OF PERSUASION

ALTHOUGH THE Soviet–Albanian split and since 1963 the Soviet–Rumanian political-organizational disagreements have been accepted as ongoing conflicts by Western scholars, today there is no such common assumption with respect to Soviet–East German "differences." There are questions as to whether such differences exist, whether the sensitivity of the Ulbricht regime was not just a convenient excuse for the Russians who want the benefits of détente without the price. Perhaps. It is not unknown for states in the East or West to prefer token concessions.

However, the depth of East German concern at bilateral negotiations with the Federal Republic—discussed in Chapter 6—has convinced me that throughout 1969 and most of 1970, Soviet–East German differences were no mirage. In 1969, the possibility of a serious Moscow-Bonn rapprochement with its probable consequences for the relations of other East Europe states to West Germany threatened what the GDR considered its survival interests. Hence the almost frantic attempts to restrict contacts to multilateral Warsaw Pact initiatives. That Ulbricht failed in this effort does not make the attempt less real or less important for evolution of the alliance. For even as he tried to use the Warsaw Pact as a brake on bilateral contacts with Bonn, the Soviets, Poles, and Rumanians utilized the joint machinery to press the East Germans into precisely such bilateral talks with the West Germans.

This chapter is the story of Ulbricht's one step forward. (It is in no sense a prediction that, given the opportunity—unlikely to happen in the atmosphere at the time of this writing, in May 1971—the East German party, now headed by Erich Honecker, will not immediately take two steps backward.) And since Moscow's German policy was undoubtedly formed with one eye to the East, it is also an attempt to untangle the meaning of the Russia-China-Germany triangle for the Warsaw Pact alliance. In so doing it becomes once again in part a story of Rumanian resistance. Thus 1970 is more than slightly problematical.

There are too many actors, and everything seems to be happening at once, which makes writing about it difficult because neither Western culture nor the English language is comfortable with problems of simultaneity. In short, 1970 is too recent to fall into any neat pattern and too important to ignore. Therefore, let us begin by returning to the sharp upswing in Moscow-Bonn relations in early February. At that time the commercial agreement involving 1.2 billion deutschmarks in West German credit was not long in finding its political counterpart.

The Politics of Inter-German Talks

Following a series of high-level Soviet–West German meetings,[1] Soviet Foreign Minister Gromyko visited East Berlin at the end of February. The resulting Soviet–East German communiqué was more moderate than most GDR pronouncements and unmistakably marked by the current Soviet interpretation of the West German scene. From Ulbricht's view the communiqué left much to be desired. Although it referred to the December Moscow meeting, it did not reaffirm the "opinion" of the participants that all states should establish relations with the GDR based on international law.

The two parties agreed only that "relations between all states should be based on the principles of sovereign equality, respect for territorial integrity, the inviolability of state borders, and internal social order." The GDR expressed willingness to shape its relations with the Federal Republic, as well as with other states, "on this basis, which is generally recognized in international practice."[2] International *practice* is not international law. The implication was that de facto recognition was the best

---

[1] Gromyko dined at the West German embassy for the first time in 15 years on February 10 and West German Foreign Minister Walter Scheel stopped in Moscow on his way to India on the 13th, the same day that Bahr unexpectedly met with Kosygin. For an excellent analysis of these developments, see *RFE Research* "Continued Improvement in Soviet-West German Relations" (April 24, 1970). It was at this time, February 12 to be exact, that Stoph replied to Brandt's letter of January 22 by agreeing to meet February 19 or 26. His reply was cold and specified that in the GDR interpretation "equality of right" meant that the two governments would recognize each other as "sovereign subjects of international law with equal rights." *Neues Deutschland*, February 13, 1970.

[2] *Pravda*, February 28, 1970.

the GDR could get. Bonn could argue that Brandt's formula of two German states within one German national was substantially the same thing. At bottom hardliners in the East German leadership could not help but have thought (as did Peking)[3] that such a formulation sold out their most vital interests.[4]

If the difficulties surrounding the East-West German talks about talks can be seen as a fair indication of Pankow's frame of mind, an outside observer might be excused for thinking that the GDR had been pushed inwardly kicking and screaming to the conference table. These technical discussions bogged down on the issue of Berlin, the East Germans insisting that Brandt not set foot in West Berlin before or after his meeting with Stoph in the eastern half of the city. Not only would yielding to such a demand have hurt Brandt's *Ostpolitik* domestically but as the former Mayor of West Berlin he would have seemed absurd. The stalemate ended when both delegations agreed to meet in the East German city of Erfurt, thereby making it possible for Brandt to bypass both sectors of Berlin.

East German unambiguous demands concerning the Erfurt meeting left no doubt that the formula of Soviet-GDR Communiqué of February 28 had been Gromyko's and not Winzer's. Two days before the meeting Ulbricht attacked the transfer of the meeting site from East Berlin and repeated his opinion that peaceful coexistence between the two German states required recognition under international law.[5] On the day of the talks, *Neues Deutschland* insisted that normal relations could come about only "according to the principles of sovereign equality, territorial integrity, and inviolability of state frontiers, according to the principles of international law. . . ."[6]

The Erfurt communiqué limited itself to a brief formal statement that the meeting had occurred. Indeed, that Stoph accepted the West German Chancellor's invitation to meet again in the West German city of Kassel

---

[3] At the time of the February 3 credit agreement, the Chinese accused "Soviet revisionist social imperialism" of "selling out the sovereignty and interests of the German people" by making this "dirty deal with West German militarism." Peking NCNA International Service in English, 1823 GMT, February 9, 1970.

[4] Then party security chief Erich Honecker's hysterical speech accusing Bonn of preparing for a third world war just five days after Stoph agreed to meet leaves little doubt as to how he must have felt on the matter. It was a controversial statement at the time, for only a brief excerpt appeared in the GDR press on February 17 with publication of the entire speech delayed until *Neues Deutschland*, February 22, 1970.

[5] Interview granted *Agence francaise d'image*, East Berlin radio in German to Germany 2042 GMT, March 17, 1970.

[6] *Neues Deutschland*, March 19, 1970.

on May 21 was more than might have been expected. Subsequently Stoph's report on the session reiterated the demand for recognition under international law and rejected any form of "special intra-German relations." Although he carefully did not make recognition a precondition for talks, the message was clear. Nor was the cold war language used by SED Politburo member Albert Norden at the People's Chamber meeting to discuss Stoph's report encouraging for future progress.[7] The GDR had no intention of backing down.

Still, Moscow's assessment of the meeting was cautiously optimistic.[8] For despite East German coldness, the thaw in Soviet–West German relations had progressed. Negotiations between Gromyko and Bahr overlapped with the technical talks setting up the Brandt-Stoph meeting, and on March 22 Brandt himself said that outlines of an agreement with Moscow were in sight.[9] Publicly the Soviets still supported Ulbricht's demand for recognition under international law, but such recognition was in no way tied to the ongoing negotiations with Bonn[10] indicating that an agreement along the lines of the February communiqué's wording "inviolability of borders and internal social order" was at least a possibility. If Soviet–West German renunciation of force agreement had been even substantially agreed upon by the May 21 meeting in Kassel, Moscow, would have had a strong interest in seeing corresponding progress in the inter-German talks. Otherwise the Soviets would be extremely vulnerable to Peking's charge of selling out GDR interests.

By the end of May, however, the situation within the Warsaw Pact itself was increasingly complex. To understand the mounting individual and collective pressures, it is necessary to look eastward.

The Role of the Enemy: Escalating Sino-Soviet Polemics

Like Janus, the Soviet Union faces in two directions, and Russian leaders have long had nightmares of a war on both fronts, fears of being squeezed between attacks from East and West simultaneously. At the end

---

[7] Norden spoke scathingly of "revanchists, neofascists, and imperialist wolves." East Berlin Domestic radio in German, 1141 GMT, March 21, 1970.

[8] For example, the trade union newspaper blamed West Germany for not having shown a real readiness to improve relations but felt that "clearly there is a certain shift forward." *Trud*, March 24, 1970.

[9] Quoted by *Bayerischer Rundfunk*, March 22, 1970. At the same time, West German sources announced that Bonn was to open a Consulate-General in Leningrad, while Moscow would establish one in Hamburg.

[10] Soviet Ambassador to the GDR Abrasimov in *Neues Deutschland*, April 1, 1970.

of World War II, Stalin went to great lengths to secure the western borders. Given 40 million Russians dead, the demand for friendly buffer states between the Soviet Union and Germany had weight among the Allies. And to this day fear of a revanchist Germany acts to consolidate Soviet interests throughout East Europe. Therefore it is not surprising that, on the one hand, Sino-Soviet border clashes pushed Moscow toward rapprochement with Bonn, or on the other, that the Soviets wanted their Warsaw Pact allies to go along in the process of redefining who is the main enemy. Even as early as 1967 and certainly by 1969 there were signs that Moscow tried to commit the East European socialist states to defend the inviolability of all borders rather than those in Europe referred to by the Warsaw Pact. Throughout 1970, as improvement in Soviet-German relations paralleled escalating Sino-Soviet tensions, such pressure increased.

Ever since the March 1969 clashes on the Sino-Soviet border, Moscow had shown an interest in collective defense in the East. Whether that interest grew out of military-political imperatives or was a part of a diplomatic campaign to pressure Peking into negotiations on the border issue is debatable, but by September there were indeed rumors that Air Force units from Poland, Hungary, and Bulgaria had been transferred to Soviet Central Asia within striking distance of China.[11]

During the winter the border talks broke down. Then in January 1970, Kuznetsov's return to Peking notwithstanding, the Soviet press began attacking the "war psychosis" in China, in some instances reporting "total mobilization" and "preparation for aggression" in the Chinese frontier provinces.[12] Seen in the context of stepped up references[13] to the Brezhnev Doctrine on the common internationalist duty of socialist countries to defend one another, such accusations had ominous implications. By March I. Aleksandrov, a pseudonym for one of *Pravda*'s most active

---

[11] Don Cook reporting from Berlin, *The New York Post*, September 13, 1969. It is questionable that the Soviet Air Defense Command would need help in countering the Chinese air threat, nor is it likely that the mobile armor of the Red Army would seriously need Warsaw Pact reinforcements despite the fact that the Chinese could put more troops on the border than the Soviets. I am grateful to Captain William A. Platte, USN, for our conversations on this matter.

[12] See *Literaturnaya gazeta*, January 14, 1970; in March the military newspaper accused China of building military roads to the Soviet border, *Krasnaya zvezda*, March 31, 1970.

[13] For example, E. P. Sitkovskiy, "Marksizm-Leninizm—edinoe internatsional'noe uchenie rabochego klassa," *Filosofskie nauki* 1 (1970) and Colonel S. Lukonin, in *Pravda*, March 7, 1970.

polemicists against the Dubček government during 1968, had joined those harping on the dangerous "sabre-rattling" in Peking.[14]

In all fairness, although the Chinese had contributed their share to the polemics, Mao may well have thought that he had reason to fear a preemptive Soviet strike. Certainly neither Soviet language nor military maneuvers in the spring of 1970 would have calmed such fears. Nor was the suggestion—even as a trial balloon—that the Soviet Ambassador to Czechoslovakia (a man obviously symbolic of the "allied socialist" invasion of that country) return to China exactly fraternal. Moscow finally appointed V. I. Stepakov, the apparently downgraded head of the Central Committee's Department of Propaganda and Agitation.[15] He could not have been a welcome choice to Peking. That he was accepted at that time showed the depth of Chinese concern to maintain contact—or perhaps to stall. For during the celebration of Lenin's birthday, Peking came forward with a monumental blast accusing the Soviets of "social-imperialism, social-fascism, and social-militarism" and attacking Brezhnev personally as a new Hitler. This outpouring rose to heights of rhetoric on the issue of the Brezhnev Doctrine:

> Now let us examine what stuff this "Brezhnev doctrine" is made of.
> First, the theory of "limited sovereignty." Brezhnev and company say that safeguarding their so-called interests of socialism means safeguarding "supreme sovereignty." They flagrantly declare that Soviet revisionism has the right to determine the destiny of another country "including the destiny of its sovereignty.". . .
> In other words, you have the right to order other countries about, whereas they have no right to oppose you; you have the right to ravage other countries, but they have no right to resist you. Hitler once raved about "the right to rule." Dulles and his ilk also preached that the concepts of national sovereignty "have become obsolete" and that "single state sovereignty" should give place to "joint sovereignty." So it is clear that Brezhnev's theory of "limited sovereignty" is nothing but an echo of imperialist ravings. . . .

Soviet leaders were charged with having concocted the theory of "international dictatorship" as

> . . . the "theoretical basis" for military intervention in or military occupation of a number of East European countries and the Mongolian

---

[14] *Pravda*, March 19, 1970.
[15] See "The New Soviet Ambassador to Peking," RFE Research Report, April 2, 1970.

People's Republic. The "international dictatorship" you refer to simply means the subjection of other countries to the new tsars' rule and enslavement. Do you think that by putting up the signboard of "aid to a fraternal country" you are entitled to use your military force to bully another country, or send your troops to overrun another country as you please? Flying the flag of "unified armed forces," you invaded Czechoslovakia. What difference is there between this and the invasion of China by the allied forces of eight powers in 1900, the 14-nation armed intervention in the Soviet Union and the "16-nation" aggression organized by U.S. imperialism against Korea!

The concept of a "socialist community" was dismissed as "nothing but a synonym for a colonial empire with you as the metropolitan state." [16]

A formal Soviet response did not come until late May,[17] but Radio Moscow retaliated with an intensely personal attack on Mao Tse-tung implying that the Chinese leader was guilty of complicity in the deaths of his first wife and his eldest son who had been educated in the Soviet Union and rejected Mao's "pseudoscientific junk." According to the broadcast, Mao's indifference to the fate of his relatives extended to "all the Chinese people"; he considered them "a mass of inanimate objects—he may arbitrarily humiliate them, force them to suffer hardships, or even let them die." [18] Seldom had intraparty polemics reached such a pitch of personal vilification. Only the external impetus of the United States' invasion of Cambodia reactivated the deadlocked border talks, bringing the Soviet First Deputy Minister of Foreign Affairs once more to Peking.[19]

Yet Kuznetsov's presence appeared to be more of symbolic gesture than any real attempt to settle differences in face of joint opposition to the American role in Indochina. For coming when it did, the Soviet-Czechoslovak Treaty's explicit reference to protection of socialist achievements as the common international duty of all socialist countries[20] was a sure sign that Moscow did not intend to deescalate seriously.

[16] "Leninism or Social-Imperialism?," *Peking Review* 13, no. 17 (April 24, 1970): 10. Stepakov did not, in fact, become the Soviet ambassador to Peking. Rather, the post was quietly filled   by V. S. Tolstikov, former head of the Leningrad party organization, five months later. *International Herald Tribune*, September 17, 1970.

[17] "Pseudorevolutionaries Unmasked," *Pravda*, May 18, 1970; *CDSP* 22, no. 20 (June 16, 1970): 1–7.

[18] Chinese language broadcast to China, April 25, 1970; quoted from *The New York Times*, May 3, 1970.

[19] See Harrison Salisbury's analysis in *The New York Times*, May 19, 1970.

[20] See Document 10, p. 231.

The Soviet-Czechoslovak Treaty of Friendship, Cooperation, and Mutual Assistance

Signed May 6, 1970, this treaty signaled the hardening of the Soviet line and a sharp worsening of Soviet-Rumanian differences. Despite support for state sovereignty, independence, equality, and nonintervention in internal affairs, it could hardly have been more offensive to Bucharest. The treaty added one more legal prop to the Brezhnev Doctrine, specifically praised "socialist economic integration within the framework of CMEA," and pledged both parties to consider an attack against the other "by any state or group of states" as an attack against itself. The general assumption in Prague and elsewhere that this meant China was not a bad guess given the timing.

From the Rumanian view, this confirmation of the Brezhnev Doctrine in a bilateral treaty of mutual assistance must have been even more threatening than Article 10 extending Czechoslovak military obligations outside of Europe. Article 10 had considerable precedent. Soviet bilateral treaties with Bulgaria and Hungary in 1967 had both contained almost identical clauses as had a number of such treaties among the East European countries themselves. The attempted legalization of Moscow's interpretation of "common international duty" was new, while Article 5 binding both parties to "undertake the necessary measures to protect the socialist achievements of the people . . . to strive for the development of all-round relations between the states of the socialist community and *to act* in the spirit of strengthening their unity, friendship and fraternity seemed to almost invite Soviet interference in Czechoslovak internal affairs. [Italics mine.]

It did not require much imagination to realize that Bucharest would be under pressure to model its own, as yet unsigned, treaty of mutual assistance along the lines of the Soviet-Czechoslovak version. The Rumanian Minister of Defense lost no time in restating the principles of Ceaușescu's February 5 speech on the nature of Rumanian obligations as as a member of the Warsaw Pact, calling for the withdrawal of all non-European troops from Europe, and drawing some interesting conclusions from the victory over fascism in World War II (a victory for which he gave the Rumanian army and people substantially more credit than is customary even in Bucharest).

The historic victory over fascism has demonstrated once again that no matter what the size of reactionary forces thrown into battle, no matter how huge the invading imperialist forces may be they cannot overcome the will of the peoples for liberty, their desire to decide their fate for themselves.[21]

In short, if pushed to the wall by anybody the Rumanians would fight to maintain their independence. And, as if this scarcely veiled warning were not enough, the Bucharest's commemoration of the Warsaw Pact's 15th anniversary showed the extent of Rumanian resistance.

The 15th Anniversary of the Warsaw Pact

The leading Rumanian papers of May 14 stressed that Bucharest continued to develop her military cooperation with the member countries of the Warsaw Pact and with *all* socialist countries—implying that such cooperation potentially extended outside the alliance to China, Albania, and Yugoslavia for example. *Scînteia* repeated the litany of the Rumanian perception of the limits of coalition politics among socialist states, i.e. the Warsaw Pact as an alliance of sovereign states with equal rights; an alliance whose "sole objective" was to defend its members against "imperialist attack in Europe." The commentator restated Ceauşescu's and Ionita's position that the leaders of the Rumanian Armed Forces were the Party, the State Council, and the Supreme National Command. Only these bodies could issue orders to the Army; only such orders would be carried out. Indeed he went further to explain that "armed formations of the people" (the Militia set up in August 1968) now played an especially important role in strengthening the country's defenses.[22]

Deputy Minister of the Armed Forces Colonel General Marin Nicolescu added emphasis, referring to "the entire population" trained "in the defense of the homeland." [23] He warned that cooperation among socialist armies did not sanction interference in the affairs of any country or army, and he repeated the *Scînteia* commentator's allusion to Bucharest's desire for military cooperation with "all socialist countries."

Such willingness would be most welcome in Peking, and it was not

---

[21] General-Colonel Ion Ionita, *Scînteia*, May 7, 1970.

[22] V. Iliescu, *Scînteia*, May 14, 1970.

[23] The Rumanian Armed Forces weekly, *Aparagea Patriei*, May 14, 1970, quoted in the RFE Rumanian situation report, May 22, 1970. Interestingly enough a somewhat emasculated version of Nicolescu's views subsequently appeared in the Soviet military newspaper *Krasnaya zvezda*, July 2, 1970.

long before a Rumanian delegation to China actively began exploring possibilities. But that is getting ahead of the story. In May, Bucharest used the Warsaw Pact anniversary primarily to caution Moscow against pushing too hard along the lines of the Soviet-Czechoslovak treaty. The Rumanians wanted no part of an even symbolic united military front against Peking. Conversely, the Soviets took the pact anniversary as an opportunity to make their desire in that direction still more explicit. Any doubts about Moscow's intent could not have survived the delayed response to the Chinese polemical broadside of April 22, charging:

> Peking is accompanying its entire campaign of the militarization of the country with appeals to prepare for war against the USSR and the *other socialist countries* [and] with appeals for a struggle to overthrow the socialist system in *these countries*. . . .[24] [Italics mine.]

This editorial, taking up several full pages of *Pravda,* came on the heels of a *Krasnaya zvezda* call for other socialist countries to face up to the necessity for "preparedness" against the threat of Chinese war psychosis.[25] Soviet preferences were clear. Whether or not Moscow could convince or pressure the other members of the alliance into accepting its interpretation of the danger from the East remained to be seen. But in any case Yakubovsky's simultaneous insistence that the new Soviet-Czechoslovak treaty was "vivid confirmation" of the "new type of relations among socialist states" must be seen as part of a systematic campaign in that direction.[26]

The Pact Commander-in-Chief's most definitive statement came in a major article for the May issue of the military-history journal. Here he underlined that the Joint Armed Forces of the Warsaw Pact faced the common task of guaranteeing "the inviolability of the state borders of the *socialist commonwealth.*" [Italics mine.] There was no hint that this obligation applied solely to Europe. Carried to its logical conclusion it not only committed the Joint Command to protect the Sino-Soviet border but implied that Warsaw Pact forces could be called upon to defend North Vietnam or Cuba should the need arise. (Indeed Castro must have been quite pleased. His only serious criticism of the invasion of

---

[24] *Pravda,* May 18, 1970.

[25] *Krasnaya zvezda,* May 14, 1970. The May 13 editorial of this newspaper had been primarily devoted to the Soviet-Czechoslovak treaty as a monument to the firm determination of both Prague and Moscow "jointly with the other Warsaw Pact states" to insure the inviolability of their frontiers against "any forces of militarism and revanchism."

[26] *Pravda,* May 14, 1970.

Czechoslovakia had been that Moscow had not extended the reasoning of the famed Warsaw letter to Havana and Hanoi.[27]) As for attempts to weaken the Warsaw Pact from within, Yakubovsky explicitly cited Hungary in 1956, the Berlin Wall in 1961, and the defeat of "counter-revolution" in Czechoslovakia in 1968 as glowing manifestations of proletarian internationalism. He did not exactly claim that these were Warsaw Pact operations. Yet he strongly implied it.[28]

The extension of the obligations of the Joint Command to defend the borders of "the socialist commonwealth" found no takers among the East European members of the pact. Even the East German anniversary article emphasized only the European nature of the alliance. For example, Stoph explicitly said that the GDR national army joined Soviet troops in "guarding peace at the *western* border of the socialist community." [29] On the issue of the importance of the Warsaw Pact during intra-Communist conflict—i.e., what was or was not a manifestation of proletarian internationalism among its member states—the East European countries split. Both Stoph and the Czechoslovak Minister of Defense Martin Dzur[30] echoed Yakubovsky's references to the saving of socialism in Hungary in 1956 and Czechoslovakia in 1968. Warsaw, like Bucharest, concentrated on the coalition's drive for European security (most especially inviolability of European borders) and ignored both incidents of internal conflict among the member states.[31]

As for Hungary, Budapest was noncommittal. There was no editorial on the anniversary, but neither was there any mention of events in 1956 or 1968 in the long report of the anniversary speech by Politburo member Lajos Fehér. Although Fehér spoke obliquely of "previous attempts against socialist countries," he did not specify. Nor did he refer to the Soviet-Czechoslovak Treaty or otherwise indirectly sanction the Brezhnev Doctrine. It was an exceedingly bland comment.[32]

[27] Robin Remington, ed., *Winter in Prague: Documents on Czechoslovak Communism in Crisis* Document 51, p. 334.

[28] I. Yakubovsky, "Na strazhe mira i sotsialisma," *Voenno-istorichesky zhurnal* 5 (May 1970): 17.

[29] *Neues Deutschland,* May 14, 1970.

[30] *Rudé Právo,* May 1, 1970.

[31] *Trybuna ludu* editorial May 14, 1970. The Poles were also careful to emphasize in somewhat milder terms than the Rumanians that military integration within the Warsaw Pact did not mean mechanically following the Red Army's model or in any way dissolving separate socialist armies. See also M. Jurek and E. Skrzpkewski, Uład warszawski (Warsaw, 1970), published under the auspices of the Polish Ministry of Defense.

[32] *Népszabadság,* May 14, 1970. I am grateful to László Urban for his summary of this article.

In general the East European commentaries emphasized national interests served by their membership in the alliance. Here, with the exception of Rumania, the Ulbricht regime far outdid the rest. In the East German view, not only the GDR but the Warsaw Pact as well was struggling to guarantee the basic prerequisites of European security among which Stoph catalogued:

- Recognition of the GDR under international law.
- Renunciation by the FRG of its claim to sole representation.
- Prevention of access of the West Germans to any form of nuclear weapons.
- Recognition of West Berlin as an independent political entity.

It was an interesting list. The East German Premier threw in recognition of the Oder-Neisse line and the invalidity of Munich to give the demands a somewhat less exclusively GDR flavor. Yet he was undeniably still attempting to restrict the ongoing bilateral negotiations with the Federal Republic by other pact members.

At the same time he violently attacked the *Ostpolitik* of "all the governments which have so far been in office in West Germany" as aiming at the "annexation of the GDR." This position contradicted the assumptions underlying negotiations on a Soviet–West German Renunciation of Force agreement. It was also out of step with the attitude toward Bonn expressed in the Soviet and other East European anniversary commentaries, which had maintained a studied silence on contemporary trends in the Federal Republic and in fact referred to West Germany only in the context of the original impetus for the Warsaw Pact. Combined with Stoph's insistence that the Western border of the GDR was directly threatened by "imperialist subversion in politics, ideology, and economics," it made prospects for the approaching second round of inter-German talks at Kassel seem slim indeed.

Kassel and the SED 13th Central Committee Plenum

The second German summit meeting opened in the West German city of Kassel on May 21.[33] Steady media attacks on West German intentions led up to the discussions that consisted primarily of a cold restatement of

[33] This meeting coincided with the second session of the Warsaw Pact Committee of Defense Ministers in Sofia, May 21–22, 1970. See Boris Kidel commentary, *The Observer*, May 24, 1970; for an excellent analysis of the East German frame of mind, Dorothy Miller, "Kassel and Thereafter," RFE Report, May 29, 1970.

the East German demand for legal recognition under international law and Stoph's refusal to so much as consider Brandt's 20-point program.[34] There was no communiqué, no date set for a future meeting, and no arrangements to maintain contact through secondary officials.

Popular response was even less helpful than at Erfurt where the cheering crowds' calls for Brandt to come to the window must have given GDR negotiators strong qualms about the domestic repercussions of increased contact. At Kassel the East German flag was torn down while clashes between Communists and right-wing extremists delayed a planned wreath laying until evening. Given these provocations, the only major surprise was that Stoph did not simply pick up his documents and go home.

Subsequently Brandt regretted the East Germans' "all or nothing" attitude which indeed verged on making de jure recognition a precondition for further contact.[35] If anything the Ulbricht regime seemed to have hardened since Erfurt. The more Bonn moved forward, the harder Pankow drew back. For as Stoph unambiguously pointed out, the Federal Republic was not willing to establish relations with the GDR as an equal, sovereign state under international law and from the East German side "settlement of a number of other questions depends on such a settlement of relations." [36] As for the attitude of other socialist states, Foreign Minister Winzer commented that common policy was coordinated on the basis of complete equality and respect for "bilateral, tripartite, or quadripartite" mutual interests; his statement stopped just short of saying that GDR negotiators had acted in accord with such a common policy at Kassel.

Despite the obvious impasse in inter-German talks, progress continued in Moscow-Bonn negotiations, as did Polish-West German discussions. And if the speeches at the SED 13th CC Plenum can be considered an indication, the East German leaders themselves were divided on whether or not the GDR could afford to remain intransigent. Opening the day after the West German cabinet's brief communiqué stating its readiness to begin formal negotiations with the Soviet Union, the plenum focused

[34] *Christ und Welt,* May 29, 1970.

[35] The GDR Foreign Minister Winzer promptly denied the charge and told a German television audience that if that were the case a socialist revolution in West Germany would have been the preconditions for negotiating with Brandt. East Berlin in German to Germany 1200 GMT, May 24, 1970.

[36] Stoph statement on returning from Kassel, *Neues Deutschland,* May 23, 1970.

on economic issues. Yet several major speakers addressed themselves directly to the problem of policy toward the Brandt Government.

Both the party ideologist Albert Norden and Premier Stoph took a hardline approach toward Bonn.[37] Norden repeated the trojan horse theory of *Ostpolitik* as an attempt to isolate the GDR for purposes of importing counterrevolution. Stoph rephrased the Foreign Minister's contention that East German demands were certainly not "all or nothing" or there would have had to be a socialist revolution in West Germany prior to talks. Both strongly attacked Brandt's 20-point proposal, with Norden insisting that the change in government in Bonn by no means reduced the danger of West German imperialism. Nor was Norden optimistic about Soviet negotiations with the Federal Republic. He mentioned them only once and then in the context of internal West German opposition to a renunciation of force agreement. Stoph did not refer to the negotiations at all.

Against this backdrop Ulbricht himself sounded remarkably conciliatory.[38] He showed some understanding for the difficulties created by Brandt's internal situation, said explicitly that "something" had changed for the better under Brandt—i.e., willingness to begin negotiations on the renunciation of force—and expressed an interest in discussing at least one of the twenty points: that concerning joint membership in the United Nations. The First Secretary had hopes for a third round of talks between the two German states despite the discouraging results at Kassel. Although he continued to insist on recognition under international law, he also saw some advantages in de facto recognition. Combined with the suggestion that Brandt was influenced by the more rational elements of the West German bourgeoisie rather than being representative of the most reactionary forces, this attitude signalled a potentially more flexible GDR response.

Why the East German leader was willing to go so far at that time is not clear. Given his careful praise of Soviet attempts to achieve an agreement with Bonn as an example of peaceful coexistence, one could suspect that Moscow was not uninvolved. However, it is also true that Ulbricht is an acute politician. Such people do not like to cut off options, and he

[37] *Neues Deutschland,* June 15, and 16, 1970, respectively.

[38] *Neues Deutschland,* June 16, 1970. For a detailed comparison of these speeches, see Dorothy Miller, "Some Political Aspects of the 13th SED CC Plenum," RFE Research Report, June 18, 1970.

may well have feared to have Soviet and Polish negotiations move forward in the face of open East German opposition. The nightmare of the GDR is isolation either international or within the socialist commonwealth. In any case, the question of joint policy toward West Germany remained a sensitive question; one that undoubtedly occupied the attention of the Warsaw Pact Foreign Ministers meeting at the end of June, appearances to the contrary notwithstanding. For, as is often the case in Communist coalition politics, the agenda of this meeting was undoubtedly longer than one would suspect from its concluding documents.

Budapest Revisited

In part a response to the NATO foreign ministers conference in Rome May 28–29, the 1970 Budapest meeting avoided direct comment on the NATO suggestion that talks on balanced mutual force reductions should take place before an all-European security conference. Rather the participants noted growing enthusiasm for such a conference and issued a memorandum to put the preparations for an ESC on a more practical basis.

Both the communiqué[39] and the memorandum[40] were free of propagandistic attacks on either Bonn or Washington. The member states unreservedly accepted US and Canadian participation; stressing that direct participation of "interested states" was desirable at all stages of preparation and organization of the conference including preparatory meetings of the representatives of these states. Such preparation should begin in the "near future." The memorandum specified that convocation of a conference must not be linked to any preconditions. Discussions on content and agenda of an ESC should continue. From the signers' point of view, however, such an agenda should include setting up a permanent body to deal with questions of European security and cooperation. Reduction of foreign armed forces on the territory of European states could be discussed. Other preferences listed were (1) problems of human environment, (2) development of cultural relations, (3) renunciation of the use of force or threats of force, and (4) broadening commercial, economic, and scientific-technical relations based on equality. It was a tall order for any one sitting. Yet one of the implications was that once general lines were established, the standing body should continue to handle the

[39] *Pravda*, June 24, 1970, Document 12, p. 239.
[40] *Pravda*, June 27, 1970, Document 13, p. 240.

issues. In many respects this position seemed genericly tied to Brezhnev's preelection speech of June 12 in which the Soviet leader had first referred to the idea of a "permanently functioning mechanism" for practical implementation of agreed upon measures.

Timing of this serious a step in the Pact's drive for an ESC was most likely influenced by multiple factors. First, the East Germans probably pressed for reassurance on the bilateral talks with Bonn. In this respect, bilateral and multilateral consultations were explicitly praised by the meeting as was the principle of renunciation of force agreements. Second, the Conservative victory in Britain combined with Brandt's losses in the June 14 provincial elections may have brought fears that favorable international conditions could fade even more quickly than they had arisen. Third, despite the exclusively European focus, there are marginally good reasons to believe that once again the conference was held under the long shadow of Sino-Soviet clashes. Certainly at least two of the participating states had cause to be simultaneously reacting to developments in China. On June 20, for example, a Hungarian correspondent reported that Kuznetsov, the leader of the Soviet delegation negotiating the border talks in Peking, had become ill and returned home.[41] His departure came virtually on the heels of former Rumanian Defense Minister Emil Bodnaras's friendship visit to China.[42] Such events do not happen in a vacuum and throughout the fifteen years of the Warsaw Pact, Rumanian trips to the East have had considerable influence on the workings of that alliance.

The Sino-Soviet-Rumanian Triangle

Since the Rumanian Party Statement of 1964, Bucharest has considered its neutrality in interparty schisms a cardinal principle. Such a policy is always threatened when Sino-Soviet relations sharply deteriorate. Therefore not surprisingly with intensified Sino-Soviet hostility in the winter and spring of 1970, Soviet-Rumanian tensions began building again. At first these differences expressed themselves in indirect polemics between

---

[41] Denes Baracs, Budapest MTI Domestic Service in Hungarian, 1935 GMT, 20 June 1970. In Summer 1970, high-level Soviet negotiators seemed quite vulnerable to sudden illness. According to reports, Stepakov's departure to Peking had been delayed by a mild "heart attack." *The New York Times*, July 31, 1970. Brezhnev stayed home with a cold rather than attend the signing of the Soviet-Rumanian Friendship Treaty in early July 1970.

[42] For speeches in honor of the Rumanian delegation, see *Peking Review* 13, no. 25 (June 19, 1970): 5–14.

Soviet and Rumanian media—primarily ideological debates on questions of "limited sovereignty" within the socialist commonwealth, the leading role of the Soviet Union, the proper mix of internationalism and socialist patriotism (i.e., nationalism).[43]

By early May, however, Moscow was being more explicit about what was wanted. The standard syndrome of sharpening Sino-Soviet polemics paralleled by stepped-up pressure for integration within CMEA and the Warsaw Pact had gone back into gear. Although the Soviets might bitterly condemn the rumors surrounding Shtemenko's article as a Western fabrication to put Warsaw Pact members at "loggerheads with one another,"[44] this time they had only themselves to blame for Bucharest's intransigence—unless the wording of the Soviet-Czechoslovak treaty, Moscow's stated goals for the May 1970 CMEA council session,[45] and Soviet preferences expressed in celebrating the 15th anniversary of the Warsaw Pact could also be considered "imperalist plots."

Despite problems created by the disastrous floods that convulsed the country throughout May, the Rumanians countered both ideologically and politically. Bucharest's cooperation at the 24th CMEA council session was correct but minimal. Maurer attended the Warsaw meeting. *Scînteia* reprinted the final communiqué and declaration without comment. However, Rumania was conspicuously absent from the list of countries par-

[43] For a detailed analysis of this period, see J. Arthur Johnson, "Rumanian-Soviet Polemics: An Escalation of Pressures on Bucharest?," RFE Research Report, April 22, 1970.

[44] *Krasnaya zvezda*, February 5, 1970.

[45] Ever since December 1968 when a Soviet economist put forward a master plan for economic integration of the Soviet bloc openly proposing supranational economic bodies, it had been clear that Moscow wanted maximum economic consolidation as well as stepped up military integration to be among the organizational components of normalization. (See G. M. Sorkin, *Voprosy ekonomiki*, December 1968.) His plan was strongly objected to in East Europe. The Rumanians came out with a whole series of polemical articles between December and the CMEA summit in April 1969. (See particularly the December issue of the RCP theoretical journal *Lupta de Clasa* and *Scînteia*, January 24, 1969, April 22, 23, 1969.) However, opposition was not limited to Bucharest. The Poles wanted no part of supranational planning either. (*Politika*, December 7, 1968). The Hungarians were unhappy, and even the Czechs protested. (*Rudé Právo*, March 13, 1969.) Faced with massive objections, Moscow backed down in April 1969; however, renewed enthusiasm (if less far-reaching) appeared in May 1970 indicating the Soviets had only put aside, not abandoned, their hopes for an eventual single economic and political entity in East Europe. I am most grateful to Michael Gamarnikow for letting me read his excellent analysis of the 1968–1969 period in his forthcoming study on the institutional and political impact of economic reform in Eastern Europe being prepared for the Columbia Research Institute in Communist Affairs.

ticipating in the planned investment bank,[46] while Ceauşescu's May 20 interview in *Le Figaro* eloquently expressed that in his opinion CMEA membership did not sanction interference in its members' economic relations.

Flat restatements of Rumanian positions of CMEA and the Warsaw Pact were followed by an intense round of international diplomacy beginning with the Chinese. It was a sure sign that Ceauşescu's visit to Moscow May 18–19 had not gone according to his satisfaction.[47]

In early June, former Rumanian Defense Minister Emil Bodnaras went off on a four-day (June 9–12) friendship trip to Peking. There he had "cordial" conversations with Mao Tse-tung and Lin Piao. He dined with Chou En-lai, toasted the everlasting friendship of the Rumanian and Chinese people, and reminded the banquet guests that as Comrade Nicolae Ceauşescu not long ago pointed out:

> We will fight resolutely for the victory of the principles of equality, mutual respect for national independence, and state sovereignty, and non-interference in each other's internal affairs so as to guarantee that the people *of every country* have the right to determine their own development *free from any foreign interference.*[48] [Italics mine.]

It was a reminder obviously designed to echo in Moscow. Even as in 1958 when Rumanian visitors to China had stressed support for the withdrawal of *all* troops.

---

[46] *Scînteia*, May 15, 1970. Later, during the sensitive period following the December 1970 change of government in Poland, Rumania joined the bank—stressing that its activity "is based on full equality of rights." *Scînteia*, January 13, 1971.

[47] That Ceauşescu would leave the country during a natural catastrophe the magnitude of the floods and the composition of the delegation, indicated the importance of this meeting. Both Party Secretary Paul Niculescu Mizil, RCP ideologist largely responsible for problems of the world Communist movement, and Suslov, who is primarily concerned with CPSU relations with other parties, took part. Their presence along with that of former Rumanian Defense Minister Emil Bodnaras currently handling Bucharest's relations with Eastern countries (plus that the delegation arrived the day of *Pravda's* voluminous attack on Peking implying that Chinese hostility threatened "other socialist countries" as well as the USSR) imply that the desired Soviet-Warsaw Pact military front against China was high on the agenda. Soviet Foreign Minister Gromyko cancelled a meeting with the West German Secretary Bahr on the renunciation of force agreement in order to be able to attend. (See RFE Rumanian Situation Report, May 22, 1970, p. 14.) Other probable topics of discussion with a good deal of latitude for disagreement included Rumania's partial alignment with the Chinese on the issue of Cambodia implicit in Bucharest's tentative recognition of Sihanouk's exile government, its rejection of the CMEA investment bank, the contents of the projected Soviet-Rumanian mutual assistance treaty, and attitudes toward West Germany and European Security.

[48] *Peking Review* 13, no. 25 (June 19, 1970): 10.

Bodnaras thanked the Chinese for their "tremendous assistance" in rehabilitating the ravages caused by flood. It was no coincidence that the next day Corneliu Bogdan, Rumanian ambassador to Washington, called a press conference to thank the US government for its aid in flood relief.[49] Nor were these diplomatic gestures unconnected with Ceauşescu's visit to France (June 16–20). Bucharest was diversifying its base of support, and in the plainest political language communicating its intention of continuing current policies.

Yet throughout the test of Rumanian intraalliance diplomacy there has been the art of balance. And that process obviously still worked. Although only Colonel General Ion Gheorghe, the First Deputy Minister of the Armed Forces and Chief-of-Staff, attended the Sofia meeting of WTO Defense Ministers Committee, May 21,[50] Foreign Minister Manescu went to the Pact Budapest meeting (June 21–22) rather than joining the virtually simultaneous Rumanian delegation to West Germany (June 22–26).[51] Then in early July Bucharest signed the Soviet-Rumanian Friendship Treaty that had been hanging fire for two years.[52] This document was a delicate compromise. But that it was signed at all did in some sense stabilize the situation of the moment.

Modelled along the lines of the Soviet-Hungarian and Soviet-Bulgarian Treaties of 1967, the mutual assistance pact reflected Rumania's special position in Eastern Europe (as indeed the Soviet-Czechoslovak treaty had done, only in a reverse direction). It contained no reference to the shared obligation of socialist countries to come to the defense of socialist achievements.[53] On the question of cooperation on foreign policy issues, both parties agreed "to consult" on all important international questions so as to reach accord. They did not, as in the early treaties, agree "to act" on that common stand or as the Soviet-Czechoslovak Treaty phrased it "proceed from their common standpoint." Like the other mutual assist-

---

[49] According to *The New York Times,* June 13, 1970, he gave figures to the effect that the United States had contributed four times the amount of flood relief given by Moscow —400,000 to 50,000 respectively.

[50] *Pravda,* May 23, 1970.

[51] Manescu then immediately left for San Francisco to take part in the ceremonies for the 25th anniversary of the UN Charter.

[52] Document 14, p. 242.

[53] This refusal to sanction the Brezhnev Doctrine may have been the cause of the Soviet Party leader's absence from the signing. Although he was reported ill, Brezhnev seems to have been well enough to go to a football match in Moscow at the time. That his signature is missing has the practical consequence of turning the Soviet-Rumanian Treaty into a governmental rather than a party document.

ance pacts, Rumanian defense obligations are extended beyond Europe in case the Soviet Union is subject to attack by *any* state or group of states (Article 8).

That Bucharest did not like the implied commitment against China was made clear by continued references to expanded Rumanian military cooperation with *all* socialist countries. This policy rapidly had unambiguous results. A Rumanian military delegation led by the Defense Minister Ionita visited first North Korea and then arrived in Peking July 23. Ionita toasted to the constant development of friendship between Rumania and China; repeated Rumanian willingness to fulfill its duties as a Warsaw Treaty state in case of "imperialist aggression in Europe"; and said categorically that Bucharest opposes all policies of aggression and domination:

> It stands for the complete elimination of colonialism and neocolonialism *in all its manifestations* and the fostering of an atmosphere of respecting national independence, sovereignty, and the sacred rights of all peoples to freedom and development.[54] (Italics mine.)

In return the Chief of General Staff of the Chinese Army pledged that Rumanian comrades can "rest assured that we are always your reliable friends when you struggle against foreign intervention, control, and aggression."[55] This was most explicit, virtually nonesoteric communication. Ionita had come to reassure Peking that Rumania would reserve the right to decide who had attacked whom in any Sino-Soviet conflict. The Chinese stopped just short of pledging assistance should there be an attempt to apply the Brezhnev Doctrine to Rumania. How militarily useful such aid would be might be doubtful, but there could be no doubt that such maneuvering had political clout. Moreover, whether or not aid conceivably would be needed in part depended on opportunities opened by the Soviet–West German negotiations at that time under way in Moscow. For East Europe is to a painfully large extent for its nationalistic peoples subject to the whims of protagonists in the European politics—Russia and Germany.

Bonn-Moscow Agreement: August 1970

Signed in Moscow August 12, this nonaggression agreement appeared to have opened a new epoch in much more than Soviet–West German

---

[54] Peking NCNA International Service in English, 0048 GMT, July 31, 1970.
[55] Peking NCNA Domestic Service in Chinese, 1857 GMT, July 30, 1970.

relations. For the Soviets it achieved one of Moscow's major postwar aims, West German recognition of the European status quo and acceptance of East Europe as a Soviet sphere of influence. For Bonn it signaled the end of postwar inhibitions that had kept West Germany a second-class political power despite the country's remarkable economic growth. For Eastern Europe, it implied increased freedom of contact with the West, always a corollary of deepening East-West detente. Indeed, the potential advantages to the smaller members of the Warsaw Pact went beyond the opportunities created for individual foreign policy initiatives. For the Bonn-Moscow agreement had significance for the mechanism of the regional defense alliance as well.

Although the Poles overstated the situation in claiming that the agreement was a result of "jointly worked out and uniform policy of the socialist countries in Europe,"[56] in fact it was concluded only after extensive bilateral and multilateral consultation among Warsaw Pact states. The text affirmed the inviolability of present borders in Europe, explicitly referring to the Polish western border at the Oder-Neisse and the frontier between East and West Germany. It did not deal with the issue of recognition of East Germany or the problem of Berlin.[57]

To the East Europeans, Bonn's concession on the question of borders was perhaps most important. Not unexpectedly the Rumanians stressed the importance for all Europe of agreements to settle differences without force or threat of force.[58] The Poles, and most likely the Czechoslovaks as well, were intensely aware of the impetus given their own bilateral discussions with the Federal Republic.[59] This was true despite reservations in Warsaw that the border formula agreed upon by Moscow did not go far enough.[60] For although the general wording of the agreement may have marginally weakened the Polish bargaining position in pushing

[56] *Dziennik ludowy*, August 31, 1970.

[57] For an unofficial translation of the Bonn-Moscow Pact and 12 pages of commentary from the West German press, see *The German Tribune*, August 27, 1970; for more detailed analysis, especially of West German policy, W. E. Griffith, *The Soviet-American Confrontation 1970 II. The East-West Confrontation in Europe, 1970: The Soviet-West German Treaty and European Security* (M.I.T. Center for International Studies, C/70–16, October 1970.)

[58] *Scînteia*, August 10 and 15, 1970.

[59] *Trybuna ludu*, August 13, 1970.

[60] See Gomułka speech of September 6, *Trybuna luda*, September, 1970, and K. Zamorski, "Poland's Insistence on Total Recognition of Oder-Neisse Frontier," *Radio Free Europe*, September 11, 1970.

for final recognition of the postwar western border, it also provided an umbrella of approval for the Warsaw-Bonn negotiations—thereby completely undercutting former East German demands that recognition of the GDR be included among preconditions for normalizing Poland's relations with the western half of Germany. That demand had proved powerful in the past, keeping Polish German policy under the thumb of East German interests for almost five years from 1964 until Gomułka's speech of May 17, 1969.

Only the East Germans had serious cause for chagrin. There had been no recognition of the GDR under international law. Even though Pankow understood full well that there would have been no pact at all had Moscow insisted on that, there is no reason to think such an outcome would not have been preferred in East Berlin. As it stood the agreement meant a considerable loss, particularly from the hardliners' point of view represented by Honecker. Attempting to make the best of a bad situation, Ulbricht immediately requested recognition first from a number of West European countries and then from the United States, France, and Great Britain as the logical extension of the Bonn-Moscow Pact.

The East German delegate to the Warsaw Pact meeting in Moscow gave no open sign that East Germany intended to balk. The political consultative committee praised the agreement as an important contribution to normalizing relations in Europe and paving the way for a European Security Conference.[61] Unlike the December 1969 Moscow summit, there was no simultaneous demand for de jure recognition of East Germany or attack on "revanchist, neo-Nazi forces" in the Federal Republic. By implication, at least temporarily the West German threat as the common denominator of the Warsaw Pact had been removed.[62]

---

[61] *Pravda*, August 22, 1970.

[62] Whether or not Moscow would continue the drive of early spring to convince the alliance to accept China as the new Enemy remained to be seen. Although on August 28 Brezhnev scoffed at the idea that the pact with West Germany had been designed to free Moscow to increase pressure on Peking (and indeed took a largely unpolemical tone), he had chosen Alma Ata on the occasion of the 50th anniversary of the Kazakh republic as the place for his major foreign policy speech including his first reference to the treaty since its signing. Alma Ata is only about 175 miles from the Chinese border; some 2000 miles from Moscow. The lull in Sino-Soviet polemics accompanying the exchange of ambassadors and trade agreement in the fall of 1970 did not survive the "December events" in

Tacit willingness to move forward with the other members of the alliance in the search for European security notwithstanding, the Ulbricht regime continued to disagree. *Neues Deutschland* combined lukewarm support of the Bonn-Moscow agreement with strong warnings about rightist opposition to the treaty in the FRG. Still more important, the official youth newspaper associated with Honecker completely rejected the idea of concessions on West Berlin.[63] And since the Brandt government has tied West German ratification to progress on Berlin, the East German regime retained the practical ability to sabotage ratification if it so decided. Which brings us straight to the heart of divided Europe, that most constant barometer of East-West tension: Berlin.

The Berlin Talks

Approaching the problem of Berlin is about like choosing which viper to take from the nest first. There is the problem of access to West Berlin, of contact between East and West Berliners, of relation to West Germany.[64] Just what the West German government would count as improvement was not clear. Washington worried that Brandt would settle for tokenism. The West German opposition attacked him for abandoning German rights. East Germany, to the surprise of many political observers, offered to reopen the East-West German dialogue that had died so abruptly at Kassel in May.[65]

It was more of a feint than a step forward, however. For with the first sign of movement in the Big-Four ambassadorial talks on Berlin, the GDR jumped back to its pre-Moscow treaty stance. Since the chief source of the rumored progress was Soviet ambassador Pyotr Abrasimov, it is unlikely that the resulting spat of hardline East German pronouncements

---

Poland. For a sharp refutation of Peking's interpretation as virtually indistinguishable from the "fact-juggling and deliberate falsehoods" of imperialist propaganda, see *Pravda*, December 31, 1970.

[63] Reported in *The New York Times*, August 23, 1970.

[64] For background on Soviet and East German policy on Berlin, see Dieter Mahncke, "In Search of a Modus Vivendi for Berlin," *The World Today* 26, no. 4 (April 1970): 137–147; Gerhard Wettig, "Die Berlin-Politik der USSR und der DDR," *Aussenpolitik* 5 (1970): 284–296, and Lawrence L. Whetton, "The Role of East Germany in West German-Soviet Relations," *The World Today* 25, no. 12 (December 1969): 507–520.

[65] *Neues Deutschland*, October 30, 1970.

had been coordinated in Moscow. Although the Soviets might gain a slight advantage in thus demonstrating to the Western allies that East German interests cannot be ignored,[66] it is doubtful that such a demonstration would have been timed on the heels of cordial reopening of the SALT talks or that Abrasimov would have repeated his prognosis in East Berlin at the reception in honor of the 53rd anniversary of the October Revolution much as if he felt that East German spokesmen had deliberately missed the point.[67]

On November 5, just one day after the first progress report in eight months and nine meetings on Berlin, an authoritative *Neues Deutschland* editorial restated East German reservations in most unambiguous terms. Couched in an attack on rightist circles in West Germany, the editorial underlined that in its view:

1. Talks between the two Germanies could proceed only on the basis of complete equality and nondiscrimination as is "common among independent states, based on the norms of international law."

2. The idea of an "inner-German" dialogue placed the GDR in a subordinate position to Bonn and was nothing but a ploy to make the borders of East Germany "permeable" for the struggle against socialism.

It went on to redefine the purpose of the Big-Four talks on Berlin as "putting an end to any activity that would contradict the legal status of Berlin" and stressed that any questions of goods and passenger traffic to West Berlin could be settled only by the GDR and the West Berlin senate directly. The same line was put forth in the next issue, November 6, both by a political commentator and in Politburo member Albert Norden's speech during the GDR celebrations of the October revolution. Then, speaking after the Soviet ambassador's public optimism, Ulbricht himself joined the discussion with a position that held little hope for meaningful contact between the two Germanies:

> The government of the GDR has stated its readiness to start negotiations with the FRG government on questions of reciprocal transit of people and goods on the condition that any activity of other states be discontinued in West Berlin which contradicts the international status of this

---

[66] A point on which I consider Dorothy Miller's generally excellent analysis of the East German and Soviet policy a bit too cautious. See Dorothy Miller, "East German Posture on the Dialogue: Old or New?," *Radio Free Europe*, November 11, 1970.

[67] *Neues Deutschland*, November 7, 1970.

city and which violates the interests of the GDR and of other socialist states. Every word in my formulation, incidentally, is significant.[68]

By making East-West German transit negotiations contingent on such conditions Ulbricht left himself a wide path for retreat. Not only was it improbable that Bonn would stop holding political meetings in West Berlin as the Federal Republic has consistently used this means to emphasize its continuing ties with that city but other *states* [plural] implied the East German leader might mean the Western allies as well. Although the point was not elaborated, it remained as a warning of just how unreasonable the East German regime could be should it so decide. Since it was a Soviet initiative that set off this particular round of intransigence, there is reason to think it was a warning intended for Moscow.

References to progress in the Berlin talks had come within a matter of days after Soviet Foreign Minister Gromyko visited West Germany. French sources hinted that Gromyko told his West German counterpart Walter Scheel that a detailed agreement on access to Berlin was possible.[69] Given East German panic at the idea of *any* Berlin agreement reached over their heads, the hurried restatement of the GDR's most extreme negotiating position had its own logic. It reinforced East German independence, put the long-cherished "three Germanies theory" (the GDR, FRG, and West Berlin as an independent political entity) squarely in the middle of the potential bargaining table, and reminded Moscow that even tentative settlements negotiated without East German participation might face practical obstacles. That Ulbricht was in no mood to modify or even discuss this stand within the framework of multilateral consultation can be assumed from his absence at the Hungarian Party Congress later in November. Moreover, between his November 9 interview and that congress he had had to absorb still another blow to East German sensitivities—the Warsaw-Bonn Treaty on normalization of relations.

---

[68] *Neues Deutschland*, November 9, 1970. Translated by Dorothy Miller, "East German Posture on the Dialogue: Old or New?," p. 5.

[69] *International Herald Tribune*, November 3, 1970. Since Gromyko's visit and the optimistic speculation on Berlin occurred shortly before the West German state elections in Hesse, where losses for Walter Scheel's Free Democratic party could have been a serious blow to Brandt's *Ostpolitik*, there is the possibility that Moscow was more interested in helping the West German chancellor over that hurdle than in making genuine concessions. The GDR response, however, indicates these moves were taken as deadly serious in East Berlin if not the West.

Polish–West German Treaty and the 10th MSZMP Congress

Initiated in Warsaw November 18, 1970, roughly a year and a half after Gomułka's major policy speech in May 1969 opened the way for bilateral talks, the treaty culminated weeks of tough negotiating.[70] For the Poles it was a major achievement, if something less than the definitive victory Warsaw claimed.[71] The text included (1) a firmer frontier formula than the August Soviet-West German agreement; (2) a renunciation of force clause; (3) a statement of intent to move toward complete normalization of relations; (4) assurance that other treaties would not be affected; and (5) an implementation clause.[72]

For the West Germans, it was a step in the right direction made possible by Polish concessions not actually written into the text. First, the Polish government provided the Federal Republic with information regarding the solution of the so-called "humanitarian problem," i.e., the plight of the German minority in Poland. Second, an explicit agreement, implied but not stated by the phrase "full normalization," to establish diplomatic relations immediately after the treaty came into force.

To the East Germans, it must have seemed a bitter continuation of the process set in motion by the Bonn-Moscow pact. For despite Polish emphasis on the similarity to the Zgorzelec treaty concluded with the GDR in 1950,[73] Poland was proceeding with a normalization that left East Germany out in the cold. There was not even the passing reference to the inviolability of the East-West German frontier that had been in the Soviet-West German agreement. Worse, ratification now became the only condition attached to formal Polish diplomatic relations with Bonn.[74] Gone was the hope for a package deal that had been the crux

[70] See especially James Feron, *International Herald Tribune*, November 4, 1970, and Hansjakob Stehle, *Die Zeit*, November 20, 1970.

[71] One well-known Polish commentator went so far as to call the treaty a "final sanctioning" of western border binding not only on the Federal Republic but "its eventual legal successors." Ryszard Wojna, *Zycie Warszawy*, November 19, 1970.

[72] See also Michael Costello "The Polish-West German Agreement: A Preliminary View," *Radio Free Europe*, November 25, 1970.

[73] *Trybuna ludu*, November 21, 1970. The article went further to conclude that after the agreements with Moscow and Warsaw, Bonn must logically recognize the GDR under international law as the next step. It was a bit of wishful thinking that had been put forward by East German commentary on the treaty, *Neues Deutschland*, November 19, 1970.

[74] Spelled out in the communiqué after the signing of the treaty and specifically alluded to in Brandt's toast. *Trybuna ludu*, December 8, 1970.

of GDR attacks on Rumanian independent recognition of the Federal Republic in 1967. The handwriting was on the wall: after Poland, Hungary and Czechoslovakia would not be far behind.[75] The long-standing East German nightmare of being isolated in the heart of Europe was, from Pankow's point of view, taking on an ugly daytime reality. Although his rumored illness seems to have been a political malaise, it was small wonder if Ulbricht felt indisposed when the Hungarian Party Congress opened November 23.

Meeting less than a week after the initialling of the Warsaw-Bonn treaty, the 10th MSZMP Congress was a logical occasion for an informal summit to discuss further coordination of policy toward West Germany. Not only was Ulbricht conspicuously absent but so were the other top members of the GDR leadership. If he were ill, that did not explain why the SED delegation was led by a second-rate political functionary, Friedrich Ebert. Ebert, in a speech that praised the Moscow-Bonn agreement for confirming the territorial integrity and sovereignty of the GDR in "a form binding under international law," took perfunctory note of the Polish-West German treaty. Pointedly referring to Brezhnev's remark that both treaties resulted from joint, agreed-upon foreign policy of the socialist countries,[76] he launched a harsh attack against "so-called intra-German relations." It was a not particularly esoteric equivalent of "don't tread on me." Joint, principled foreign policy of the socialist countries must stop short of demanding intra-German relations between socialism and imperialism, for such relations "do not exist and will never exist." [77]

Never is a long time. However, for the moment, Gromyko's visit to East Berlin (November 25, while the Congress was still in session) did not seem to soften the GDR line. Ebert's speech appeared in *Neues Deutschland* the very day East-West German talks resumed. It was followed by a stringent denial of all ties between West Berlin and the Federal Republic.[78] Then on November 29 another series of traffic delays on the autobahn to West Berlin began in retaliation for a West German political meeting in that city.

To all appearances, jointly coordinated policies notwithstanding, the East Germans were continuing to back into the atmosphere of détente so

---

[75] See the Czechoslovak newspaper *Rudé Právo*, November 25, 1970.
[76] *Pravda*, November 25, 1970.
[77] *Neues Deutschland*, November 27, 1970.
[78] *Neues Deutschland*, November 28, 1970.

enthusiastically greeted by other East European leaders at the Hungarian Congress.[79] As so often with Rumania in the past, the party forum of consultation had broken down. Given established patterns of intra-organizational maneuvering, it was not surprising that Moscow should turn to the Warsaw Pact. Only this time the alliance moved with unaccustomed speed.

Warsaw Pact Meeting in East Berlin

Reportedly at Gomułka's suggestion, the political consultative committee met December 2 in East Berlin. Rumors of Ulbricht's heart condition stopped when he personally welcomed the arriving delegations. Although the meeting issued four statements covering the trouble spots of Indochina, the Middle East, and Guinea as well as the situation in Europe, its timing left little doubt that the PCC had convened primarily to talk about what next vis-à-vis Brandt's *Ostpolitik*—i.e., Berlin. And, despite standard claims of full unanimity, the statement "On Questions of Strengthening Security and Developing Peaceful Cooperation in Europe" read very much like a piecemeal product of compromise.

It contained the favorite Rumanian formula for strict observance of independence, sovereignty, territorial integrity, equality, and noninterference in internal affairs. It recognized the significance of the Moscow-Bonn agreement and the Warsaw-Bonn treaty. It supported the Czechoslovak demand that West Germany renounce the Munich agreement.

As for East Germany, the participants expressed solidarity with the "peace-loving policy" of the GDR. Recognition of East Germany by those states that had not yet done so as well as the GDR's full-fledged membership in the U.N. was considered a contribution to the cause of peace. However, once again such recognition was not made a precondition for anything. Most certainly not for a European security conference, for which the statement claimed sufficient preconditions had already been created. On the whole the tone was unpolemical. Less than half a sentence was devoted to "revenge-seeking, militaristic forces" in the Federal Republic, and that was followed by assurances that the forces of peace would overcome all obstacles.

On Berlin the statement expressed hope that a solution meeting the

---

[79] See Gomułka's speech, *Trybuna ludu*, November 25, 1970; Zhivkov, *Rabotnichesko delo*, November 25, 1970; Kádár, *Népszabadság*, November 25, 1970; and the Rumanian delegate Paul Niculescu-Mizil, *Scînteia*, November 27, 1970.

interests of détente in Europe, the requirement of the population of West Berlin (Brezhnev's recent contribution in his speech in Armenia) and the sovereign rights of the GDR. Not surprisingly, there were no details on what such a solution might entail.[80]

The meeting was extensively covered in both Soviet and East European press with about the difference of emphasis that could have been expected. Moscow divided attention between stressing the importance of coordinated foreign policy among socialist states and pressing for a European security conference "without delay or preconditions"—the latter point undoubtedly directed towards the NATO Council meeting in Brussels.[81] The Rumanians concluded experience had shown the correctness of Bucharest's independent recognition of West Germany in 1967.[82] Warsaw saw the meeting as a confirmation of its treaty with the Federal Republic.[83] The East German's quoted its warnings against provocative actions by West German "revanchists." [84]

If Pankow privately agreed with the Albanian analysis that the PCC meeting, like the NATO Council in Brussels, demonstrated a US–Soviet "holy alliance" to persuade East Germany to open its doors to ideological subversion from the West,[85] it gave no sign. For the moment, the GDR appeared to bend before intraalliance pressure.

Harassment of traffic to West Berlin ceased. Then December 9, one day after the signing of the Warsaw-Bonn treaty, Ulbricht reluctantly indicated that talks on Berlin might get going. Despite his claim of complete conformity with the position of the Warsaw Pact declaration on the Berlin talks, the East German leader gave a remarkable reinterpretation of the PCC documents. According to his version, the joint consultations emphasized the solidarity of the socialist states with the GDR, considered recognition of East Germany to be the central issue in normalizing the European situation and agreed to resolutely resist all attempts by Bonn to

---

[80] *Pravda*, December 4, 1970 and Document 15, p. 245.

[81] *Pravda*, December 4, 1970 and *Izvestia*, December 5, 1970. If so it was a fruitless gesture, for the NATO Council announcement of December 4 firmly tied the ESC to concessions on Berlin.

[82] *Scînteia*, December 5, 1970.

[83] Gomułka's speech at Zabrze, *Trybuna ludu*, December 4, 1970; *Zeri i Popullit*, December, 1970.

[84] *Neues Deutschland*, December 8, 1970.

[85] Tirana ATA International service in French, December 7, 1970. *Zeri i Popullit*, December, 1970. However one should remember there was strong feeling in the GDR about just such dangers with respect to "intra-German" talks.

invent any intra-German principles of relations between the GDR and the FRG. Ulbricht continued to stress the dangers of "imperialist forces" and an "intensified anti-Communist campaign" in West Germany. He alluded to the need for Warsaw Pact documents to be considered by "parties and mass organizations in discussions with GDR citizens," a frank admission of intent to mobilize popular support for his regime's stand. In conclusion he made a hardly veiled declaration of independence:

> The Berlin session of the Warsaw Pact political consultative committee has engendered clarity in many respects and answered complicated questions. Our central task, the cardinal task of the GDR worker-peasant regime . . . remains the political, economic, cultural, and military strengthening of the GDR.[86]

The SED Plenary session that ended December 11, in the words of the earlier PCC statement "hoped" the current Big-Four talks would lead to an acceptable solution. The simultaneous election of Hermann Axen, a hardliner reportedly close to Honecker, to the 15-man Politburo indicated such hopes might have stiff sledding.

Moreover, within a matter of days events coalesced to take much of the steam out of pressure on the East Germans. Rioting followed by a rapid change of government in Poland brought the spectre of internal disorders. Leaders in Warsaw suddenly faced the fact "for the first time in 300 years" there was not a single state in Europe to question Poland's frontiers might prove a mixed blessing.

Undoubtedly the forces in Moscow to push hardest on the path of rapprochement with West Germany were shaken. Any nagging voices echoing Molotov's reservations about the effects of wooing Tito back into the bloc in 1955 to warn about potential disadvantages of West German bedfellows were strengthened. At the very least it must have required a reassessment in which speedy ratification of the Bonn-Moscow agreement lost considerable attractiveness.

In these circumstances, it appeared that Ulbricht might well have been allowed to take his two steps back while Moscow sat out the next round. For despite the initial appearance of willingness to let the Polish regime

---

[86] *Neues Deutschland,* December 10, 1970. Although Western press coverage tended to imply that Ulbricht had yielded to Soviet pressure, any reading of the complete text of his December 9 speech makes it doubtful that such concessions in fact amounted to much. Indeed his main point was cryptically repeated by Honecker at the 15th SED CC Plenum: "Our main attention will be focused on the further all-around strengthening of the GDR. . . ." *Neues Deutschland,* January 31, 1971.

restore order in its own house, there is the disquieting memory of Czecho-slovakia. In 1968 the Soviets first opted for noninterference followed by attempts at polemical persuasion that ended in invasion. And in 1971? It remains an open question in which much hangs on the fate of Poland—the future of détente, East Europe, and the Warsaw Pact.

8
CONCLUSIONS

"The Warsaw Pact has been, and remains, the main center for coordinating the fraternal countries' foreign policy." Brezhnev to the 24th CPSU Congress, March 30, 1971

The Political Balance Sheet

In retrospect, as it was set up, the Warsaw Treaty served multiple Soviet and to a lesser extent East European purposes. For the Soviets the treaty constituted another move in their German policy—although East German participation was carefully restricted—legalized the presence of Soviet troops which otherwise should have been withdrawn from Hungary and Rumania, and provided a propaganda-prestige counterpart to the North Atlantic Alliance. As with NATO, the Warsaw Treaty Organization was not intended to fight but to gain another bargaining card in the cold war.

The treaty formalized Soviet influence in East Europe without sacrificing the outward equality of East European Communist states. It accomplished this by conveniently limiting independent foreign policy maneuver on the part of the people's democracies in that (1) the members pledged not to join other conflicting alliances, and (2) no withdrawal procedures were specified. Thus, although this treaty set forth a reality existing long before 1955, its timing lent it a much broader diplomatic and political importance for Moscow.

As for the smaller member states, there was, admittedly, little choice. However, in that the pact was directed against the possibility of renewed German aggression, it did serve a fundamental East European interest. And in some cases the treaty met specific national interests. For the Poles it was another prop to the Oder-Neisse boundary. For the East Germans it strengthened the GDR's position in pushing for German reunification in that despite the lack of general withdrawal procedures, it was accepted that East Germany could withdraw into a democratic united Germany from the beginning. Also, and perhaps most important to the East European representatives actually signing the treaty, the presence of Soviet troops provided vital support for their regimes.

Thus, the Warsaw Treaty Organization was established—a formally egalitarian military and political institution with prescribed rules regulating both its own operation and the member states' relations to each other and to nonmember states. Given this institutional structure and the post-Stalin Soviet leadership's desire to change at least the world image of relationships within the socialist camp, it is not surprising that the speeches at the founding Warsaw Treaty Conference and those at the first political consultative committee meeting were characterized by a fair measure of diversity, focusing on some issues of specific interest to East European Communist leaders as well as supporting Soviet policies.

The Polish and Hungarian events in 1956 sharply interrupted this trend, while if the document detailing the reorganization of Hungarian armed forces is at all an accurate description of Soviet intentions, the initial phase of diversity (like the "coalition" period of consolidating power within the people's democracies) may well have been intended as a prelude to increased centralization, at least militarily. Albeit, under the pressure of major conflict within the socialist camp, the formal organization set up by the Warsaw Treaty was in effect abandoned. The rules were thrown out. The Soviet Union intervened in the internal affairs of Hungary, thereby violating both the preamble to the Warsaw Treaty and Article 8.

Ex post facto justifications of Soviet military intervention in Hungary further emphasized the USSR's obligation under the Warsaw Treaty. The members' promise "to take the agreed upon measures necessary to strengthen their defense, to protect the peaceful labor of their peoples, guarantee the integrity of their borders and territories, and guarantee defense from possible aggression" (Article 5) was cited. No mention was made of when and by whom the measure of Soviet intervention in Hungary was agreed upon. As noted, there had been no meeting of the political consultative committee after January in 1956, nor even mention of East European leaders convening for any purpose immediately prior to or during the rebellion in Hungary. Much later the Soviets stressed even more positively that the "active strength of the Warsaw Treaty manifested itself in the days of the counterrevolutionary events in Hungary." Although individual East European governments sanctioned the invasion, this Soviet interpretation has never been repeated in an official Warsaw Pact document—an unmistakable sign that even at the time of the May 1958 political consultative committee meeting the alliance had become more than an echo of Soviet formulations.

By the early 1960s, Moscow faced open defiance from Albania and stubborn, if cautious, resistance from Rumania on ideological and political issues both within the Warsaw Pact and in the broader context of the "socialist commonwealth."

In the Albanian case the situation was one of sustained defiance on the part of a small member-state to Soviet wishes. And despite Khrushchev's criticisms of Stalin's failure to deal realistically with Yugoslavia, Soviet responses to such defiance did not differ markedly between 1948 and 1960. Both Stalin and Khrushchev publicly denounced the offending state. Names were called, economic sanctions applied, treaties broken. Individual East European Communist regimes followed the Soviet example with varying degrees of dedication.

Yet the effect of the Soviet-Albanian dispute upon Soviet–East European joint organizations was decidedly less than that of the Soviet-Yugoslav conflict upon either the Soviet–East European bilateral treaty system or the cominform. For although de facto exclusion of Albanian representatives from both the Warsaw Treaty Organization and CMEA had resulted, Albania was never formally expelled.

These differences between 1948 and 1961 were due largely to changes in the political environment. First, a reordering of priorities had occurred. From the 1940s until Stalin's death, the cold war had occupied first place as a justification for the sacrifices demanded of the Soviet people and for the subordination of other Communist parties and states to Soviet will. In the period of the post-Stalin succession struggle the Soviets changed their perception of nuclear war; as a result Khrushchev became committed to détente with the West and internal considerations took on increased importance.

Second, the myth of Soviet infallibility, badly damaged by the Soviet-Yugoslav rapprochement in 1955, was not strong enough to survive the combined blows of Khrushchev's "secret speech" and the October 30, 1956 Declaration admitting Soviet mistakes in dealing with other socialist countries.

Third, and perhaps most important, Khrushchev was confronted with problems that Stalin never faced, sustained innerparty conflict complicated by an openly recalcitrant China intent on influencing socialist policy-making and the events within the East European Communist states. Regardless of the exact chronology of the Sino-Soviet rift (the Soviets originally dated it from the Chinese article *Long Live Leninism* of April 1960 and now favor 1958;[1] the Chinese claim that differences began in 1956), it was obviously a consideration in Communist thinking long before Westerners took the issue seriously. Consequently, East European support within the international Communist movement became increasingly important to Moscow. As a corollary, the maneuverability of these states increased, and Soviet political control over the area became more and more difficult.

Khrushchev had no more success at controlling Tirana than Stalin had had with Belgrade. Nor did he seem able to cope with Rumanian recalcitrance. The attempt to do so by upgrading military consolidation within the Warsaw Pact and economic integration via CMEA met with little success. That this was the case does not negate the importance of such an attempt for European Communist coalition politics however, for with the increased emphasis on military and economic content, the political requirement of affirming Soviet policy positions declined.

When Brezhnev and Kosygin came to power in 1964, their attitude toward the Warsaw Pact was formed against the background of Khrushchev's failure to control the Albanians and successful Rumanian resistance to Soviet plans for economic integration within CMEA. Khrushchev sank into obscurity but his emphasis on the Warsaw Pact as a valuable instrument for socialist consolidation was, if anything, intensified. Moreover, whereas Khrushchev had treated the alliance as a vehicle for Soviet power and appeared to value it primarily as a stepping stone to more universal forms of Communist organization,[2] the new collective leadership came to use the mechanism of the coalition for consultation and conflict containment. At first this was part of a largely unsuccessful effort to mollify Rumania. For Moscow obviously wanted to treat its dif-

---

[1] Suslov's report to the CPSU CC Plenum, *Pravda*, April 3, 1964, and W. E. Griffith, *Sino-Soviet Relations 1964–1965* (Cambridge, Mass.: The MIT Press, 1967), Document 19, p. 204.

[2] Khrushchev, "Vital Questions of the Development of the World Socialist System," p. 9.

ferences with Bucharest as a product of Khrushchev's tactless handling of the matter, that is, to assume the problem was one of personalities rather than a genuine conflict of interests. That proved not to be the case. Yet the attempt itself magnified the importance of the Warsaw Pact in Soviet eyes. In turn, this changing perception of the value of the alliance was reinforced in 1965 by Rumanian willingness to participate in Warsaw Pact meetings, while pointedly abstaining from other forms of interparty consultation.

Even Albania was invited to the January 1965 political consultative committee session which seems to have focused on the members' differences vis-à-vis West Germany. In 1966, weeks of intensive intra-alliance negotiations preceded the July Bucharest meeting, and the resulting Declaration had all the earmarks of compromise. Then in 1967 Moscow worked to contain the heated debate over Rumanian independent recognition of West Germany within the alliance rather than excluding the Bucharest from the pact. Thus, by 1967 the Warsaw Pact had appeared to be evolving into an alliance that functioned as an increasingly genuine channel for conflict resolution among European Communist states rather than as an echo of Moscow policy initiatives. The relationship of command that existed between the Soviet Union and smaller member states throughout the 1950s had given way, at least with respect to Rumania, to a relationship of bargaining.

In 1968, this evolution could not survive the combined impact of Bonn's new Eastern policy and liberalization in Prague. As early as the Dresden meeting, Moscow must have decided that controlling Czechoslovakia had priority over retaining the Soviet-Rumanian balance in part made possible by the Warsaw Pact. In short, this time Bucharest was to be isolated rather than mollified. The result was that as the conflict intensified between Czechoslovakia, the Soviet Union, and more orthodox East European regimes, the Warsaw Pact served as a weapon against Prague. It was an instrument of pressure, particularly with respect to the demand for Pact maneuvers on Czechoslovak territory.

The fact of this difference in handling Soviet-Rumanian and Soviet-Czechoslovak conflicts of interest is history. But to return to the questions raised in the introduction of this study: why? Any form of conflict resolution, Communist or not, moves along a continuum of persuasion to force. By 1967, the Soviets had obviously decided that containing Soviet-

Rumanian differences within the alliance had advantages over either invading as they had done in Hungary in 1956 or excluding the Rumanians as they had done with the Albanians after 1961.

Brezhnev had declined to interfere at the time of the Czechoslovak plenum that deposed Novotný as party chief. The initial Soviet reactions to reforms in Prague were not overtly hostile. Dubček went to Moscow in late January; the Sofia meeting of the Warsaw Pact PCC on March 8 showed only slight signs of strain. Subsequently the delay, intensive bilateral and multilateral consultations in the months before the invasion, and the fact that virtually the entire Soviet Politburo picked up and went to the Čierná talks all indicate that the leadership was undoubtedly divided and not anxious to use troops.

Moscow might well have preferred the Rumanian model. To understand what went wrong, it is important to look at the differences between the Soviet-Rumanian and Soviet-Czechoslovak conflicts.

First, the area of conflict was not the same. Rumania had (1) balked at Soviet goals for "perfecting" the Warsaw Pact and CMEA; (2) insisted on neutrality in the Sino-Soviet dispute; and (3) refused to coordinate its foreign policy vis-à-vis West Germany and Israel with that of Moscow and the more orthodox members of the alliance. Czechoslovakia had gone to great pains not to be too far out of line with joint foreign policies (although there were signs of differences in approach toward the Federal Republic and Israel) and had taken care to follow Soviet initiatives with respect to Peking—all the while assiduously emphasizing its loyalty to the Warsaw Pact. The problem was that its domestic developments brought Moscow and certainly Warsaw and Pankow as well to question two things: (1) whether Czechoslovak "socialism with a human face" was an ideologically acceptable model for a socialist state (2) whether Dubček could in fact maintain control. Both questions that had undoubtedly been asked about Hungary in 1956.

Second, the timing. Soviet-Rumanian differences developed over a period of years. As had been the case with Albania, there was never a really convenient moment to intervene. In Czechoslovakia, the Prague spring lasted eight months (exactly the same amount of time between the forming the Petöfi clubs in Budapest and the first Soviet intervention in Hungary). Moreover, in Czechoslovakia once the draft statutes were published on August 10, it was clear that unless the intervention took place before the Slovak Party Congress scheduled for August 26 the nature of Czechoslovak communism might be irrevocably changed.

Third, the leading role of the party. The Rumanian Communist Party (again like the Albanians) had kept complete control over the political, economic, and social life of the country. All levers of power remained exclusively in the hands of the party. In Czechoslovakia, as in the Hungarian case, this was not so. Of course, the situation in Prague in 1968 differed from Budapest in 1956.[3] But certain fundamentals were the same. Nagy had intended to bring major representatives of non-Communist parties into his government. Dubček appeared willing to go even further. In Prague there was talk of pluralism, of the role of interest groups in a socialist society, even of opposition parties. Once censorship had been removed, the number of conflicting views on both what was possible and what was optimal must have been confusing even within the KSČ, to say nothing of to Moscow and East European political leaders unused to coping with a free press.

Fourth, alternative support. Ever since the late 1950s Rumania had been cautiously implying that should the Soviets push too hard Bucharest would turn for protection to China. To Moscow this cannot have been an empty threat. Albania had already become an island of Chinese influence in East Europe; the Chinese were openly anxious to expand the number of their supporters in the area.[4] In some ways Prague might have profited by wooing Peking.[5] However, ideologically the Chinese and Czechoslovak positions in 1968 were completely incompatible. If Peking considered the Soviet leaders revisionist renegades, Dubček and company were beyond the pale. Therefore the best the Czechoslovaks could do within the Communist world was ally themselves with the Rumanians, the Yugoslavs, and some of the more flexible parties such as the Italian and British. It was not enough. As for other allies, the West Germans

[3] Bela K. Király, "Budapest 1956—Prague 1968," *Problems of Communism* 17, nos. 4–5 (July–October 1969): 52–60.

[4] Hemen Ray, "China's Initiatives in Eastern Europe" *Current Scene* 7, no. 23 (December 1, 1969): 1–17 and M. Kamil Dziewanowski, "Communist China and East Europe," *Survey* 77 (Autumn 1970): 59–74.

[5] Many quite ordinary Czechs and Slovaks appear to have taken this notion perhaps more seriously than the Dubček government. In the post-invasion period one of the slogans written on buildings in Prague roughly translated "We are close to the Chinese," while one of the stories I was told by a member of an institute of international politics in the summer of 1969 was that during the invasion a delegation of workers came to the institute to ask whether or not they should make a direct appeal to China.

who even prior to the Brandt government would have been the most interested in both economic and potentially political contact, were unacceptable on two counts. The issue of Munich had to be settled. And, indeed, the more contacts Prague had with Bonn the more justified Moscow could feel about intervening. The United States kept a hands-off attitude that went to the extent of a news leak from a "high official" at the time of the Čierná talks that although Washington would be upset if the Soviets invaded Czechoslovakia there was basically nothing that could be done about it.[6]

Fifth, the attitude of the other member states was much less ambiguous with respect to Czechoslovakia than had been the case with Rumania. It was one thing to sanction foreign policy initiatives that other East European governments might even want to imitate in the future; quite another to watch domestic developments in Czechoslovakia take a turn that could threaten the stability of their own regimes. The unfortunate fact was that the issue of the Prague spring had become a matter of symbolic concern in the innerparty politics of both East Germany and Poland. Not only did these two countries have a genuine fear that relaxation in Czechoslovakia might be contagious within key sectors of their own populations but for internal purposes the dangers of the Czechoslovak model became a weapon in the hands of hardliners. Bucharest's firm stand against discussing the internal affairs of another party at joint meetings meant that Czechoslovakia's most natural supporter within the alliance was excluded from multilateral consultation on this topic from the beginning. As for Hungary, the Kádár regime may well have been unenthusiastic, but was equally unwilling to jeopardize the future of Budapest's extensive economic reforms by refusing to participate in collective measures against Prague.

In short, the picture that seems to emerge is one in which all the cards, including the international situation, were stacked against Prague. As one high placed KSČ member said to me in June 1969, the wonder was not that the Soviets invaded but that they waited so long. For this would seem to be the crux of the ideological component of the Warsaw Pact alliance. The question is what is an acceptable model of socialist construction and who decides—the country in question, Moscow, or a collectivity in which the Soviets have the loudest but not the only voice.

[6] Tom Wicker, *The New York Times*, August 1, 1968.

In Hungary in 1956, clearly it was a Soviet action and a Soviet decision. Or to be more precise, in 1956 ideology provided the framework in which historical conditions were analyzed and Moscow's decision-making supported to the advantage of the Soviets. There is a good deal of evidence that this is what the Soviets had in mind for 1968 as well. Thus the early attempts to justify the "allied socialist" invasion of Czechoslovakia reinterpreted the function of the Warsaw Pact alliance so as to support the military intervention and implicitly a return to Soviet hegemony in as much of Eastern Europe as possible. Such an interpretation put Rumania in a most untenable position. The Albanians denounced the Warsaw Treaty as a "treaty of enslavement" and formally withdrew from the Pact. Moscow did not invade Albania, a clear signal that the deciding factor in Hungary in 1956 and Czechoslovakia in 1968 was not only formal membership in the alliance.

Seen in perspective one could say that liberalization in Prague and the resulting Soviet-Czechoslovak conflict caused Moscow to revert to the Molotov theory of the Warsaw Pact. For even in 1954, the Soviet leadership had been divided on the purpose of that alliance.

In Molotov's view, its primary function was to safeguard the borders of the socialist camp. Yet, for the most part, his interpretation was pushed aside. Initially, emphasis appeared to be on the international significance of the Warsaw Pact, that is, its importance for Soviet policy toward the West. The text of the Treaty did not mention the socialist camp. Its formally open-ended membership policy was contrasted to NATO's exclusion of the USSR; willingness of Warsaw Treaty members to dissolve the Pact in favor of a general European security system was reiterated. Warsaw Treaty Organization meetings dovetailed with East-West confrontations.

Yet, even in 1955, Soviet analyses of the Warsaw Treaty had used "participants of the Warsaw Pact" and "members of the socialist camp" interchangeably. Within this context Moscow clearly perceived the substance of the Warsaw Pact as derived not from its stated aims but from the political system of its member states. With each successive East European challenge to Soviet authority, the implications of that duality became more explicit. To Molotov the Warsaw Pact had been a vehicle of socialist consolidation. He lost in the 1950s. However, the Molotov theory of the Warsaw Pact is, in fact, one of the fundamental assumptions underlying the current Brezhnev Doctrine. Ironically in May 1968, one finds Pact Commander-in-Chief Yakubovsky repeating almost word for word Molotov's pledge of 1954:

> There is no power on earth that can turn back the wheel of history and prevent the building of socialism in our countries.[7]

Whether or not Moscow can reimpose control is doubtful. For as Molotov himself so eloquently said, the wheel of history has its own inertia. Despite similarities 1968 was not 1956, nor is the situation in 1970 that of 1947. Khrushchev may have outlined the maximum Soviet goal for Eastern Europe in 1959 when he spoke of the question of borders as eventually becoming a "pointless question."[8] But in 1970 the Soviet leaders are caught in a paradoxical situation of being among the most ardent defenders of the "inviolability of borders."

In sum, current parallels to postwar development of the people's democracies are misleading. As Brzezinski has correctly pointed out,[9] there was no intrinsic reason why the initial diversity among the East European regimes ended so abruptly or why the "transitional period" was so brief. Rather the consolidation of Communist power in and Soviet control over the states of East Europe during the postwar years depended on a series of fortuitous circumstances favoring the Soviets, that is, rapid Western disengagement in the area, the proximity of Soviet power, and the weakness of the non-Communist opposition. Nor were East European Communists unmindful of the protection Soviet power gave to their own positions in face of popular hostility.

Also the psychological setting of the late 1940s worked against manifestations of East European independence. The men who took power in postwar East Europe were, on the whole, Comintern-bred Communists steeped in the obsequious Comintern attitudes toward the Soviet Union. For years they had been physically supported by Soviet funds and emo-

---

[7] Yakubovsky on the 13th anniversary of the Warsaw Pact stressed that the Pact would continue "to reliably defend" the countries of socialism, adding, "And there are no forces capable of turning back the wheel of history or arresting the relentless movement of nations toward socialism. . . ." *Pravda*, May 14, 1968. His formula was not much different from Brezhnev's blunt justification of the subsequent "allied socialist" invasion of Czechoslovakia to the 24th CPSU Congress, "revolutionary gains will not be given up, the frontiers of the socialist community are inviolable. . . ." *Pravda*, March 30, 1971.

[8] March 27, 1959.

[9] Brzezinski, *The Soviet Bloc: Unity and Conflict* (Cambridge, Mass.: Harvard University Press, 3rd ed., 1967).

tionally nourished by Soviet myths. The Soviet Union was the "fatherland," the leader, the vanguard. Proletarian internationalism equated with imitation, and even love of all things Soviet. The accounts of Yugoslav leaders' responses to the 1948 break with Stalin are classic examples of this pattern. Even with the assumption of power many of these attitudes remained the same, while the cold war replaced the war against Fascism as the external threat necessitating complete conformity with Soviet goals.

Thus until Stalin's death East Europe was much like the periphery of a national empire in which the Soviet Union had effective decision-making power and military control. Despite the formally sovereign East European states, the foreign policy of those states, and to an abnormal extent their domestic policy as well, was centrally directed from Moscow and largely to the benefit of the Soviet Union.

At the present time, objective political conditions are much less favorable for rapid consolidation. For some twenty years Communist states, highly conscious of their boundaries, have existed in East Europe. Popular nationalism has infected the regimes. In Rumania, Gheorghiu-Dej died only to have Ceauşescu continue his independent policies. Kádár, a Soviet installed puppet in 1956, has become the symbol of a "Hungarian way." Dubček fell, but despite his current role Husák can be expected to go the way of Kádár. Ulbricht spoke of his regime's primary task as "strengthening" the GDR. And when the dust settles in Warsaw, we may again see a Polish national communism. Despite Moscow's drive for economic integration through CMEA, East European trade is turning Westward which can be expected to further limit, or at least modify, these countries' dependence on the Soviet Union. The continued pitch and intensity of the Sino-Soviet dispute has increased East European leverage in the Communist world.

Moreover, Moscow's temporarily abandoned attempt to substitute China for West Germany as the external threat necessitating constant vigilance within the alliance had no natural basis. Germany is a danger East European leaders and peoples alike have experienced, understand, and fear. China is not. West Germany is within a few days march of any East European border. China is not. Also, Soviet attacks on Mao Tse-tung notwithstanding, China is a socialist country and a variety of attitudes toward Peking continue to be acceptable within the international Communist movement.

In these circumstances, the Soviets may find that although they still have the power of negative definition, that is, Moscow can say what *is not* an acceptable model of socialism, the "wheel of history" is making it harder for the Soviet leadership to retain control over what is permissible within the context of "the leading role of the Communist party." Already Albania, and to some extent East Germany, have graphically demonstrated the problem raised by small Communist states who differ from Moscow on the side of dogmatism rather than reform—a reminder that any universal movement whether theological or ideological has difficulties with members who would be more catholic than the pope (and even in the Soviet Union the historic Russian idea of Moscow as the Third Rome is not dead).

In studying coalition politics, however, it is important not to forget that the increased number of players always subtly modifies the game—a fact true of Communist as well as non-Communist alliances. Despite wide areas of accepted agreement, each member-state has a difference of emphasis in reflecting any spectrum of interests. And within the Warsaw Pact there seems to be a growing understanding in both Moscow and the East European capitals that compromise is preferable to open conflict unless (as was the case with Albania) there is no desire to return to talk another day. Therefore, much is contingent on the collective evolution in Eastern Europe—whether Husák can hold his own against the extremists in Prague, the importance of the Hungarian experiments with what is basically Sik's economic model, progress or the lack of it in moving the East Germans one step closer to a solution on Berlin and, most important, the direction taken in Poland.

If there is any topic that warrants caution it is what has happened and is happening in Poland. Yet despite the hazards of dealing with events as recent as yesterday that will still be happening tomorrow, I could not allow a book on the Warsaw Pact to be published in 1971 without a preliminary discussion. Briefly, on December 17, 1970, the Polish Council of Ministers passed a resolution declaring a nationwide state of emergency and calling on the militia to shoot, if necessary, to restore order in Gdansk and other coastal cities where rioting had broken out following steep increases in food prices. Although the initial impulse was to blame "adventurers and instigators" for exploiting the workers' protest,[10] by De-

---

[10] Premier Cyrankiewicz speech, *Trybuna ludu,* December 17, 1971. Subsequent reports indicate that Kliszko and Gomułka as well favored the counterrevolutionary interpretation of events, i.e. Soviet intervention to keep Gomułka in power.

cember 19 it was admitted that the price changes were badly timed and that not only hooligans had gone into the streets.[11] On December 20, Gomułka fell, as a result of the demonstrations and, reportedly, of a plot by Gierek and Moczar against him. His post went to Edward Gierek, head of the Katowice Voivodship, known for his successful economic management of that region.

Gierek had no mean job. Domestically he faced continuing strikes and work stoppages, a declining economy with little or no reserves, an admitted credibility gap between the Communist party and the Polish people, and a delicate internal political balance in which his own position at least to some extent depended on the support of Mieczysław Moczar, the leader of the nationalistic partisan faction.[12] It is much too soon to judge how well he will succeed. However, in the short run one can say something about the steps along the way.

At home the new government promised economic reform, attacked the "bureaucratic inertia" of the Gomułka leadership for allowing the situation to deteriorate, and step by step made concessions. First the unpopular incentive plan that the workers (most likely rightly) feared would cut real wages by threatening the bonus system was postponed. On December 23, Gierek announced that seven million zloty had been allotted to improving the situation of families in the lowest income category and promised a freeze on food prices for the next two years. Then in mid-February the December price increases were cancelled a reversal made possible by credit assistance from the Soviet Union.[13]

These economic measures were combined with high-speed political maneuvering. Polish Politburo members began a whirlwind of internal (and external) travel. Gierek personally went to two of the most serious trouble spots, Gdansk and Szczecin, on January 24–25, and Primer Jaroszewicz went to Łódz to talk with women textile workers whose massive strike seems to have led directly to a mid-February price cutback. On all

[11] *Trybuna ludu*, December 19, 1971.

[12] At this time, May 1971, there are at least some signs that Moczar's influence has slipped for the time being. He did not attend the CPSU 24th Congress at the end of March, nor an important reception in honor of Soviet-Polish friendship in mid-April. It is unclear whether he has fallen. For a report that he has, see *The Sunday Telegraph* (London), May 2, 1971.

[13] *Trybuna ludu*, February 15, 1971. Subsequently Jaroszewicz revealed that this aid amounted to 100 million dollars worth of hard currency. *Zycie Warszawy*, April 16, 1971.

levels, the Polish party began a massive fence-mending campaign. It was a time of almost continuous meeting of regional and local party conferences. There were many hard questions, much self-criticism, and a still difficult-to-evaluate turnover of middle-level cadres.[14] Simultaneously Gierek attempted to consolidate his position by at least partially satisfying identifiably important sectors of society, a move in which he was particularly conciliatory toward the potentially powerful Polish Catholic church.[15]

As for intera-alliance politics, the new leader of the Polish party could not have been more explicit:

> An unshakeable canon of our foreign policy is, and always has been, our fraternal alliance and friendship with the Soviet Union, constituting decisive guarantees of our security and independence.[16]

Nor was there any reason to think that the new government was in any way unacceptable to the Soviet Union despite Moscow's formerly close relationship with Gomułka. Katowice had long ranked high among Polish regions hosting visiting Soviet delegations; and the solid eastward orientation of the new premier Piotr Jaroszewicz, who had spent World War II in the USSR and returned as defense minister in the Moscow sponsored government of National Unity in the 1940s, was reassuring. As the other strong contender, Moczar could not have looked much better from the Soviet view. Perhaps more important, the speed with which the changeover took place limited the extent of outside influence.[17]

On December 17, *Pravda* printed a Polish Press Agency report on the riots in Gdansk without comment. This was followed by other reprints from the Polish press, including Cyrankiewicz' appeal and the resolution of the Council of Ministers. The first direct Soviet comment came in the form of Brezhnev's congratulatory telegram to Gierek on December 21, followed by a biography of the new Polish leader.

Thus it would seem that when Gierek went to Moscow on January 5, the Soviet leadership was informed rather than consulted about changes that had already taken place. Certainly, keeping on good terms with

[14] By mid-February eight regional party chiefs had been replaced. *International Herald Tribune*, February 19, 1971.

[15] The state tacitly accepted the church's conditions for "normalization" of church-state relations (English text in the *International Herald Tribune*, January 2–3, 1971) and on January 25 announced the government's willingness to turn over property titles to churches and other ecclesiastical buildings in the western territories to the church.

[16] *Trybuna ludu*, December 24, 1970.

[17] *Pravda*, December 22, 1970.

Moscow played an important role in what the new Warsaw government felt free to do or say. For stated or unstated, the analogy to Czechoslovakia was in peoples minds,[18] a consideration that may have had much to do with the heavy schedule of intrabloc travel by many of the Polish politburo members during January.[19] In his speech to the 8th CC Plenum, Gierek himself referred to these trips, claiming:

> In the talks held we enlisted complete understanding for our situation and our current activity.[20]

Whether or not he was indulging in politically expedient optimism, that such consultations were held during what must have been judged in Moscow and also East European capitals as an ongoing crisis was a departure from the norm within the Warsaw Pact. That such talks involved independent visits to other East European leaders, rather than being

[18] On January 30 Reuters reported that *Głos Szczeciński*, the official Communist party newspaper in Szczecin, warned workers against political gamblers wanting to set Poland on the path of Czechoslovakia in 1968. At the same time *Pravda* attacked reports by UPI Vienna correspondent Richard C. Longworth that Russia was ready to invade Poland if new riots broke out as "an impudent UPI lie," in *Pravda*, January 30, 1971. Gierek, speaking in Katowice warned against numerous enemies who "would like to weaken Poland . . . . to undermine the forces of the entire socialist camp." Therefore, "every political step we take must be aimed at strengthening socialism and barring the ways of action to its enemies." *Trybuna ludu*, March 7, 1971.

[19] On January 5 Gierek and Jaroszewicz were in Moscow; on the 11th they were in East Berlin, on the 16th in Prague. January 6–9 Polish Foreign Minister Stefan Jedrychowski held talks with Stoph, Winzer, and Ulbricht. Politburo member Stefan Olszowski conferred with Ceaușescu in Bucharest and also went to Hungary. Moczar was in Bulgaria; Kociołek in Czechoslovakia. Then on January 14, Politburo member Jozef Tejchma and Stanisław Kania, head of the CC administrative department, were in Belgrade exchanging information. It is quite likely that the state of affairs in Poland was also discussed both at the Warsaw Pact foreign ministers meeting, February 18–19, and at the metting of the Defense Ministers Committee, March 2–3, 1971. Although the February meeting was officially another step in the pact's campaign for a European security conference without preconditions, its timing seemed much more related to events in Poland, i.e., the Łódź strike and reversal of the December price increases. As for the Defense Ministers meeting, the fact that Rumanian Defense Minister Ionita went to Budapest, in my opinion, was anything but a sign that Bucharest had returned to the Warsaw fold. Rather Rumanian policy during the first half of 1971 should be viewed in the perspective of 1968. (See Dan Morgan, *Washington Post*, March 14, 1971). In the months leading up to the invasion of Chechoslovakia, the Rumanians had been isolated, unable to influence joint councils. In February and March 1971, the Rumanian leadership was undoubtedly willing to bend over backwards to prevent replaying that scenario. That a Chinese trade delegation signed the Rumanian-Chinese exchange of goods for 1972–1975 the day the foreign ministers' meeting opened in Bucharest said plainly that even though the Rumanians did not want to be dealt out, they were also intent on maintaining their neutrality in the Sino-Soviet split. *Scînteia*, February 19, 1971.

[20] *Trybuna ludu*, February 8, 1971. There were signs that the understanding was less than complete in Czechoslovakia, where by February 25 the minister of interior was reported to have told members of his ministry about dangerous developments in Poland and suggested that "international aid" might be necessary. *The Times* (London), April 6, 1971.

limited to bilateral discussions between Moscow and Warsaw or a multilateral meeting called by the Soviets, can be seen as an index of the changing nature of Communist coalition politics. At the minimum, it indicates that Gierek perceived that the security of his regime required more than immediate Soviet sanction. It is indirect evidence that East European voices were more than echoes in the months leading up to the decision to invade Czechoslovakia.

At the same time, the Polish leader frankly admitted that the "December Crisis" should be called a "crisis of confidence" between the party and the working class, an explanation not surprisingly missing from Soviet excerpts of his speech.[21] It was, he maintained, a crisis that could be overcome. And although here Gierek was vague, the prescription was generally for reform both of the economy and the style of party work.[22] Such reforms would draw on the experiences of other socialist countries, but Gierek concluded that in the end the Poles must create their own system for themselves, for it must be adapted to their conditions.

In terms of the Warsaw Pact, the new Polish system is not important in itself. Rather the salient fact is the change in Moscow's attitude toward intrabloc crisis. For when rioting followed by strikes and work stoppages caused the fall of Gomułka's government and threatened the stability of his successor during January and February 1971, the Soviets had three choices. They could have denounced the strikers as counterrevolutionaries, declared Polish socialism in danger, and intervened militarily. Or, as in Czechoslovakia in 1968, they could have adopted a hands-off approach and watched the situation deteriorate until invasion seemed inevitable. Or they could buy time by giving Gierek enough aid to act as a finger in the dike while he consolidated. That Moscow opted for number three has long-term implications for Communist coalition politics in Europe.[23] This

---

[21] *Pravda*, February 1, 1971.

[22] At this time Gierek at least implied that institutional reform was needed. As in his December 23 speech he spoke of "renewal" of the party and "dialogue." However it is this aspect upon which there has been the least progress and by April 20 the Polish leader had scaled down his suggestion to "constructive discussion."

[23] As an indication, one should note the rapid change in Soviet ambassadors in Poland, Rumania, and Hungary. The new ambassadors are Stanislav Pilotovich, 49; Vasily Drozdenko, 47; and Vladimir Pavlov, 48. All three men are under 50 years old and deputies in the USSR Supreme Soviet. Pavlov is a member of the CPSU CC; Drozdenko is an alternative member of the CC; and Pilotovich is a secretary of the Byelorussian CC. Even more important, however, is the shift in emphasis to consumer goods in the new Soviet five-year plan presented at the 24th Congress, a shift paralleled throughout East Europe. If the promises in the new economic plans are carried out, it means that for the first time Communist regimes are assuming an obligation to see that some of the rewards of socialism

was the first test of the Brezhnev Doctrine on other than an ex post facto basis. And it was a classic case. That the Soviets chose to recognize that the grievances of the working class were justified, instead of claiming that counterrevolutionaries were at work on the Polish coast, speaks volumes. In short, the Brezhnev Doctrine had been interpreted to include economic intervention. Polish socialism could be saved by hard currency as well as guns.

Whether or not it will work is another question and the answer depends in part on developments in the more dogmatic East European countries. In Czechoslovakia Presidium member Vasil Bilak has sent messages to regional party organizations criticizing Gierek's concessions.[24] Although the East Germans currently support the Polish solution, one should not forget that Ulbricht pushed relentlessly toward the invasion of Czechoslovakia,[25] and there is reason to think that he was even more enthusiastic than Moscow about the Soviet duty to protect each single "link" of the socialist commonwealth.[26] Yet how much influence the East Germans have in Moscow, in turn, depends on the political climate in Europe, progress in Soviet-American talks (here the extent of Soviet nervousness at stepped-up US–China contact is also a factor) and perhaps most of all, on innerparty maneuvering within the CPSU. For example, it is likely that the forces behind the August 1970 Bonn-Moscow renunciation of force agreement are not overly enthusiastic about the GDR interpretation of the "main danger in Europe" and what should be done about it.

But as a caveat, there are signs that the Soviet leadership is again undergoing an internal struggle analogous to the process that brought Khru-

are reaped today rather than tomorrow. Such a recording of priorities, if it continues, could radically change the nature of European Communist states. It could alter the relationship of the party to the people in these countries and (although less so) their relationship to each other within CMEA and the Warsaw Pact.

[24] *The Times* (London), April 6, 1971.

[25] Fetjö, "Moscow and Its Allies," p. 36, refers to an internal East German memorandum that apparently called for an invasion of Czechoslovakia to be justified by the Warsaw Pact as early as May 1968.

[26] For example, the East German press did not simply repeat Soviet Foreign Minister Gromyko's pledge that Moscow would not allow "one link to be snatched" from the socialist commonwealth. Speech to the UN, *The New York Times,* October 4, 1968. *Neues Deutschland* strengthened the stance by adding "never and nowhere," *Neues Deutschland,* October 10, 1968. This pattern haas continued throughout 1970. In the first few months of 1971, it took the form of repeated warnings against imperialist attempts to undermine socialism from within and reference to how Warsaw Pact troops fulfilled their internationalist duty in August 1968. See GDR Defence Minister Heinz Hoffmann's speech on the 53rd anniversary of the Soviet armed forces for example. *Neues Deutschland,* February 24, 1971.

shchev to power in the late 1950s and then produced the Brezhnev-Kosygin leadership in 1964. The 24th CPSU Congress was postponed. It was finally held at the end of March 1971. Despite Brezhnev's stated willingness to fulfill obligations undertaken in connection with the August 1970 agreement,[27] press leaks before the congress[28] support the suspicion that the Soviet leadership remained divided on the vital question of how far it could safely respond to Brandt's *Ostpolitik* without jeopardizing East Europe. There may be an orthodox faction in the Soviet military, for example, only too happy to accept the East German view of the dangers of rapproachement.[29] If, and in what manner, these differences are resolved, could have a profound effect upon Soviet behavior toward the Warsaw Pact alliance.

On the Military Side

Moscow is still intent on "continually perfecting" the Warsaw Pact, and "continually perfected" has come to cover a great deal of military activity among Pact member states. The extent of actual command integration within the joint armed forces remains to date largely a matter of conjecture. In 1962, the first comprehensive work on military strategy to appear in the Soviet Union since 1926 speculated that in modern conditions:

> Operational units including armed forces of different socialist countries can be created to conduct joint operations in military theaters. The command of these units can be assigned to the Supreme High Command of the Soviet Armed Forces, with representation of the Supreme High Commands of the Allied countries. In some military theaters, the operational units of the Allied countries will be under their own supreme high command. In such cases, these units can be commanded according to joint concepts and plans of operation and by close co-ordination of troop operations through representatives of these countries.[30]

[27] Brezhnev speech to the 24th CPSU Congress, *Pravda*, March 30, 1971. There were also signs that the East Germans might have a very different view of Moscow's obligations. Ulbricht did not follow the Soviet example and attack the Chinese at the congress. His restraint could indicate that the SED would consider extending it maneuvering to issues other than intra-German relations.

[28] Following claims of criticism of Brandt by Soviet embassy employees in Washington and Stockholm, the Soviet embassy in West Germany denied the charge. Kosygin then assured Bonn of Moscow's concern to improve relations. *International Herald Tribune*, February 10, 11, 1971.

[29] See the interesting article by GDR Defense Minister Hoffmann in *Krasnaya zvezda*, February 28, 1971.

[30] V. CO Sokolovskii, ed., *Soviet Military Strategy*, translated with an analytical introduction, annotations, and supplementary material by Herbert S. Dinerstein, Leon Goure, and Thomas W. Wolfe, a RAND Corporation Research Study (Englewood Cliffs, N.J.:

As a historical precedent for such a procedure the book recalled that Polish, Czech, Rumanian, Bulgarian, and Hungarian units were incorporated into Soviet existing front formations "by agreement with the governments" of their states during World War II. These units fought under the operational command of Soviet commanders at the front.[31]

One consideration indicating that Sokolovskii's postulation of the future incorporation of operational units of the armed forces of various socialist states into the Soviet High Command was even at that time a better measure of Soviet preferences than the actual evolution of the Joint Command can be seen by looking at the joint maneuvers conducted by Warsaw Treaty member states. By October 1962 these training exercises were being carried out under the command of the minister of the armed forces of the country where the maneuvers were taking place, and this pattern seems to have been followed with some regularity to date (May 1971).[32] Nor, apparently, was the East European command limited to the upper-military hierarchy, with control at operational unit level falling back into the hands of the Soviets. At least according to a Berlin radio broadcast speaking of the September 1963 maneuvers, coordination extended to the battalion level with officers of the East German forces commanding Polish, Czechoslovak, and Soviet units.[33]

In 1966, a Soviet naval handbook on international law specified that the ministers of defense who command national contingents assigned to the joint command are subordinate to the commander-in-chief only in this capacity, retaining complete independence on questions relating to the armed forces of their own countries. The joint command exercises leadership only of those contingents that have been put under its control. "Its

---

Prentice-Hall, 1963), p. 495. See also Thomas W. Wolfe, *Soviet Strategy at the Crossroads,* pp. 210 ff.

[31] Sokolovskii, p. 494.

[32] Prior to this time there was no specific data released on the question of command of the joint maneuvers. In April 1962, for instance, the TASS communiqué announcing the maneuvers simply said that they involved Hungarian, Rumanian, and Soviet troops and "took place according to the plan of the headquarters of the joint armed forces of the Warsaw Treaty states." *Pravda,* April 21, 1962.

[33] Military-political lecture by Guenther Seidel, East Berlin Domestic Service in German, 2110 GMT, September 16, 1963. Interestingly enough, the broadcast also noted that German was the language of command and that "various possibilities" are being tried out in the communications field. This is the only reference I have seen to the language used during Warsaw Treaty Organization joint maneuvers, although Váli emphasizes that even during the initial Sovietization of the Hungarian Army, Russian was never used as a command language and all instructions from the Soviets were translated into Hungarian. Váli, *Rift and Revolt in Hungary* (Cambridge, Mass.: Harvard University Press, 1961).

competence does not extend to the armed forces of the Treaty's member states which are not part of the United Armed forces. . . ."[34] This reference leaves open the question of whether such contingents are assigned temporarily for the period of the joint maneuvers or on a more permanent basis and (despite the speculation caused by Shtemenko's article in January, 1970) there has been no formal announcement that WTO member states do, in fact, assign contingents to the joint command. Rather, according to a more recent Soviet source, the East European troops allotted to the Warsaw Pact joint command would be under the military command of the pact commander-in-chief only in case of a generalized war. In all other cases these forces are supervised by the defense minister of the country in question.[35] Political considerations make it most unlikely that this situation will change. The rule of unanimity and the extent of Rumanian objections would seem to preclude the establishment of an actually integrated command. Certainly Yakubovsky has taken pains to stress that within the joint command each army preserves "its national characteristics and historical tradition."[36]

For the purposes of this study, however, the operational details of joint military activity under the Warsaw Pact are much less important than its extent. Joint maneuvers were first publicized in 1961. Since that time they have been held with increasing regularity; giving the impression that the Soviets are, indeed, bent on perfecting the defensive mechanism of the Warsaw Pact.[37]

Summary

Most of the following points are included in the text. Yet there is always the danger of trends getting buried in facts. And although facts are important, I want to make clear for the convenience of the reader, the general direction of events in the evolution of intra-alliance conflict within the Warsaw Pact, an example of the development of Communist conflict

[34] *Voenno-morskoy mezhdunarodno-pravovoy spravochnik* (Moscow: Voennoe izdatelstvo, 1966), pp. 410–414. I am grateful to Fritz Ermarth of RAND for calling this handbook to my attention.

[35] *Sovremennyye problemy razoruzheniya* (Moscow: Mysl' Publishing House, (1970); for analysis, R. Waring Herrick, "Contingents for Warsaw Pact Involve No Integration," Radio Liberty Research, CRD 374/70 (October 27, 1970). More recently, Col. A. Ratnikov, *Krasnaya zvezda* March 24, 1971.

[36] Yakubovsky, I., "Na strazha mira i sotsialisma," *Voenno istoricheskii zhurnal* 5 (May 1970): 70.

[37] For a detailed analysis see J. Pergent, "Le pacte de Varsovie et l'inventaire des forces de l'Est," *Est et Ouest* 19, no. 387 (July 1967): 16–19.

resolution within an institutional framework similar to that of non-Communist regional defense coalitions.

Poland and Hungary, October–November 1956

The role of the pact in the conflicts was extremely limited. There was an indication in the October 30 declaration on relations among socialist states that Moscow initially considered trying to make the conflict with Hungary multilateral when it sought to make the withdrawal of Soviet troops in Hungary dependent on all Warsaw Treaty states. There were no PCC meetings during the conflict. Bilateral consultation between the Soviet Union and Hungary did include references on both sides to responsibility under the Warsaw Pact. In Hungary, the conflict was solved by Soviet resort to force. The Warsaw Pact was used as ex post facto justification of the resort to force.

Albania

By March 1961, difference on intraparty matters were directly affecting Albanian participation in pact meetings. The Albanians took independent positions on policy issues, specifically on the German question. Albania was de facto excluded from the pact after 1961. There was some slight indication that the Soviets attempted to use the January 1965 PCC meeting to try to improve Soviet-Albanian relations. After the invasion of Czechoslovakia in 1968 Tirana formally withdrew from the Warsaw Pact. Differences continue.

Rumania

Most data on the Warsaw Pact and Rumania are available from about 1963 to date. In 1958 Soviet troops left Rumania, a decision approved by the PCC. Subsequent Soviet-Rumanian differences over foreign policy and intraparty issues were to some extent contained within the pact. The Soviets attempted to use the alliance to press for consolidation, the Rumanians to increase their freedom of maneuver and their influence on joint policy. There was conscious and deliberate balancing on both sides. Although this did not affect Rumanian participation in PCC meetings, it sometimes did affect the level of representation. Differences continue.

Czechoslovakia

From January to August 1968 the Warsaw Pact was intimately involved in conflict with Czechoslovakia. The Soviets continued to refer to Prague's obligations under the pact, both as a means of pressuring for a multilateral meeting in the summer of 1968 and as an excuse for maneuvers on Czechoslovak territory. Prchlík expressed dissatisfaction with the lack of East European opportunities to participate in decision-making within the Warsaw Pact. The Dubček government tried unsuccessfully to use the issue of loyalty to the alliance to ward off direct interference in Czechoslovak internal affairs. The PCC met once on March 8, 1968. This meeting was followed by extensive bilateral and multilateral consultation dealling with the conflict, but not by official Warsaw Pact meetings. The conflict was resolved by multilateral invasion of Czechoslovakia, which was condemned by one member of the coalition, Rumania. Moscow used the provisions of the Warsaw Pact as an ex post facto justification of the invasion of Czechoslovakia.

East Germany

From 1969 to date, the Soviets attempted to use the Warsaw Pact to bring East German policy into line with Moscow's desire for rapprochement with Bonn. The Ulbricht regime attempted to use the alliance to keep control over other East European initiatives toward West Germany. Its organizational maneuvering was very similar to the Rumanian pattern. PCC meetings increased greatly, combined with extensive bilateral consultation. Differences appear to be contained explicitly within the framework of the Warsaw Pact alliance. There are signs that the pressure is temporarily off (May 1971), but it may very well be resumed.

DIFFERENCES BETWEEN THE ROLE OF THE ALLIANCE IN THE RUMANIAN,
CZECHOSLOVAK, AND EAST GERMAN CASES, AND THE
ROLE PLAYED IN EARLIER CRISES

The extent of coalition involvement in the conflict itself was much greater in the three cases under discussion.

Both the superpower and the East European state involved perceived the joint institution as a channel of conflict containment, if not of conflict resolution. This is also true in the case of Czechoslovakia, despite the eventual resort to force.

Although the Czechoslovak and Hungarian crises both led to invasion, there was considerable difference in the decision-making process leading up to that act, and in the number of invaders. In 1956, the Soviets used force unilaterally, without consultation. In 1968, five members of the Warsaw Pact invaded after extensive consultation among one another and with the Dubček government.

Soviet-Albanian differences led to the complete exclusion of Albania from the Warsaw Pact. In contrast, no formal PCC meeting was held to which Rumania, Czechoslovakia, or East Germany were not invited. Instead, these countries' differences with Moscow affected only their participation in nonpact meetings.

EFFECT ON THE SUPERPOWER'S PERCEPTION OF THE COALITION AND ON THE EXPECTATIONS OF THE SMALLER MEMBER STATES

In the cases of Rumania, Czechoslovakia, and East Germany, Moscow's awareness of the importance of the Warsaw Pact for accomplishing policy objectives in East Europe seems to have increased. With respect to Soviet–East German tensions, the pact appears to have served as a vehicle for a broader Soviet policy toward Europe.

Successful Rumanian maneuvering within the alliance certainly heightened the sensitivity of other East European states to the opportunity to do likewise. Czechoslovakia's failure did not encourage further experiments, or at best signaled the advisability of extreme caution. However, both Polish policy in 1969 and 1970 and East German refusal to put "joint coordinated policy" above what the current regime considers its own vital interests indicate that the invasion of Czechoslovakia may have increased rather than ended the sophistication of such East European attemps.

CHANGES IN THE ALLIANCE ITSELF DUE TO THE CONFLICT

1956

The conflicts of 1956 contracted the activities of the coalition, in that no meetings were held for two years. However, the joint treaties concluded with Hungary, Poland, Rumania, and East Germany on the stationing of Soviet troops in those countries was in some sense an extension of the Warsaw Pact. The conflict spurred Moscow to renew its emphasis on the socialist nature of the alliance.

Albania

Albanian membership in the Warsaw Pact was de facto limited. At the same time military activity increased. These phenomena initially seemed to have caused a decline in the political content of the pact.

Rumania

The conflict with Rumania increased the importance of representation in the pact and the number of meetings. The intraorganizational issue was brought forward as a continuing problem in Soviet–East European relations. The Warsaw Pact assumed increased political importance both in Soviet–East European and world Communist affairs. An example is the Rumanians' insistence that the alliance not be used as a forum to attack China or even to completely side with Moscow in the Sino-Soviet dispute.

Czechoslovakia

The formal activity of the Warsaw Pact seemed to lessen in the months leading up to the invasion. However the invasion, uncommendable as it was, met not only Soviet but at least East German and Polish interests. And there is some hope that its multilateral nature might make such acts more difficult in the future. Immediately after "normalization," activity of the pact resumed at a higher level.

East Germany

East Germany repeats the Rumanian pattern. There has been a marked increase in the political activity of the Warsaw Pact.

The Comparative Focus

By 1970 (unlike the early 1960s), this upgrading of the Warsaw Pact militarily had been paralleled by more high-level bilateral and multilateral consultation among WTO member states and greatly expanded representation at Political Consultative Committee meetings.[38] Consequently, against the background of successful Rumanian maneuvering, the obvi-

---

[38] For example, in January 1956 the political consultative committee meeting was attended by the chief or deputy chief of Government and defense ministers of the member states. By the February 1960 meeting the delegations were led by the first secretaries of the Communist parties and included the chairman of council of ministers, defense ministers, and foreign ministers. See *The Warsaw Pact: Its Role in Soviet Bloc Affairs*, pp. 32–38. By July 1966 PCC conference in Bucharest this list had been expanded to the extent that some delegations included other members of the Politburo, representatives of the chiefs-of-staff,

ously heightened Soviet perception of the importance of the pact after the multilateral invasion of Czechoslovakia, and the postinvasion pattern in which Moscow reverted to the 1967 Rumanian model of using the alliance to contain not only its conflicts with Rumania but Soviet-East German differences as well, the Warsaw Pact can be expected to reflect a more genuine balance of interests in the future.

Given such an evolution, it becomes increasingly necessary to reevaluate the stereotyped images of Communist and non-Communist alliance systems. Traditionally, emphasis has been upon ideology and its imperatives as definitively separating Communist and non-Communist organizations. In large part this interpretation has relied on the nature of Soviet-East European relationships during Stalin's lifetime. Yet from the beginning the OAS, NATO, and the Warsaw Pact followed similar organizational patterns. Both Communist and non-Communist groupings were created in the face of a commonly recognized external threat. And, as this study has shown, conflicts of interest and attempts to influence the joint organization in line with national policies occur within the Warsaw Pact as well as in non-Communist organizations.

Thus, in my opinion it would be useful to shift the emphasis from ideology (recognizing that ideology itself can serve as an element of power) to power relationships in comparing Communist and non-Communist coalitions. From this perspective a comparative analysis of the Warsaw Pact and the Organization of American States has the most possibilities. For in both the WTO and the OAS a number of significantly less powerful states share membership with one of the most powerful, highly-industrialized nations in the world. As Brzezinski and Huntington have described the interaction process in both coalitions:

> This relationship was one of indirect colonialism by means of satellite regimes. Both major powers, in their expansionist phase, had asserted their domination over a contiguous divided and weak region, and imposed upon it their own political supremacy and economic mastery.[39]

and the ambassador to the USSR. *Pravda*, July 7, 1966. In August 1970, central committee secretaries in charge of interparty relations (with the exception of Hungary and Czechoslovakia) took part in the discussions. *Pravda*, August 21, 1970; for Yugoslav commentary, *Politika*, August 20, 1970.

[39] Zbigniew Brzezinski and Samuel P. Huntington, *Political Power: USA/USSR* (New York: The Viking Press, 1967), p. 38. There is an interesting, as yet unpublished, work comparing the two alliances. I am grateful to William Zimmerman for letting me look at his draft manuscript, "Hierarchical Regional Systems and the Politics of System Boundaries."

Although there may have been significant differences in the pattern of domination, the parallel is sufficient to provide evidence as to what are the relevant questions to ask about regional alliance systems. Is the determining factor ideology or is ideology only one aspect of a relationship largely defined by the power configuration of member states? Is the criterion for behavior tied up with whether these states are Communist or non-Communist, or is it rather a question of whether they are big or small, powerful or weak? One indicator may well be the pattern of response during intra-alliance conflict. And here there is at least some reason to believe that ideological acceptability of governments within the OAS has been important to the United States as the "correct form of socialist construction" is to the Soviet Union in East Europe. For the US invasion of the Dominican Republic in 1965 had much in common with the Soviet action against Czechoslovakia three years later.

Santo Domingo and Prague

This is not the place for a detailed recounting of the Dominican crisis.[40] Yet in an analysis of how conflicts are resolved in Communist coalition politics, it is instructive to note how similar instances of intra-alliance strife are dealt with in more ideologically heterogeneous coalitions. That is one way of getting at what is unique about communism when it comes to influencing state behavior at the international level. This book has not attempted to answer that question. But it does raise it and hopefully provides a basis on which further comparative work can build.

For when stripped to the skeleton of motive, response, and justification,

[40] For a carefully researched analysis of the Dominican case, see Jerome Slater, *Intervention and Negotiation: The United States and the Dominican Republic* (New York: Harper and Row, 1970). Other more journalistic, book-length studies are Tad Szulc, *Dominican Diary* (New York: Doubleday and Co., 1965), and Dan Kurzman, *Santo Domingo: Revolt of the Damned* (New York: G. P. Putnam's Sons, 1965). Not surprisingly much of the material on this topic is polemical. The former US Ambassador to the Dominican Republic who acted as President Johnson's first envoy during the crisis has written his account. John Bartlow Martin, *Overtaken by Events* (New York: Doubleday and Co., 1966). For an official administration version, see "The Dominican Crisis: Correcting some Misconceptions," *State Department Bulletin* (November 8, 1965). The most articulate antiadministration interpretation that, as Slater points out, has come "to be almost unquestioningly accepted by most serious students of American foreign policy" is that of Theodore Draper: "The Dominican Crisis," *Commentary*, December 1965, "U.S. Power and Responsibility—the New Dominican Crisis," *New Leader*, January 31, 1966, "A Case of Political Obscenity," *New Leader*, May 9, 1966, *The Dominican Revolt*, Commentary Report, 1968, and "The Dominican Intervention Reconsidered," *Political Science Quarterly* 86, no. 1 (March 1971): 1–36.

great power "crisis management" in the Dominican Republic in 1965 and in Czechoslovakia in 1968 had a depressing sameness.[41] Both cases involved a conflict of interest between one of the most powerful, highly industrialized countries in the world and a small state within the superpower's sphere of influence. In both fear of a potentially unacceptable change in the political structure of the small neighbor precipitated invasion. Both superpowers maneuvered to get token participation from other members of the joint defense alliance, although in the case of US intervention the OAS forces were involved only on an ex post facto basis.[42] Both justified resorting to force by a return to blatant cold war cliches. That the rationale behind the decision to act was more complicated than the explanation is not the point. It always is.

Briefly, when the Dominican military junta collapsed in April 1965 beneath the exigencies of the International Monetary Fund austerity program and prolonged drought, the streets filled with people screaming for the return of President Juan Bosch and the constitution of 1963. Within Santo Domingo, two groups sought power—the young officers, headed by Colonel Juan Caamaño, wanted Bosch to return; and the older officers led by General Wessin y Wessin, an extreme rightist, were determined to prevent the former president from setting foot on Dominican soil. Both groups appealed for US support.

At first Washington preferred inaction. The United States had originally supported Bosch when he came to power in February 1963 as the first democratically elected president of the Dominican Republic in over thirty years. However during his few months in office, the US Ambassador John Bartlow Martin became convinced that at best the new president was incompetent and soft on communism, at worst a "deep cover Communist"[43] hiding under nationalism and commitment to social

[41] I do not mean to imply that there were not differences between the Dominican crisis of 1965 and Czechoslovakia of 1968. There were differences of which to my mind the most important have been (1) that the United States did not discredit all alternatives on the side of reform in the process of intervention (2) that U.S. forces subsequently withdrew. However, these are not differences in either motive for intervention, choice of alternative methods for influencing the situation, or subsequent rationalizations.

[42] For a detailed discussion of OAS involvement, see Jerome Slater, "The Limits of Legitimization in International Organizations: The Organization of American States and the Dominican Crisis," *International Organization* 23, no. 1 (Winter 1969): 48–72.

[43] Martin, *Overtaken by Events*, p. 347. One can assume that this assessment grew from Bosch's resistance to Martin's suggestion that the Dominican president eliminate agrarian reform involving land confiscation, close leftist schools, illegally harass or detain Dominicans

reform. Thus there had been little regret in Washington when Bosch fell in September. The military junta that replaced him was soon controlled by Donald Reid Cabral, a wealthy conservative from a powerful Dominican family, a Yale man with whom the new American ambassador William Tapley Bennett, Jr., got along smoothly. Bennett himself was out of town when the junta fell, but his telegram to Assistant Secretary of State For Economic Affairs, Thomas C. Mann in early April leaves few doubts as to his opinion of the situation:

> Little foxes some of them red are chewing at the grapes. . . . A dimunition of our effort or failure to act will result in bitter wine.[44]

In short, US policymakers did not want Bosch back, nor did they want to intervene. If possible Wessin y Wessin would pull the chestnuts out of the fire, making the Dominican Republic relatively simple to deal with again. So US diplomats turned a deaf ear to the rebels. They underestimated Caamaño's resistance, the attachment to constitutionalism, and the people's hatred of the corrupt Dominican military.

When it looked as if the constitutionalists might win, however, that was another matter. On May 2, President Johnson himself declared that the revolution had been "taken over and really seized and placed in the hands of a band of Communist conspirators." [45] The American Embassy in Santo Domingo began passing out lists varying from 53 to 70 "known and active" Communists alleged to be working with Caamano. Ambassador Bennett described sickening but impossible to verify atrocities. Military moves to wipe out Caamaño were made secretly and followed by false explanations. The U.S. troops ostensibly in Santo Domingo only to protect American lives and property were increased to 32,000.

A ratio of one U.S. soldier to every hundred Dominicans can fairly be called overreaction to 53 or even 70 Communists. In Latin America it was taken as a matter of course that these troops had other purposes. As one diplomat said, "you don't need a cannon to kill a fly." Seen in perspective it is hard to challenge the opinion that American marines moved in to support a U.S. sponsored junta against a vastly more popular constitutionalist movement.

---

travelling to Cuba, and imprison or deport both the extreme right and left. *Ibid.*, pp. 487, 510, 562.

[44] Quoted by Barnard L. Collier in his eyewitness accounts and analysis, *New York Herald Tribune*, May 16, 1965.

[45] Quoted by Slater, *Interventions and Negotiations*, p. 39.

As for Czechoslovakia, the "Prague Spring" was in its most fundamental aspect a program of reform necessitated by Novotný's disastrous
economic policies. Although rooted in a desperate need for economic reorganization, the program did not stop at economics. Domestically it at
least initiated a partial reordering of institutional relationships. For the
Communist party this meant turning the phrase "inner-party democracy"
into something more than pious cant; for the writers, an end to censorship; for the Slovaks, a chance to achieve political and economic equality
with the Czechs; for nonparty people, a means to some genuine political
participation via previously forbidden clubs. The men intent on making
these changes in the quality of Czechoslovak political life were dedicated
Communists. They did not think of themselves as abandoning communism, but rather as fulfilling its highest ideals.

Throughout Dubček held to what he considered the three essentials of
communism: (1) alliance with Moscow via the Warsaw Pact; (2) continuing nationalization of industry; and (3) the leading, if limited role
of the Communist party. Nevertheless as early as the end of March,
Soviet anxiety at the possible consequences of democratization in Prague
had ended all but the flimsiest pretense of noninterference in Czechoslovak internal affairs. And as the spring progressed it became more and
more evident that a significant part of the Soviet leadership did not trust
Dubček to hold the line.

Like the United States with respect to Santo Domingo, the USSR
would have preferred not to intervene. But Soviet polemicists tried to
make clear early in the game that Moscow took its own version of the
domino theory with the utmost seriousness.

Subsequently, the famous Warsaw letter sent by the Central Committees of the U.S.S.R., GDR, Poland, Hungary, and Bulgaria to Prague
was an ultimatum outlining the rationale for invasion. More ominous
yet, it specified a concrete program for getting the situation back in hand:
complete repression of antisocialist, rightist forces; the banning of political clubs; reimposition of censorship; and reorganization of the KSČ
along "fundamental Marxist-Leninist lines." Dubček's defense was
brushed aside, and the Soviet press set the stage for invasion with de-
scriptions of hooligans attacking the Czechoslovak Central Committee
building and honest workers being subjected to "frenzied persecutions."
Moscow claimed that unidentified party and government leaders in
Czechoslovakia had requested urgent assistance. However, Soviet and

East European troops could not find the object of their search. The comrades they had come to assist did not materialize.

Again as in the case of Santo Domingo, after-the-fact explanations relied heavily on an external Enemy. But Moscow was more ambitious than Washington. The Soviet "White Book" on events in Czechoslovakia drew together conspiracy theories tying the Czech Club of Committed Non-Party Members to anti-Communist activities in West Germany, the British Intelligence Service, and "an international Zionist organization." By comparison Ambassador Bennett's fewer than 100 Communists seemed an unimaginative effort indeed.

The invasion of Santo Domingo and Prague are important not for the sake of academic parallelism. Rather they point to the unpleasant reality that as the political fabric of the cold war wore thin during the 1960's, decision-makers in Washington and Moscow alike still clung to familiar patterns of hostility as a rationale for forcing their will on other nations. As Slater has succinctly put it:

> In 1965 the United States was a prisoner, both at home and abroad, of its own oversimplifications, myths, and outmoded policies, particularly the Monroe Doctrine and its ramifications. Indeed, one of the more revealing aspects of the Dominican crisis was the way in which it highlighted the inflexibility and obsolescence of the operating framework of assumptions of so many U.S. policy makers.[46]

Minus the reference to the Monroe Doctrine, the same could have been said about the Soviet Union in 1968. (And indeed, one could make a case for the idea that despite its more inclusive terminology, the Brezhnev Doctrine was propounded to serve as a socialist version of the Monroe Doctrine in Eastern Europe.)

Both superpowers recognized the need for reform in what it is now fashionable if somewhat misleading to call the "client" state. Both first supported the leader of those reforms, then lost faith in his ability to control the situation at what the superpower considered the minimal acceptable solution. Both acted in the shadow of recent history within its sphere of influence. Lyndon Johnson felt he could not tolerate a "second Cuba." Soviet leaders may well have been equally unwilling to "lose" Czechoslovakia when Khrushchev had "saved" Hungary, or to see Czechoslovakia become "another Yugoslavia" (Gomułka specifically re-

---

[46] Slater, *Intervention and Negotiation*, p. 201.

fers to that danger, for example, in his speech defending the Brezhnev Doctrine at the 5th Polish Party Congress in November 1968).

Thus in the case of both the United States and the Soviet Union a sense of threat to the superpower's international credibility combined with fear of intra-alliance problems and domestic reaction (undoubtedly much greater in the Soviet Union but which Slater makes clear was also a consideration in the American decision) led to military invasion of a small ally in instances where the great power had, in my view, neither legal right nor objective reason to intervene. When the chips were down Washington showed as little respect for the principle of nonintervention as Moscow did for socialist noninterference in internal affairs. That both superpowers organized token multilateralization of their resort to force cannot constitute legitimization—although as a precedent one can hope it might make such interventions more difficult in the future. It only damaged the legitimacy of the regional defense alliance associated with the intervention.[47]

Neither invasion was as disastrous as it might have been had the superpower been met with organized military resistance or prolonged guerrilla warfare. Yet both have had recognizably destructive consequences.[48]

Certainly anti-American nationalism in Latin America did not decrease as a result of the Dominican intervention. Faith that the Alliance for Progress could bring about non-revolutionary social reform weakened. Castro's scornful description of the OAS as Washington's "Ministry of Colonies" gained credibility in wider circles, while according to Slater, "radical-extremist" if not Communist strength in the Dominican Republic is stronger today than in 1965. Moreover domestically that intervention added to the alienation and shame many American students, intellectuals,

[47] Thus although it is an oversimplification of the institutional relationship involved in the invasion of Czechoslovakia, Robert O. Keohane's conclusion that the Warsaw Treaty Organization "might well be labeled an "Al Capone alliance" in which remaining a faithful ally protects one not against the mythical outside threat but rather against the great-power ally itself, just as, by paying "protection money" to Capone's gang in Chicago, businessmen protected themselves not against other gangs but against Capone's own thugs" had a point that was made, in equally colorful if somewhat different wording, by Communist parties and states as well as other non-Communist scholars. Robert O. Keohane, "Lilliputians! Dilemmas: Small States in International Politics," *International Organization* 23, no. 2 (1969):302. It is a point that unfortunately applies to the OAS as well.

[48] Which is not to say that there may not be some positive results also. If a desire to avoid another such intervention helped keep the lid on U.S. interpretations of the 1970 election of Marxist President Allende in Chile, or prevented Moscow from defining striking Polish workers as counterrevolutionaries in December 1970, it is a step in the direction of sanity.

and ordinary citizens feel as a result of the foreign policy of their government in Vietnam. It deepened the splits in American society, thereby, in
my opinion, making the normal operation of internal politics more difficult by intensifying such problems as the racial issue and student demonstrations and contributing to an atmosphere of continual confrontation.
For example, the sometimes unfortunate tactics of those opposing military
intervention as a means of exerting political influence in such countries
as the Dominican Republic and Vietnam interacted with the, also unfortunate, tactics of the Chicago police to create the violence surrounding
the Democratic Party National Convention in 1968. Similarly, the invasion of Cambodia led to massive student demonstrations, which, in turn,
heightened concern for internal stability (i.e., law and order) in the
divisive 1970 congressional elections, during which highly emotional
charges and countercharges further strained domestic political consensus.

As for Czechoslovakia, the invasion and subsequent Soviet pressure
started the KSČ on a path of corruption and decline that there are some
signs even Moscow has come to regret. It split still further the international Communist movement, strained relations among socialist states,
and led to the Brezhnev Doctrine which is a return to the philosophy of
Soviet diktat that marked Zhdanov's two-camp theory in the late 1940s
and the Molotov line on the Warsaw Pact in 1954. It weakened the attrac-
tion of the Soviet model for developing countries, strengthened NATO,
and at best delayed prospects for détente and arms control. Domestically
it led to the almost unheard-of public demonstration in Red Square that,
along with the many private conversations with Westerners, testifies to
the despair with which the Soviet intellectual community viewed the implications of that invasion for domestic developments in the Soviet Union.

Why?

John Burton has succinctly summarized the stated rationale:

Communism (or Capitalism) is an actual threat to the independence of
all non-Communist (or Communist) States because Communism (or
Capitalism) as a system is aggressive; it must, therefore, be contained at
some point. Social and political change is desirable, but in the process
of change, power vacuums occur that play into the hands of local and
foreign-inspired minorities. It is therefore necessary to help existing governments to maintain themselves in office if they are generally in support,
and meanwhile to persuade them to induce changes. Opposition to all
forms of Communism (or Capitalism), whether they be aggressive or not,

is a responsibility of the United States (or the Soviets) in its defence of the rest of the world; any weakening of its opposition anywhere would both encourage aggression and discourage resistance to it. The United States and the Soviet Union must oppose the alternative ideology even though there is no direct threat to their territories and even though the nature of the threat were no more than that which arises out of the competition of ideas.[41]

I don't think so. These arguments have lost force even among the decision-makers who still refer back to them. The United States recognizes differences among Communist states. There is the comparatively good communism of Yugoslavia, or the not too dangerous communism in the USSR or (despite the recent flurry of ping-pong diplomacy) the more dangerous communism of China. The Soviets recognize realistic forces within capitalism, consider a treaty with the Brandt government in West Germany quite all right, and conduct the SALT negotiations with the Americans.

Is it, as Burton goes on to maintain, a means of avoiding challenges to political and social institutions within a state by identifying those making the challenge with foreign ideologies, i.e., an attempt to avoid the burden of internal change? In part, yes. There is certainly evidence that internal considerations were important. Yet since at the time those decisions were taken neither the US nor the USSR faced an internal crisis that could be called a "what if" factor in the decision to invade, one should be cautious about assuming it tipped the scaled. Or there is the provocative notion that such alliances represent human pecking orders in which the superpowers channel aggressions against a smaller ally because it is too dangerous for them to attack one another.[50] However, being unable to make a coherent judgment on that idea given the current state of my knowledge, I would rather say the following.

It is probably correct to say that decision-makers in Moscow and Washington suffered from faulty analysis, that they acted rashly without understanding the best interests of their nations "in the long run." One can build a case that the Dominican Republic would not have become a Second Cuba or that if it had no vital interest of the United States would

[49] John W. Burton, *Systems, States, Diplomacy and Rules* (Cambridge, Eng.: Cambridge University Press, 1968), pp. 116–117.

[50] Based on Robert Ardrey, *The Territorial Imperative* (London: Collins, The Fontana Library, 1966).

have been damaged as badly as it was damaged by the fact of that intervention.[51] And there are persuasive arguments that Czechoslovak "socialism with a human face" would not have abandoned communism, that a more responsive communism might have met some needs in Moscow as well as Prague.

Yet in my view factual refutations are not the point (not when it is still a common, if undemonstrated, assumption that informed observers in Washington considered the Castroite danger the deciding factor in Santo Domingo). For such faulty analysis is not the product of sloppy research. Rather in both superpowers it is a habit of thought, a reflex based on cold war interpretation in which international events are still tallied in terms of a political competition that has little bearing on the internal dynamic of the event. It is a dangerous game in which the question of who "won" or "lost" can all too easily be a self-fulfilling prophecy with domestic factions convinced that their internal political position hangs in the balance.

In this sense there is some truth to the proposition that militarists in both Moscow and Washington have a reinforcing relationship that goes deeper than their ideological differences. And it becomes difficult not to conclude that at least throughout the 1960s (as the Chinese have stated cryptically if in a different context) what has been important in the operation of Communist and non-Communist coalitions alike is a process whereby

The time-worn habits of big countries in their relations with small countries continue to make their influence felt in certain ways.[32]

[51] Jerome Slater's *Intervention and Negotiation* has done an admirable job of just that.
[52] "More on the Historical Experience of the Dictatorship of the Proletariat," *Jen-min Jih-pao* (December 29, 1956), *Current Background*, 433 (January 2, 1957).

DOCUMENTS

DOCUMENT 1

THE WARSAW TREATY

COMPLETE TEXT

New Times 21 (May 21, 1955), Moscow

TREATY

of Friendship, Cooperation and Mutual Assistance Between the People's Republic of Albania, the People's Republic of Bulgaria, the Hungarian People's Republic, the German Democratic Republic, the Polish People's Republic, the Rumanian People's Republic, the Union of Soviet Socialist Republics and the Czechoslovak Republic

The Contracting Parties, reaffirming their desire for the establishment of a system of European collective security based on the participation of all European states irrespective of their social and political systems, which would make it possible to unite their efforts in safeguarding the peace of Europe; mindful, at the same time, of the situation created in Europe by the ratification of the Paris agreements, which envisage the formation of a new military alignment in the shape of "Western European Union," with the participation of a remilitarized Western Germany and the integration of the latter in the North-Atlantic bloc, which increases the danger of another war and constitutes a threat to the national security of the peaceable states; being persuaded that in these circumstances the peaceable European states must take the necessary measures to safeguard their security and in the interests of preserving peace in Europe; guided by the objects and principles of the Charter of the United Nations Organization; being desirous of further promoting and developing friendship, cooperation and mutual assistance in accordance with the principles of respect for the independence and sovereignty of states and of noninterference in their internal affairs, have decided to conclude the present Treaty of Friendship, Cooperation and Mutual Assistance and have for that purpose appointed as their plenipotentiaries: the Presidium of the People's Assembly of the People's Republic of Albania: Mehmet Shehu, Chairman of the Council of Ministers of the People's Republic of Albania; the Presidium of the People's Assembly of the People's Republic of Bulgaria: Vulko Chervenkov, Chairman of the Council of Ministers of the People's Republic of Bulgaria; the Presidium of the Hungarian People's Republic: Andras Hegedüs, Chairman of the Council of Ministers of the Hungarian People's Republic; the President of the German Democratic Republic: Otto Grotewohl, Prime Minister of the German Democratic Republic; the State Council of the Polish People's Republic: József Cyrankiewicz, Chairman of the Council of Ministers of the Polish People's Republic; the Presidium of the Grand National Assembly of the Rumanian People's Republic: Gheorghe Gheorghiu-Dej, Chairman of the Council of Ministers of the Rumanian People's Republic; the Presidium of the Supreme Soviet of the Union of Soviet Socialist Republics: Nikolai Alexandrovich Bulganin, Chairman of the Council of Ministers of the U.S.S.R.; the President of the Czechoslovak Republic: Viliam Široký, Prime Minister of the Czechoslovak Republic, who, having presented their full powers, found in good and due form, have agreed as follows:

Article 1

The Contracting Parties undertake, in accordance with the Charter of the United Nations Organization, to refrain in their international relations from the threat or use of force, and to settle their international disputes peacefully and in such manner as will not jeopardize international peace and security.

Article 2

The Contracting Parties declare their readiness to participate in a spirit of sincere cooperation in all international actions designed to safeguard international peace and security, and will fully devote their energies to the attainment of this end.

The Contracting Parties will furthermore strive for the adoption, in agreement with other states which may desire to cooperate in this, of effective measures for universal reduction of armaments and prohibition of atomic, hydrogen and other weapons of mass destruction.

Article 3

The Contracting Parties shall consult with one another on all important international issues affecting their common interests, guided by the desire to strengthen international peace and security.

They shall immediately consult with one another whenever, in the opinion of any one of them, a threat of armed attack on one or more of the Parties to the Treaty has arisen, in order to ensure joint defence and the maintenance of peace and security.

Article 4

In the event of armed attack in Europe on one or more of the Parties to the Treaty by any state or group of states, each of the Parties to the Treaty, in the exercise of its right to individual or collective self-defence in accordance with Article 51 of the Charter of the United Nations Organization, shall immediately, either individually or in agreement with other Parties to the Treaty, come to the assistance of the state or states attacked with all such means as it deems necessary, including armed force. The Parties to the Treaty shall immediately consult concerning the necessary measures to be taken by them jointly in order to restore and maintain international peace and security.

Measures taken on the basis of this Article shall be reported to the Security Council in conformity with the provisions of the Charter of the United Nations Organization. These measures shall be discontinued immediately the Security Council adopts the necessary measures to restore and maintain international peace and security.

Article 5

The Contracting Parties have agreed to establish a Joint Command of the armed forces that by agreement among the Parties shall be assigned to the Command, which shall function on the basis of jointly established principles. They shall likewise adopt other agreed measures necessary to strengthen their defensive power, in order to protect the peaceful labours of their peoples, guarantee the inviolability of their frontiers and territories, and provide defence against possible aggression.

Article 6

For the purpose of the consultations among the Parties envisaged in the present Treaty, and also for the purpose of examining questions which may arise in the operation of the Treaty, a Political Consultative Committee shall be set up, in which each of the Parties to the Treaty shall be represented by a member of its Government or by another specifically appointed representative.

The Committee may set up such auxiliary bodies as may prove necessary.

Article 7

The Contracting Parties undertake not to participate in any coalitions or alliances and not to conclude any agreements whose objects conflict with the objects of the present Treaty.

The Contracting Parties declare that their commitments under existing international treaties do not conflict with the provisions of the present Treaty.

Article 8

The Contracting Parties declare that they will act in a spirit of friendship and cooperation with a view to further developing and fostering economic and cultural intercourse with one another, each adhering to the principle of respect for the independence and sovereignty of the others and non-interference in their internal affairs.

Article 9

The present Treaty is open to the accession of other states irrespective of their social and political systems, which express their readiness by participation in the present Treaty to assist in uniting the efforts of the peaceable states in safeguarding the peace and security of the peoples. Such accession shall enter into force with the agreement of the Parties to the Treaty after the declaration of accession has been deposited with the Government of the Polish People's Republic.

Article 10

The present Treaty is subject to ratification, and the instruments of ratification shall be deposited with the Government of the Polish People's Republic.

The Treaty shall enter into force on the day the last instrument of ratification has been deposited. The Government of the Polish People's Republic shall notify the other Parties to the Treaty as each instrument of ratification is deposited.

Article 11

The present Treaty shall remain in force for twenty years. For such Contracting Parties as do not at least one year before the expiration of this period present to the Government of the Polish People's Republic a statement of denunciation of the Treaty, it shall remain in force for the next ten years.

Should a system of collective security be established in Europe, and a General European Treaty of Collective Security concluded for this purpose, for which the Contracting Parties will unswervingly strive, the present Treaty shall cease to be operative from the day the General European Treaty enters into force.

Done in Warsaw on May 14, 1955, in one copy each in the Russian, Polish, Czech and German languages, all texts being equally authentic. Certified copies of the present Treaty shall be sent by the Government of the Polish People's Republic to all the Parties to the Treaty.

In witness whereof the plenipontentiaries have signed the present Treaty and affixed their seals.

For the Presidium of the People's Assembly of the People's Republic of Albania

MEHMET SHEHU

For the Presidium of the People's Assembly of the People's Republic of Bulgaria

VULKO CHERVENKOV

For the Presidium of the Hungarian People's Republic

ANDRAS HEGEDÜS

For the President of the German Democratic Republic

OTTO GROTEWOHL

For the State Council of the Polish People's Republic

JOZEF CYRANKIEWICZ

For the Presidium of the Grand National Assembly of the Rumanian People's Republic

GHEORGHE GHEORGHIU-DEJ

For the Presidium of the Supreme Soviet of the Union of Soviet Socialist Republics

NIKOLAI ALEXANDROVICH BULGANIN

For the President of the Czechoslovak Republic

VILIAM ŠIROKÝ

ESTABLISHMENT OF A JOINT COMMAND
of the Armed Forces of the Signatories to the Treaty of
Friendship, Cooperation and Mutual Assistance

In pursuance of the Treaty of Friendship, Cooperation and Mutual Assistance between the People's Republic of Albania, the People's Republic of Bulgaria, the Hungarian People's Republic, the German Democratic Republic, the Polish People's Republic, the Rumanian People's Republic, the Union of Soviet Socialist Republics and the Czechoslovak Republic, the signatory states have decided to establish a Joint Command of their armed forces.

The decision provides that general questions relating to the strengthening of the defensive power and the organization of the Joint Armed Forces of the signatory states shall be subject to examination by the Political Consultative Committee, which shall adopt the necessary decisions.

Marshall of the Soviet Union I. S. Konev has been appointed Commander-in-Chief of the Joint Armed Forces to be assigned by the signatory states.

The Ministers of Defence or other military leaders of the signatory states are to serve as Deputy Commanders-in-Chief of the Joint Armed Forces, and shall command the armed forces assigned by their respective states to the Joint Armed Forces.

The question of the participation of the German Democratic Republic in measures concerning the armed forces of the Joint Command will be examined at a later date.

A Staff of the Joint Armed Forces of the signatory states will be set up under the Commander-in-Chief of the Joint Armed Forces, and will include permanent representatives of the General Staffs of the signatory states.

The Staff will have its headquarters in Moscow.

The disposition of the Joint Armed Forces in the territories of the signatory states will be effected, by agreement among the states, in accordance with the requirements of their mutual defence.

DOCUMENT 2

SESSION OF POLITICAL CONSULTATIVE COMMITTEE
OF WARSAW TREATY STATES COMMUNIQUÉ
COMPLETE TEXT

Pravda, January 22, 1965, quoted from *CDSP* 17, no. 3 (February 10, 1965): 14–15

❦

The Political Consultative Committee of the partners to the Warsaw Treaty on Friendship, Cooperation and Mutual Aid, which was in session in Warsaw on Jan. 19 and 20, 1965, discussed the new situation arising in connection with the plans of several North Atlantic Pact states to form a NATO multilateral nuclear force, as well as the possible consequences for the world that a realization of these plans would entail.

The major tendency of the present-day development of international events is a growth of the forces that favor the preservation and strengthening of peace. The might of the socialist countries, which consistently pursue a peace-loving policy, is growing constantly. The Communist Parties and popular masses of the states of Europe and other countries fight resolutely for improvement in the international atmosphere. The independent states of Asia, Africa and Latin America actively contribute to the strengthening of peace.

At the same time, imperialist forces manifest considerable energy and stubbornness in their attempts to aggravate the international atmosphere in various regions of the world. The hostile policy of the U.S.A. against the Republic of Cuba has not ceased. The dangerous provocations of the U.S.A. against the Democratic Republic of Vietnam continue. This aggressive policy is resolutely condemned by the Warsaw Treaty states, as well as all other socialist countries.

The imperialist forces interfere in the domestic affairs of independent states and use methods of economic, military and political pressure. They use their military grouping for the suppression of national-liberation movements. Examples are provided by the continuing war against the people of South Vietnam, the intervention in the Congo and the aggressive actions of the colonialists in Malaysia. The Warsaw Treaty states declare their solidarity with the peoples who are fighting for their freedom and independence or for the strengthening of their independence.

The plans for creating a NATO multilateral nuclear force are to play a special role in implementing the aggressive policy of imperialism. The Warsaw

Treaty states regard the plans for creating a NATO multilateral nuclear force, which are favored by the ruling circles of the U.S.A. and of West Germany, as a grave threat to peace in Europe and the world over. The formation of a multilateral nuclear force in any form would mean a proliferation of nuclear weapons and, in particular, the presentation of these weapons to the West German militarists.

This applies to the U.S. plan for a multilateral nuclear force, supported by the F.R.G., as well as to the British plan for an "Atlantic nuclear force." Both variants are incompatible with the desires of the peoples and of the peace-loving states, which favor a cessation of the nuclear arms race, elimination of the threat of nuclear war and the realization of general and complete disarmament. They are incompatible with the efforts of many states toward creating nuclear-free zones in various regions of the world.

A NATO multilateral nuclear force aims at the consolidation of a separate American-West German bloc within the North Atlantic Alliance. It is a sort of a deal, through which the U.S.A. wants to ensure its military and political hegemony in Western Europe and the F.R.G., in return for its willingness to support this American line, will gain access to nuclear weapons.

F.R.G. access to nuclear weapons, whether within the framework of the "multilateral" or the "Atlantic" nuclear force, is viewed by the West German militarists merely as a step on the way to obtaining their own nuclear weapons.

When the F.R.G. became a member of the North Atlantic Pact, it gained an opportunity to create, in violation of the Potsdam Agreements concluded after the unconditional surrender of Hitlerite Germany, an aggressive military force. Access to nuclear weapons would undoubtedly stimulate the desire of the West German revanchist forces to change the situation that came about in Europe after the end of the second world war and to realize territorial claims upon the German Democratic Republica and other states. No assurances from the Western powers can serve as a guarantee against this threat to peace.

The true intentions of the F.R.G. are indicated by facts such as the provocational plan, proposed by the leadership of the Bundeswehr, for creating an atomic-mine belt along the eastern frontiers and by the announcement of the so-called "frontline strategy," which requires the use of nuclear weapons from the very outset of any military conflict in Central Europe. This attests to the desires of the F.R.G. revanchist forces to make the U.S.A. and other NATO countries party to their adventurous plans.

But any attempts to effect the West German revanchist demands with the help of nuclear weapons are of the greatest danger to the German people, because such attempts would inevitably lead to a nuclear war, resulting not in the reunification of Germany but in its reduction to an atomic desert.

The Warsaw Treaty states resolutely oppose giving nuclear weapons to the Federal Republic of Germany in any form whatever—directly or indirectly, through groupings of states, for its exclusive use or in any form of participation in the use of these weapons.

The Warsaw Treaty states fully support the peace-loving policy of the German Democratic Republic and consider that participation by the Federal Republic of Germany in creating a NATO multilateral nuclear force to mean that the F.R.G. government is writing off the unification of Germany. A relaxation of tension and effective agreements on disarmament in Germany and in Europe are the only ways to create conditions for the unification of the two existing sovereign and equal German states in the spirit of the principles of the Potsdam Agreements.

The formation of a NATO multilateral nuclear force is aimed not only against the interests of peace and security in Europe. It would also increase imperialist and neocolonialist pressure on the newly liberated peoples and those fighting for their independence.

The basic interests of all peoples demand a renunciation of the plans for creating a NATO multilateral nuclear force. But if the NATO states, acting contrary to the interests of peace, realize their plans for creating a multilateral nuclear force, no matter in what form this may be done, then the Warsaw Treaty states, faced with the grave dangers this would entail for peace and security in Europe, will be compelled to take the necessary defensive measures to ensure their security.

The chief goal of the policy of the Warsaw Treaty states is to ensure peaceful conditions for building socialism and communism in their countries and for the liberation of mankind from the threat of a nuclear world war through the joint efforts of all the peace-loving peoples.

The Soviet Union and the other Warsaw Treaty states have submitted a whole series of proposals for improving the international situation. The Warsaw Treaty states will continue to support measures leading toward an easing of international tension and the creation of favorable conditions for a cessation of the arms race and the attainment of general and complete disarmament.

The Political Consultative Committee of the Warsaw Treaty states considers that an urgent demand of our time is to ensure European security, which is threatened by the plans for creating a multilateral nuclear force. This goal would be served by the realization of the proposal for freezing nuclear armaments and the proposal for creating an atom-free zone in Central Europe.

Supporting the initiative of the Polish People's Republic, the Political Consultative Committee proposes the convocation of a conference of European states to discuss measures ensuring collective security in Europe.

The Warsaw Treaty states remain willing to conclude a nonaggression pact with the NATO states that would greatly contribute to a relaxation of tension in Europe and the world over.

The Warsaw Treaty states support the efforts toward attaining a German peace settlement in the interests of ensuring peace in Europe. The attainment of this goal would be furthered by legal recognition of the existing frontiers, the liquidation of the remnants of the second world war and pledges by the two German states not to add nuclear weapons to their armed forces and to carry out measures toward disarmament.

The Political Consultative Committee of the Warsaw Treaty states also supports the proposal of the G.D.R. that the two German states renounce nuclear weapons.

The Warsaw Treaty states support the proposal of the government of the Chinese People's Republic for calling a conference of world heads of state on the complete prohibition and complete destruction of nuclear weapons and, as a first step, on prohibiting the use of these weapons.

The Warsaw Treaty states also support the convocation of a world conference on disarmament, which was proposed by the Cairo conference of non-aligned states.

The Political Consultative Committee declares that the socialist countries are in complete unity and solidarity in the face of the imperialist threat and that any attempts by imperialist circles to undermine this solidarity are doomed to failure.

The Warsaw Treaty states will continue to exert their efforts toward universally contributing to a relaxation of tension, to disarmament, to peaceful coexistence and to ensuring a peaceful future to all the peoples.

Warsaw, Jan. 20, 1965.

DOCUMENT 3

BUCHAREST DECLARATION ON STRENGTHENING PEACE
AND SECURITY IN EUROPE
COMPLETE TEXT

Pravda and *Izvestia,* July 9, 1966, quoted from *CDSP* 18, no. 27 (July 27, 1966): 3–7

The People's Republic of Bulgaria, the Hungarian People's Republic, the German Democratic Republic, the Polish People's Republic, the Socialist Republic of Rumania, the Union of Soviet Socialist Republics and the Czechoslovak Socialist Republic—the member states of the Warsaw Treaty of Friendship, Cooperation and Mutual Aid represented at the Bucharest conference of the Political Consultative Committee—adopt the following Declaration:

I.

The ensuring of lasting peace and security in Europe accords with the ardent desires of all peoples of the European continent and with the interests of universal peace.

The peoples of Europe, who have made and are making an immense contribution to the cause of the progress of mankind, can and must create in that part of the world a climate of detente and international mutual understanding that will make it possible to utilize in full measure the material and spiritual resources of each people, of each country in conformity with their will and decision.

The state of the relations between the European countries exerts a great influence on the state of affairs throughout the world. It should not be forgotten that two world wars, which cost tens of millions of human lives and caused vast devastation, arose on the European continent.

The problem of European security did not arise today or yesterday. Half a century ago it was placed on the agenda with the outbreak of World War I. It rose before the peoples in all its vital significance two decades later, when Europe and the world came face to face with a brutal fascism that crushed one country after another under its feet.

The peoples who entered the mortal combat imposed on them were inspired by the hope that they were fighting the last world war.

In 1945 the goal of ensuring European security appeared close; the roads to it seemed open. German fascism had been defeated and was awaiting judgment. Justice was celebrating victory. The peoples who had just lived through a war of unprecedented savagery with Hitler's Germany were demanding that everything possible be done to prevent the forces of militarism and aggression from ever again disrupting the peaceful life and creative labor of the present and future generations.

The Potsdam Agreement, which crowned the allied relations of the powers of the anti-Hitler coalition, proclaimed a broad program, aimed at the future, for establishing peace. For the first time in history Europe had a real chance of solving the problem of its own security. It was generally recognized that the chief condition for security in Europe was to prevent a resurgence of German militarism and Nazism and to ensure that Germany would never again threaten its neighbors or the preservation of peace throughout the world. Nor was there any disagreement that the fulfillment of this chief condition called for honest and friendly cooperation among the states of Europe, among all states interested in the preservation of European and universal peace.

But events did not justify these aspirations. The hopes of the peoples of Europe did not materialize, their desire for a life free of the fear of war has not been realized to this day. The responsibility for this devolves on the powers which immediately after the defeat of the German aggressors renounced the cooperation that had been forged in the great anti-Hitler coalition, which did not follow the common path of building peace in Europe and, moreover, became themselves the bearers of an aggressive policy.

Now, two decades after the end of World War II, its consequences have not yet been liquidated in Europe; there is no German peace treaty, there are hotbeds of tension, abnormal situations in the relations between states.

The socialist states that have signed the present Declaration believe that if this situation is to be eliminated and a firm foundation is to be laid for peace and security in Europe, relations between states must proceed from the renunciation of the threat of force or the use of force, from recognition of the need to solve international disputes only through peaceful means, on the principles of sovereignty and national independence, of equality and non-interference in domestic affairs, on respect for territorial inviolability. The European states must strive for the adoption of effective measures for preventing the danger of the outbreak of armed conflict in Europe and for strengthening European collective security. The realization of the common desire of all European nations presupposes the responsibility of and a contribution from each state, big or small, irrespective of its social and political system, in establishing worthy cooperation between sovereign, independent and equal states.

In the opinion of the states participating in the present conference, today's situation requires of all the peoples of Europe, of all peace-loving forces even greater determination and vigor in the struggle for strengthening peace and security in Europe.

II.

One of the decisive features of the present-day international situation is the growth of the forces that favor the preservation and strengthening of peace. Against the imperialist policy of aggression and for ensuring the security of peoples are resolutely ranged the socialist states with their vast economic, political and military might, the international working class headed by its Communist Parties, the national-liberation movement, the new states that have attained independence in the last few years, the progressive and democratic forces of the whole world. Tendencies are increasingly arising and developing in Europe toward liquidating the sediment of the cold war and the obstacles standing in the way of the normal development of all-European cooperation, toward solving disputed issues through mutual understanding, toward the normalization of international life and the rapprochement of peoples.

This course is opposed by imperialist reactionary circles, which, pursuing aggressive goals, are striving to fan tensions, to poison relations between European states.

A direct threat to peace in Europe and the security of the European peoples is presented by the present policy of the United States of America, that same policy which in another part of the world—Southeast Asia—has already led to the unleashing of an aggressive war against the Vietnamese people and which in recent years has more than once exacerbated relations between states to the point of international crises. The United States interferes in the domestic affairs of other states, violates the sacred right of each people to decide its own destiny, resorts to colonial repressions and armed interventions, stages plots in various parts of Asia, Africa and Latin America, and everywhere supports reactionary forces and venal regimes hated by the peoples.

There can be no doubt whatsoever that the goals of U.S. policy in Europe have nothing in common with the vital interests of the European peoples, with the tasks of Europe's security. The American ruling circles would like to impose their will on their allies in Western Europe with a view to making Western Europe a tool of the global policy of the U.S.A., which is based on a desire to halt or even turn back the historical process of the national and social liberation of peoples. Hence the attempts to draw some West European states into military ventures even in other regions of the world, in particular Asia.

The aggressive circles of the U.S.A., which are supported by the reactionary forces of Western Europe, are trying, with the help of the North Atlantic military bloc and the war machine it has created, to deepen ever further the division of Europe, to fan the arms race, to increase international tension and to frustrate the establishment and development of normal ties between the West European and East European states.

In pursuit of these ends, which are alien to the genuine interests of the security of the European peoples, troops of the United States are still kept in Europe, their military bases are located in West European countries, stockpiles of nuclear weapons are being created, nuclear submarines are sent to the seas that wash Europe, the American Sixth Fleet sails in the Mediterranean Sea and planes carrying nuclear bombs fly in the skies over European countries.

The policy pursued by the U.S.A. in Europe in the postwar decades is all the more dangerous for the European peoples in that it is increasingly based on collusion with the militarist and revanchist forces of West Germany. These forces are directly prodding the U.S.A. to a still more dangerous course in Europe.

This policy finds its expression in the projected creation of a sort of alliance between the American imperialists and the West German revanchists.

The militarist and revanchist forces of West Germany refuse to consider the vital interests of the German people themselves and are pursuing aggressive goals that manifest themselves in all their actions in the switching of the country's economic potential to military rails, in the creation of a 500,000-strong Bundeswehr, in the glorification of the history of German conquests, and in the nurturing of hatred against other peoples, whose lands are again coveted by the above-mentioned circles of the Federal Republic of Germany.

At present this policy is focused on the demand for nuclear weapons. In the F.R.G. the creation of a scientific-technological and industrial base that could at some time serve for the production of its own atomic and hydrogen bombs is being openly and secretly pushed. The combined efforts of the peace-loving countries and peoples have so far succeeded in delaying the creation of a joint NATO nuclear force that would give the F.R.G. access to nuclear weapons. However, plans to this effect have not been abandoned.

The fundamental interests of all peoples demand the renunciation of plans for creating a NATO multilateral nuclear force. But if the NATO members, acting in disregard of the interests of peace, embark on the path of implementing the plans for creating a multilateral nuclear force or for giving West Germany access to nuclear weapons in any form whatsoever, in that case the Warsaw Treaty member-states, faced with the grave consequences that this would entail for the cause of peace and security in Europe, would be compelled to carry out the necessary defensive measures to ensure their security.

The territorial demands of the West German revanchists must be decisively rejected. They are totally unfounded and hopeless. The question of the frontiers in Europe has been solved finally and irrevocably, and the peoples of Europe will know how to bar the path to revanchism.

One of the chief conditions for ensuring European security is the inviolability of the existing borders between the European states, including the borders of the sovereign German Democratic Republic, Poland and Czechoslovakia. The states represented at this conference reaffirm their resolve to crush any aggression against them on the part of the forces of imperialism and reaction.

The Warsaw Treaty member-states declare for their part that they have no territorial claims with respect to any state in Europe.

The policy of revanchism and militarism pursued by German imperialism has always suffered bankruptcy. Given the present correlation of forces in the world arena and in Europe, it not only will fail to bring any advantages or benefits to the F.R.G. but is fraught with irreparable consequences for the Federal Republic of Germany.

The interests of peace and security in Europe and in the whole world, like the interests of the German people, demand that the ruling circles of the Federal Republic of Germany take into account the actually existing situation in Europe. And this means that they must proceed from the fact of the existence of two German states, renounce their claims for the redrawing of the map of Europe, their claims to the exclusive right to represent the whole of Germany and the attempts to exert pressure on states that recognize the German Democratic Republic, renounce the criminal Munich *diktat* and recognize that it has been invalid from the very beginning. They must prove in deeds that they are really taking the lessons of history to heart, are putting an end to militarism and revanchism and will pursue a policy of normalizing relations between states and developing cooperation and friendship among peoples.

The German Democratic Republic, which is an important factor in ensuring peace in Europe, has addressed constructive proposals to the F.R.G. government and the Bundestag: to renounce nuclear arms on a reciprocal basis, to reduce the armies of both German states, to pledge not to use force against each other, to sit down at a table and confer on the solution of urgent national questions of interest to both the G.D.R. and the F.R.G. However, the F.R.G. government has displayed no interest in these proposals. The states that have signed the present Declaration support the above-mentioned initiative of the G.D.R.

Having comprehensively reviewed the present situation in Europe and weighed the basic factors determining its development, the states represented at the conference arrived at the conclusion that in Europe, where almost half of the states are socialist, there are chances for preventing an undesirable development of events. The problem of European security can be solved through the joint efforts of all the European states, of all social forces that are for peace, regardless of their ideological views and religious and other persuasions. The more quickly the influence of the forces that would like to continue kindling tension in relations between European states is paralyzed, the more successfully will this task be solved.

In the postwar years it has more than once been possible to thwart plans aimed at undermining peace in Europe. Of decisive importance in this have been the unity and solidarity of the European socialist states, of all the countries of socialism, their pursuit of a peace-loving foreign policy while maintaining vigilance with respect to potential violators of peace, their willingness to cooperate with all states that are ready to make their contribution to the strengthening of European security. The efforts of the working class of the West European countries, of its advanced detachments, of democratic progressive organizations and the movement of peace partisans, which mold the public opinion of the broad working masses, are directed with all vigor to the same end.

A major factor that is increasingly complicating the implementation of military ventures in Europe is the growing influence of forces in the West European states that are aware of the need to rise above differences in political views and convictions and to take steps toward a relaxation of international tension, toward the all-round development of mutually advantageous relations among all the states of Europe without discrimination, toward the complete independence of their countries and the preservation of their national identities.

The states that have signed the present Declaration note as a positive phenomenon the presence in the Federal Republic of Germany of circles that oppose revanchism and militarism, demand the establishment of normal relations with the countries of both West and East, including normal relations between the two German states, and strive for a relaxation of international tension and the ensuring of European security so that all Germans may enjoy the blessings of peace.

The influence of those who are for peace and security in Europe is becoming more marked each day, while the proponents of an aggressive course are beginning to lose their positions. More and more European countries and peoples are coming to understand the real source of the threat to each of them and to Europe as a whole and what is needed to protect the security of all European states.

The participants in the conference proceed from the premise that each European state is called upon to play a worthy role in international affairs and to become a full-fledged partner in building in Europe a system of relations between peoples and relations between states whereby the security of each would at the same time be the security of all. The European states are capable of solving questions of the relations among them without outside interference.

The socialist countries believe that one of the basic conditions for the realization of European security is the affirmation and development of normal relations between states based on observance of the principles of sovereignty and national independence, equality, noninterference in internal affairs and mutual advantage. The situation in Europe proves that, despite various obstacles, these principles are being more and more broadly recognized as a reasonable basis for cooperation between peoples and for improving the international situation.

It is very important to strengthen political relations between states, regardless of their social systems, aimed at the defense of peace.

The European countries, bound by traditional trade relations, can only gain from the development of their economic cooperation on a reciprocal basis. A broadening of economic relations between European states, and the elimination of the discrimination and obstacles existing in this area, is an especially important factor for rapprochement and for the establishment of an atmosphere of trust and mutual understanding among peoples. The development of economic relations among European countries makes it possible to broaden their trade with partners in other parts of the world. These relations, together with the all-round development of scientific, technical and cultural cooperation which makes possible the better mutual acquaintance of peoples, may provide as they develop a material base for European security and for the strengthening of peace throughout the world.

Despite all the differences in social-political systems, ideologies and political views, the European states and peoples have a common cause, conforming to the vital national interests of all—it is the task of preventing a disturbance of peace in Europe, of curbing the forces of aggression.

III.

The states that have signed the present Declaration believe that the situation as it is now developing demands of all European states vigorous actions toward strengthening European peace.

The governments of the European states cannot rely on the soothing assurances of those who are hatching plans of aggression, cannot take on faith the declarations of those who want to revise the results of World War II while claiming that they need nuclear weapons for their own security, cannot remain passive, thereby willingly or unwillingly encouraging the forces that are preparing for Europe the fate of being a springboard for a devastating nuclear conflict.

Conscious of their lofty responsibility before the peoples, the governments of the European states must undertake steps capable of ensuring a turn toward a relaxation of tension in Europe, the strengthening of security and the development of peaceful mutually advantageous cooperation among the European states.

This is not the first time Europe has been confronted with this task. The first and second world wars were prepared by the aggressive forces in deep secrecy, under the cover of deceptive declarations about peaceful intentions. A gigantic apparatus of propaganda and misinformation was used each time to lull the vigilance of the peoples. The peoples' eyes did open, but not before millions of people were already dying, and flourishing cities and villages lay in ruins. This cannot be permitted to happen for a third time—in the age of nuclear energy and mighty rockets.

The countries participating in the conference resolutely favor the speediest implementation of constructive measures for strengthening security in Europe. They are convinced that in present-day conditions it is actually possible to undertake such steps. To this end they are ready to cooperate with other states.

The creation of stable guarantees for the cause of peace and security in Europe is an important task demanding the participation of all European states, the patient and constructive discussion of points of view with the aim of reaching decisions that would enjoy general approval.

The European socialist countries have repeatedly submitted well-grounded proposals constituting a concrete program of action.

The states that have signed the Declaration believe that measures for strengthening security in Europe can and must be carried out above all in the following chief directions:

First. The states participating in the conference appeal to all European states to develop good-neighbor relations on the basis of the principles of independence and national sovereignty, non-interference in internal affairs and mutual advantage—on the basis of the principles of the peaceful coexistence of states with different social systems. Proceeding from this premise, they favor the strengthening of economic and trade ties and the multiplication of contacts and forms of cooperation in the fields of science, technology, culture and art, as well as in other fields that provide new opportunities for the cooperation of European countries.

There is no field of peaceful cooperation where the European states could not find opportunities for undertaking further mutually advantageous steps.

The development of all-European cooperation demands from all European states the renunciation of any kind of discrimination and pressure, whether it be economic or political in nature, aimed against other countries, equal cooperation among them and the establishment of normal relations between them, including the establishment of normal relations with both German states.

The establishment and development of good-neighbor relations between European states that have different social systems could intensify their economic and cultural ties and thus increase the possibilities of the European states for making an effective contribution to the cause of the improvement of the atmosphere in Europe and the development of mutual confidence and respect.

Second. The socialist countries have always consistently stood against the division of the world into military blocs and alliances and for the elimination of the dangers for universal peace and security stemming from this.

In reply to the formation of the military aggressive NATO grouping and to the inclusion in it of West Germany, the Warsaw Treaty of Friendship, Cooperation and Mutual Aid—a defensive pact of sovereign and equal states that is an instrument for the defense of the security of the treaty's member-states and of peace in Europe—was concluded.

But the members of the Warsaw Treaty have been and are of the opinion that the military blocs imposed by the imperialist forces and the presence of military bases on the territories of other states constitute an obstacle to cooperation among states. The security and progress of each European country can be genuinely guaranteed not by the existence of military groupings, which do not correspond to the present-day healthy tendencies of international life, but by the establishment in Europe of an effective security system based on relations of equality and mutual respect among all the states of the continent, on the joint efforts of all the European nations.

The countries that have signed the present Declaration believe that the necessity for measures toward the easing first of all of military tension in Europe has become ripe. A radical way to achieve this would be the simultaneous dissolution of the existing military alliances, and the present situation makes this possible. The governments of our states have pointed out more than once that should the North Atlantic alliance halt its activities the Warsaw Treaty will become invalid, and that the two would be replaced by a system of European security. They now formally reaffirm their readiness for the simultaneous liquidation of the above-mentioned alliances.

If, however, the members of the North Atlantic alliance are not yet ready for the simultaneous dissolution of the two groupings, the states that have signed the present Declaration consider it feasible even now to reach agreement on the liquidation of the military organizations of both the North Atlantic pact and the Warsaw Treaty. At the same time they declare that as long as the North Atlantic bloc exists and the aggressive imperialist circles jeopardize peace throughout the world, the socialist countries represented at the conference, maintaining high vigilance, are fully resolved to strengthen their might and defense capability.

At the same time we consider it necessary that all the member-states of the North Atlantic pact and the Warsaw Treaty, as well as countries that do not participate in any military alliance, undertake bilateral and multilateral efforts to advance the cause of European security.

Third. At present it is also very important to adopt such partial measures toward a military detente on the European continent as:

the liquidation of foreign military bases;

the withdrawal of all foreign troops from other countries' territories to within their national frontiers;

a reduction, in agreed-upon numbers and according to agreed-upon schedules, of the armed forces of the two German states;

measures aimed at eliminating the danger of a nuclear conflict: the creation of denuclearized zones, a pledge by all powers possessing nuclear weapons not to use these weapons against states belonging to these zones, etc.;

the cessation of flights by foreign aircraft carrying atomic and hydrogen bombs over the territories of European states and of the entry into these states' ports of submarines and surface vessels with nuclear weapons on board.

Fourth. In view of the danger to the cause of peace in Europe of the F.R.G.'s nuclear claims, states must direct their efforts to precluding the possibility of the F.R.G.'s access to nuclear arms in any form whatever—directly or indirectly through groupings of states, of its exclusive command or its participation in any form in command over such arms. The way in which this question is solved will to a large extent decide the future of the European, and not only the European, peoples. And half-hearted solutions to this question are impermissible.

Fifth. The inviolability of frontiers is the foundation of a durable peace in Europe. The interests of a normalization of the situation in Europe demand that all states, both those in Europe and those outside the European continent, base their foreign-policy actions on the recognition of the actually existing frontiers between European states that were established after the most devastating war in the history of mankind, including the Polish frontier along the Oder-Neisse and the frontiers between the two German states.

Sixth. A German peace settlement accords with the interests of peace in Europe. The socialist states represented at the conference are willing to continue searches for the solution to this problem. This solution must take into account the interests of the security of all the countries concerned, the security of Europe as a whole.

A constructive approach to this question, as to other aspects of security in Europe, is possible only proceeding from reality, in the first place the existence of the two German states—the German Democratic Republic and the Federal Republic of Germany. At the same time such a settlement calls for recognition of the existing frontiers and for the renunciation by both German states of the possession of nuclear weapons.

The equal participation of the two German states in efforts aimed at the development and strengthening of relations of all-European cooperation in various fields of activity—political, economic, scientific-technical, cultural— will enable their working class, peasantry and intelligentsia, their entire population, to make their contribution, to the measure of their possibilities and creative abilities, to progress and peace jointly with the other European peoples.

As for the unification of the two German states, the road to this goal lies through a relaxation of tension, a gradual rapprochement of the two sovereign

German states and agreement between them, through agreements on disarmament in Germany and Europe and on the basis of the principle that once the unification of Germany is achieved, the united German state will be genuinely peace-loving and democratic and will never again pose a threat to its neighbors or to peace in Europe.

Seventh. It is of great positive importance to convene an all-European conference to discuss questions of ensuring security in Europe and establishing all-European cooperation. The accord reached at the conference could be expressed, for example, in the form of an all-European declaration on cooperation for the maintenance and strengthening of European security. This declaration could provide for pledges on the part of the signatory states to be guided in their relations with one another by the interests of peace, to settle disputed questions only by peaceful means, to hold consultations and exchange information on questions of mutual interest and to assist in the comprehensive development of economic, scientific-technical and cultural ties with one another. The declaration should be open for all interested states to join.

The convocation of a conference on questions of European security and cooperation could promote the creation of a system of collective security in Europe and would be a major landmark in contemporary European history. Our countries are ready to participate in such a conference at any time convenient for the other interested states, both North Atlantic and Treaty members and neutrals. The neutral European countries could also play a positive role in the convocation of such a conference.

Naturally, the agenda and other questions relating to the preparation of such a meeting or conference should be established jointly by all the participating states, keeping in mind the proposals submitted by each one of them.

The countries represented at the present conference are also prepared to employ other possible methods for discussing problems of European security: negotiations through diplomatic channels, meetings of Foreign Ministers or special representatives on a bilateral or multilateral basis, and contacts at the highest level. They believe that the considerations presented above cover the chief and most important aspects of ensuring European security. They are also prepared to discuss other proposals for the solution of this problem that have been or may be advanced by any state.

As for the participants in such a discussion, the Warsaw Treaty states make no exceptions. It is for each state to decide whether or not to participate in the discussion and solution of European problems.

The peoples, of course, are not indifferent to the political course this or that state may choose—one corresponding to the interests of peace and security or one running counter to these interests.

The participants in this conference are convinced that the countries of other continents as well cannot be indifferent to the direction in which affairs in Europe develop. The flames of two world wars broke out on European soil, but they scorched almost the whole planet. Devastation and death was visited on many countries, including some on continents far from Europe. Therefore any government that is concerned for the destiny of the world cannot but welcome each step that leads to a detente and to an improvement of the situation in Europe, cannot but support such efforts.

In expressing this concern for the strengthening of European security and their willingness to participate in the implementation of appropriate steps directed toward this goal, our countries are convinced that it is the duty of all European states to contribute to the solution of problems of worldwide significance, the adjustment of which will unquestionably have a beneficial effect on the situation in Europe as well. These include the problems of ensuring noninterference in the internal affairs of states, the prohibition of the use of force or the threat of force in international relations, disarmament, the prohibition of the use of nuclear weapons and other major measures aimed at eliminating the danger of a nuclear conflict, the final liquidation of colonialism in all its forms and manifestations, the dismantling of foreign military bases on other countries' territory and the development of international economic cooperation on equal terms. For their part, the states represented at this conference will continue to do everything in their power to promote the earliest possible solution of these world problems. They attach great importance to the strengthening of the United Nations on the basis of strict observance of its Charter, ensuring the universality of the U.N. and bringing its activity in line with the changes that have taken place in the world, and will help in every way to raise the effectiveness of the organization with a view to the preservation of universal peace and security and to the development of friendly relations among peoples.

The states that have signed the present Declaration express a readiness to seek jointly with other states for mutually acceptable ways to strengthen peace in Europe. They are fully resolved to defend in the international arena the line of peace, the international cooperation of states and the rallying of all freedom-loving and progressive forces, to fight against imperialist aggression and a policy of diktat and violence, to support the cause of freedom, national independence and social progress.

The participants in the conference appeal to all European governments and nations, to all the forces of peace and progress on our continent, regardless of their ideological, political or religious persuasion, to join forces in making Europe—one of the most important centers of world civilization—a continent of all-round and fruitful cooperation between equal nations, a mighty factor for the stability of peace and of mutual understanding throughout the world.
—[Signed] *For the People's Republic of Bulgaria:* Todor ZHIVKOV, First Secretary of the Central Committee of the Bulgarian Communist Party and Chairman of the Council of Ministers of the People's Republic of Bulgaria; *for the Hungarian People's Republic:* János KÁDÁR, First Secretary of the Central Committee of the Hungarian Socialist Workers' Party; Gyula KALLAI, Chairman of the Hungarian Revolutionary Workers' and Peasants'

Government; *for the German Democratic Republic:* Walter ULBRICHT, First
Secretary of the Central Committee of the Socialist Unity Party of Germany
and Chairman of the German Democratic Republic State Council; Willi
STOPH, Chairman of the Council of Ministers of the German Democratic
Republic; *for the Polish People's Republic:* Władysław GOMUŁKA, First
Secretary of the Central Committee of the Polish United Workers' Party;
Józef CYRANKIEWICZ, Chairman of the Council of Ministers of the Polish
People's Republic; *for the Socialist Republic of Rumania:* Nicolae CEAU-
ŞESCU, General Secretary of the Central Committee of the Rumanian Communist Party; Ion Gheorghe MAURER, Chairman of the Council of Ministers
of the Socialist Republic of Rumania; *for the Union of Soviet-Socialist Republics:* L. I. BREZHNEV, General Secretary of the Central Committee of
the Communist Party of the Soviet Union; A. N. KOSYGIN, Chairman of
the Council of Ministers of the Union of Soviet Socialist Republics; *for the
Czechoslovak Socialist Republic:* Antonín NOVOTNÝ, First Secretary of
the Central Committee of the Communist Party of Czechoslovakia and President of the Czechoslovak Socialist Republic; Jozef LENART, Chairman of
the Government of the Czechoslovak Socialist Republic.
Bucharest, July 5, 1966.

DOCUMENT 4

IN THE INTERESTS OF EUROPEAN SECURITY
COMPLETE TEXT

Pravda, February 11, 1967, quoted from *CDSP* 19, no. 6
(March 1, 1967)

A conference of Foreign Ministers of the Warsaw Treaty member-countries
was held in Warsaw Feb. 8 through Feb. 10, 1967.

Taking part in the meeting were Ivan Bashev, Foreign Minister of the
People's Republic of Bulgaria; Janos Peter, Foreign Minister of the Hun-
garian People's Republic; Otto Winzer, Foreign Minister of the German
Democratic Republic; Adam Rapacki, Foreign Minister of the Polish People's
Republic; Mircea Malice, Deputy Foreign Minister of the Socialist Republic of
Rumania; A. A. Gromyko, Foreign Minister of the Union of Soviet Socialist
Republics; and Vaclav David, Foreign Minister of the Czechoslovak Socialist
Republic.

At the conference a friendly exchange of opinions took place on questions
related to the efforts of the socialist countries aimed at easing international

tension and strengthening peace, security and cooperation in Europe and to the development of the situation on the European continent since the adoption of the declaration on strengthening peace and security in Europe in Bucharest in July, 1966.

The conference took place in an atmosphere of comradely cooperation and complete mutual understanding.

DOCUMENT 5

COMMUNIQUÉ OF THE CONFERENCE
OF THE POLITICAL CONSULTATIVE COMMITTEE
OF THE WARSAW PACT STATES
COMPLETE TEXT

Pravda March 9; *Izvestia* March 10, 1968, quoted from *CDSP* 20, no. 10 (March 27, 1968): 5–6

Sofia, March 7—A regular conference of the Political Consultative Committee of the member-states of the Warsaw Treaty on Friendship, Cooperation and Mutual Aid took place on March 6 and 7, 1968, in Sofia.

The following took part in the conference:

from the People's Republic of Bulgaria—Todor Zhivkov, First Secretary of the Bulgarian Communist Party Central Committee, Chairman of the P.R.B. Council of Ministers and head of the delegation; Stanko Todorov, member of the Politburo of the B.C.P. Central Committee and Secretary of the Central Committee; Zhivko Zhivkov, member of the Politburo of the B.C.P. Central Committee and First Vice-Chairman of the Council of Ministers; Ivan Bashev, Minister of Foreign Affairs; General of the Army Dobri Dzhurov, Minister of National Defense;

from the Hungarian People's Republic—János Kádár, First Secretary of the Hungarian Socialist Workers' Party Central Committee and head of the delegation; Jenö Fock, Chairman of the Revolutionary Workers' and Peasants' Government; Janos Peter, Minister of Foreign Affairs; Lieut. Gen. Lajos Czinege, Minister of Defense;

from the German Democratic Republic—Walter Ulbricht, First Secretary of the Central Committee of the Socialist Unity Party of Germany, Chairman of the G.D.R. State Council and head of the delegation; Willi Stoph, Chairman of the G.D.R. Council of Ministers; Erich Honecker, member of the Politburo of the S.U.P.G. Central Committee and Secretary of the Central Committee; General of the Army Heinz Hoffmann, Minister of National Defense; Gunter Kort, State Secretary and First Deputy Minister of Foreign Affairs;

from the Polish People's Republic—Władysław Gomułka, First Secretary of the Polish United Workers' Party Central Committee and head of the delegation; Josef Cyrankiewicz, Chairman of the P.P.R. Council of Ministers; Zenon Kliszko, member of the Politburo of the P.U.W.P. Central Committee and Secretary of the Central Committee; Adam Rapacki, Minister of Foreign Affairs; Marshal of Poland Marian Spychalski, Minister of National Defense; Marian Naszkowski, Deputy Minister of Foreign Affairs; Lieut. Gen. Wojcech Jaruzelski, Deputy Minister of National Defense; Ryszard Neszporek, P.P.R. Ambassador to the People's Republic of Bulgaria;

from the Socialist Republic of Rumania—Nicolae Ceauşescu General Secretary of the Rumanian Communist Party Central Committee, Chairman of the S.R.R. State Council and head of the delegation; Ion Georghe Maurer, Chairman of the S.R.R. Council of Ministers; Corneliu Manescu, Minister of Foreign Affairs; Lieut. Gen. Ion Ionita, Minister of the Armed Forces; Nicolae Blejan, S.R.R. Ambassador to the People's Republic of Bulgaria;

from the Union of Soviet Socialist Republics—L. I. Brezhnev, General Secretary of the Central Committee of the Communist Party of the Soviet Union and head of the delegation; A. N. Kosygin, Chairman of the U.S.S.R. Council of Ministers; A. A. Gromyko, U.S.S.R. Minister of Foreign Affairs; Marshal of the Soviet Union A. A. Grechko, U.S.S.R. Minister of Defense; K. V. Rusakov, First Deputy Director of a C.P.S.U. Central Committee department; A. M. Puzanov, U.S.S.R. Ambassador to the People's Republic of Bulgaria;

from the Czechoslovak Socialist Republic—Alexander Dubček, First Secretary of the Central Committee of the Communist Party of Czechoslovakia and head of the delegation; Jozef Lenárt, Chairman of the C.S.R. government; General of the Army Bohumir Lomský, Minister of National Defense; Václav David, Minister of Foreign Affairs; Pavol Majling, C.S.R. Ambassador to the People's Republic of Bulgaria.

Marshal of the Soviet Union. I. I. Yakubovsky, Commander-in-Chief of the Joint Armed Forces of the Warsaw Pact states, also took part in the work of the conference.

The participants in the conference examined all aspects of the situation that has taken shape as a result of further intensification of U.S. aggression against the Vietnamese people and its influence on the overall international situation. They noted that the U.S. government is continuing its adventurist policy of expanding the scale of the war and refuses to halt the bombing and other aggressive actions against the D.R.V., thereby obstructing the creation of conditions for talks aimed at a political settlement of the Vietnam problem.

In this connection the participants in the conference expressed unanimous condemnation of the criminal actions of the American imperialists, who are trying by force of arms to suppress the national-liberation struggle in South Vietnam and to hinder the construction of socialism in the Democratic Republic of Vietnam.

The participants in the conference adopted a Declaration on the Threat to Peace Created as a Result of Expansion of American Aggression in Vietnam. The text of the declaration has been published separately.

A thorough exchange of opinions on the problem of the nonproliferation of nuclear weapons took place at the conference.

The participants in the conference, proceeding on the basis of the position collectively elaborated by the Warsaw and Bucharest Conferences of the Political Consultative Committee, confirmed the special significance of preventing the spread of nuclear weapons and the importance of solving this problem. They examined the draft treaty on nonproliferation of nuclear weapons that was drawn up in the course of talks and discussion in the 18-Nation Disarmament Committee, and expressed their respective positions on this question.

The conference proceeded in a candid, comradely atmosphere.

DOCUMENT 6

STATEMENT ON THE NONPROLIFERATION TREATY
OF THE WARSAW PACT STATES, MARCH 7, 1968
COMPLETE TEXT

Pravda, March 9; *Izvestia* March 10, 1968, quoted from *CDSP* 20, no. 10
(March 27, 1968): 5–6

❧

Sofia, March 7—The People's Republic of Bulgaria, the Hungarian People's Republic, the German Democratic Republic, the Polish People's Republic, the Union of Soviet Socialist Republics and the Czechoslovak Socialist Republic, in a spirit of full unanimity, set forth their position on the question of nonproliferation of nuclear weapons as follows.

Proceeding on the basis of the socialist states' policy in the struggle to strengthen international peace and security, the said countries believe that the task of preventing the further proliferation of nuclear weapons is an urgent one and is of pressing importance for the cause of strengthening peace. They are convinced that settlement of the question of nonproliferation of nuclear weapons and conclusion of a corresponding international treaty will create more favorable conditions for the further struggle to halt the arms race, especially the nuclear arms race, and to implement effective measures for banning and destroying nuclear weapons. They express their resolve to continue the struggle to achieve these goals.

The above-named states believe this task is fulfilled by the draft treaty on nonproliferation of nuclear weapons that was submitted by the Soviet Union on Jan. 18, 1968, for the consideration of the 18-Nation Disarmament Committee and that was, at various stages of the talks, the subject of intensified consultations among many states. They declare their support for this draft and favor terminating the talks in the Committee of 18 by the established deadline (March 15, 1968), gaining the approval of the elaborated draft by the United Nations General Assembly and signing and putting into effect the treaty on nonproliferation of nuclear weapons.

The above-named states express the hope that all countries will make their contribution to the solution of the important problem of nonproliferation of nuclear weapons and, thereby, to the consolidation of international peace.

DOCUMENT 7

THE BUDAPEST APPEAL: MESSAGE FROM WARSAW PACT STATES
TO ALL EUROPEAN COUNTRIES
COMPLETE TEXT

Pravda, March 18, 1969, quoted from *CDSP,* 21, no. 11
(April 2, 1969): 11–12

The People's Republic of Bulgaria, the Hungarian People's Republic, the German Democratic Republic, the Polish People's Republic, the Socialist Republic of Rumania, the Union of Soviet Socialist Republics and the Czechoslovak Socialist Republic—the member-states of the Warsaw Pact and participants in a conference of the Political Consultative Committee—expressing the aspirations of their peoples to live in peace and good-neighbor relations with the rest of the peoples of Europe, as well as their firm resolve to further the cause of establishing an atmosphere of security and cooperation on our continent, address the following appeal to all the European states for multiplying efforts to strengthen peace and security in Europe.

The present and future of the peoples of Europe are indissolubly linked with the preservation and consolidation of peace on our continent. Genuine security and lasting peace can be ensured if the thoughts, deeds and energies of the European states are directed toward the goals of reducing tension, solving pressing international problems in the light of the realities and setting up multilateral cooperation on an all-European basis.

The way of good-neighbor relations, trust and mutual understanding depends on the wills and efforts of the peoples and governments of all the European countries. Each of the more than 30 large and small states of present-day Europe emerged from the second world war with its own distinct social structure, geography and interests. But they were destined by the will of history to live side by side, and no one can alter this fact.

Increasing numbers of governments, parliaments, parties and political and public figures are coming to understand their responsibility to present and future generations for preventing a new armed conflict in Europe. However, forces also continue to operate in Europe that consider as assets to European development not the settlement of disputes and peaceful agreements, but rather additional divisions and rockets and new military programs calculated decades in advance. They operate together with those who have not drawn the requisite lessons from the second world war, which resulted in the destruction of German militarism and Nazism. Their schemings are a source of tension and complicate international relations.

The states participating in the conference consider it their duty to continue doing everything in their power to protect Europe from the danger of new armed conflicts and to allow scope for the development of cooperation among all the European states, regardless of their social structures, on the basis of the principles of peaceful coexistence.

However complex the still-unsolved problems may be, their resolution must be achieved by peaceful means, by negotiations, not by force or the threat of force.

In analyzing the situation in Europe, the Warsaw Pact states think there is a real possibility of ensuring European security through common efforts, taking into consideration the interests of all the states and peoples of Europe.

Almost three years ago, the Warsaw Pact states proposed in Bucharest that an all-European conference be summoned to discuss problems of European security and peaceful cooperation. Subsequent contacts have indicated that not a single European government openly opposes the idea of an all-European conference and that real possibilities for such a conference exist.

The states of Europe have not gathered together once since the second world war, although a great number of questions await their consideration at the negotiating table. If one proceeds from the interests of consolidating peace, there are no compelling reasons whatever to postpone the convocation of an all-European conference.

Such a conference would be in the interests of all the European states. It would afford an opportunity for finding together the ways and means to eradicate the division of Europe into armed groupings and to implement peaceful cooperation among European states and peoples.

However, there are forces in the world that seek to preserve the division of our continent, pursue a policy of arousing tensions and refuse to organize peaceful cooperation among states and people; these forces openly oppose both the convocation of such a conference and other measures to strengthen European security.

The Warsaw Pact states are convinced that the development of all-European cooperation has been and remains the only real alternative to a dangerous military confrontation, to the arms race and to the further discords that aggressive forces—the forces seeking to demolish the results of the second world war and to redraw the map of Europe—are trying to foist upon Europe.

The Warsaw Pact states reaffirm their proposals directed against the division of the world into military blocs and against the arms race and the threats to world peace and the security of peoples resulting from it, as well as other measures and propositions contained in the Declaration on Strengthening Peace and Security in Europe, which was adopted in Bucharest in 1966. The vital need of the peoples of Europe is to avert new military conflicts and to strengthen political, economic and cultural ties on a basis of equality and respect for the independence and sovereignty of states. A firm system of European security creates the objective possibility and necessity of carrying out large-scale projects through joint efforts in fields directly related to the well-being of the entire continent's population: power engineering, transport, the condition of the air and water, and public health. It is this area of common concern that can and must become the foundation of European cooperation.

Among the basic prerequisites for ensuring European security are the inviolability of existing boundaries in Europe, including the Oder-Neisse line, as well as the boundary between the German Democratic Republic and the Federal Republic; recognition of the fact of the existence of the German Democratic Republic and the Federal Republic of Germany; renunciation by the Federal Republic of Germany of its claims to represent all the German people; renunciation of the possession of nuclear weapons in any form. West Berlin has special status and does not belong to West Germany.

A practical step in the direction of strengthening European security would be a meeting at the earliest possible date of the representatives of all interested European states for the purpose of establishing, by mutual agreement, both the procedure for convening the conference and the questions on its agenda. We are ready to examine at the same time any other proposal concerning the means of preparing for and convening this conference.

The states participating in the conference of the Political Consultative Committee appeal to all the countries of Europe for their cooperation in convening an all-European conference and creating the necessary prerequisites to see that the conference will be successful and will justify the hopes that the peoples associate with it.

In order to carry out this important operation—which could be a historic moment in the life of the continent—the states participating in the conference solemnly appeal to all European states to strengthen the climate of trust and, to this end, to refrain from any actions that might poison the atmosphere in relations among states. They appeal for a transition from general statements about peace to concrete detente and disarmament actions and measures, and for the development of cooperation and peace among nations. They appeal to all the European states to unite their efforts so that Europe may become a continent of fertile cooperation among equal nations and a factor in worldwide stability, peace, and mutual understanding.—[Signed] *For the P.R.B.*: Todor Zhivkov, First Secretary of the Bulgarian Communist Party Central Committee and Chairman of the P.R.B. Council of Ministers. *For the H.P.R.*: János Kádár, First Secretary of the Hungarian Socialist Workers' Party Central

Committee; and Jenő Fock, Chairman of the Hungarian Revolutionary Workers' and Peasants' Government. *For the G.D.R.:* Walter Ulbricht, First Secretary of the Central Committee of the Socialist Unity Party of Germany and Chairman of the G.D.R. State Council; and Willi Stoph, Chairman of the G.D.R. Council of Ministers. *For the P.P.R.:* Władysław Gomułka, First Secretary of the Polish Unitew Workers' Party; and Józef Cyrankiewicz, Chairman of the P.P.R. Council of Ministers. *For the S.R.R.:* Nicolae Ceauşescu, General Secretary of the Rumanian Communist Party Central Committee and Chairman of the S.R.R. State Council; and Ion Georghe Maurer, Chairman of the S.R.R. Council of Ministers. *For the U.S.S.R.:* L. I. Brezhnev, General Secretary of the C.P.S.U.; and A. N. Kosygin, Chairman of the U.S.S.R. Council of Ministers. *For the Č.S.R.:* Ludvik Svoboda, President of the Č.S.R.; Alexander Dubcek, First Secretary of the Central Committee of the Czechoslovak Communist Party; and Oldřich Cernik, Chairman of the Č.S.R. Federal Government.

DOCUMENT 8

STATEMENT OF THE CONFERENCE OF FOREIGN MINISTERS
OF THE WARSAW PACT MEMBER-STATES
CONDENSED TEXT

Pravda November 1; *Izvestia* November 1, quoted from *CDSP* 21, no. 44
(November 26, 1969): 18–19

The governments participating in the conference emphasized their desire and readiness to take new steps, both individually and in conjunction with other states, toward the relaxation of tensions, the strengthening of security and the development of peaceful cooperation in Europe. They reaffirmed the points, which have demonstrated their vitality, made in the Budapest Message of the Warsaw Pact member-states and directed to all European countries on March 17, 1969.

In this regard, the conference participants gave special attention to preparations for convening an all-European conference on questions of European security and cooperation. They noted with satisfaction the broadly favorable response to the proposal for an all-European conference on the part of the majority of European states. The proposal has become the subject of a lively and serious debate in Europe in the course of which concrete proposals have been voiced on various questions relating to preparing the conference, creating real possibilities for the conference and for the achievement of European security through joint efforts, which would be in the interests of all the states and peoples of Europe.

The valuable initiative of May 5, 1969, of the government of Finland, stating a readiness to assist in preparing and conducting the all-European conference, met with a favorable response. All signatories to the Budapest Message replied affirmatively to this declaration.

For their part the Foreign Ministers of the Warsaw Pact member-states, acting on the instructions of their governments, have suggested that the following questions be on the agenda of the all-European conference:

1. European security and the renunciation of the use of force or threats of force in relations between European states.

2. The expansion of trade, economic and scientific and technical ties, on basis of equality, with the aim of fostering political cooperation between the European states.

The socialist states that have endorsed the present statement are profoundly of the view that a fruitful discussion of these questions and the attainment of agreement on them would promote the relaxation of tensions in Europe, increase mutual understanding, foster peaceful and friendly relations between the states and, by so doing, would ensure that security in which all the peoples of Europe have a vital interest. A successful all-European conference would be an event of historic importance in the life of our continent and for the peoples of the entire world. It would pave the way to an eventual examination of other problems of interest to the European states, the solution of which would assist the strengthening of peace in Europe and would promote the development of broad, mutually advantageous cooperation between all the European states and promote the reliable security of Europe as it has taken shape and as it exists today—a security founded on collective principles and on the joint efforts of the states participating in the all-European conference.

The governments of the member-states participating in the present conference propose bilateral or multilateral consultations between interested states to discuss these points in preparation for an all-European conference. They are, of course, ready to examine all other proposals concerning the practical preparation for and success of an all-European conference.

In the name of their governments, the Foreign Ministers expressed confidence that, despite several difficulties that have not yet been surmounted, all questions of the preparation for and the actual conduct of an all-European conference—whether they are questions of the agenda, the participants to be included or the schedule for convening—can be resolved, if goodwill and a sincere desire for mutual understanding are displayed.

The governments of the Bulgarian People's Republic, the Hungarian People's Republic, the German Democratic Republic, the Polish People's Republic, the Socialist Republic of Rumania, the Union of Soviet Socialist Republics and the Czechoslovak Socialist Republic appeal to all the European states in the interests of the future peace of the continent to bend their efforts toward the speedy convocation of an all-European conference that, they believe, could be held in Helsinki during the first half of 1970. . . . —Oct. 31, 1969.

DOCUMENT 9

MOSCOW SUMMIT MEETING OF THE LEADERS
OF THE FRATERNAL COUNTRIES
CONDENSED TEXT

Pravda and *Izvestia,* December 5, 1969, quoted from *CDSP* 21, no. 49,
(January 6, 1970): 24–25

🌱

A meeting of the party and state leaders of the Bulgarian People's Republic, the Hungarian People's Republic, the German Democratic Republic, the Polish People's Republic, the Rumanian Socialist Republic, the Union of Soviet Socialist Republics and the Czechoslovak Socialist Republic was held in Moscow on Dec. 3 and 4, 1969. . . .

The participants in the meeting exchanged opinions on a wide range of problems connected with strengthening peace and international security, giving special attention to questions of European security.

Satisfaction was expressed that the proposals collectively worked out by the socialist countries for the preparation and holding of an all-European conference of states have met with widespread international support. The socialist countries will continue strenuously to seek to achieve conditions in which good-neighbor relations replace tension in Europe, peaceful coexistence becomes the universal norm for relations among European states with different social systems, and the peoples' desire for security and progress takes shape in concrete deeds and in the solution of the urgent problems of this part of the world.

The socialist countries participating in the meeting favor expansion and development of relations among all states on the basis of the principles of equality, noninterference in internal affairs and respect for sovereignty, territorial integrity and the inviolability of existing frontiers. They are fully determined to develop their relations with other European states that wish to cooperate on the basis of these principles. They reaffirmed their view that the interests of peace and security require that all states establish relations of equality with the G.D.R. on the basis of international law and that they recognize existing European frontiers as final and unchangeable, including the Oder-Neisse frontier.

It was noted during the exchange of opinions on urgent international questions that the results of the elections in the Federal Republic of Germany and the formation of a new government there reflect changes in a segment of the F.R.G. public and the growth among the public of tendencies oriented toward a realistic policy of cooperation and mutual understanding among states. The signing by the Federal Republic of Germany of the Treaty on the Nonproliferation of Nuclear Weapons was termed a positive factor. However, the participants in the meeting expressed their unanimous opinion that the unceasing and dangerous manifestations of revanchism in the F.R.G. and the stepped-up activity of neo-Nazi forces must be kept in mind and constant and sober vigilance must be maintained.

If the new West German government learns from history, rids itself of the ballast of the past and, in the spirit of the times, displays a realistic approach to the problems caused by tension in the relations among the European states, the socialist countries and all peace-loving peoples will welcome this.

Attaching great importance to having the Treaty on the Nonproliferation of Nuclear Weapons serve the cause of the strengthening of peace to the fullest extent, the Bulgarian People's Republic, the Hungarian People's Republic, the German Democratic Republic, the Polish People's Republic, the Rumanian Socialist Republic, the Union of Soviet Socialist Republics and the Czecho-slovak Socialist Republic favor adherence to the treaty by the largest possible number of states and the ratification and entry into force of the treaty as soon as possible.

The conviction was unanimously expressed that, in order to ensure a stable and lasting peace, it is necessary to proceed along the path of ending the arms race and of universal and complete disarmament, including nuclear disarma-ment. The socialist countries, which have repeatedly made concrete proposals in this area, call on all states to display goodwill and a readiness to undertake genuine disarmament in practice.

The countries that participated in the meeting reaffirmed their desire to continue to consult one another on the most important problems of inter-national life with an eye to coordinated execution of joint actions in the struggle for peace and security for the peoples, including European secu-rity. . . .

DOCUMENT 10

TREATY OF FRIENDSHIP, COOPERATION, AND MUTUAL AID
BETWEEN THE UNION OF SOVIET SOCIALIST REPUBLICS
AND THE CZECHOSLOVAK SOCIALIST REPUBLIC
COMPLETE TEXT

Pravda and *Izvestia*, May 7, quoted from *CDSP* 22, no. 18
(June 2, 1970): 5–6

The Union of Soviet Socialist Republics and the Czechoslovak Socialist Republic,
affirming their fidelity to the aims and principles of the Soviet-Czechoslovak

Treaty of Friendship, Mutual Aid and Postwar Cooperation, concluded on Dec. 12, 1943, and extended on Nov. 27, 1963, a treaty that played a historic role in the development of friendly relations between the peoples of the two states and laid a solid foundation for the further strengthening of fraternal friendship and all-round cooperation between them,

profoundly convinced that the indestructible friendship between the Union of Soviet Socialist Republics and the Czechoslovak Socialist Republic, which was cemented in the joint struggle against fascism and has received further deepening in the years of the construction of socialism and communism, as well as the fraternal mutual assistance and all-round cooperation between them, based on the teachings of Marxism-Leninism and the immutable principles of socialist internationalism, correspond to the fundamental interests of the peoples of both countries and of the entire socialist commonwealth,

affirming that the support, strengthening and defense of the socialist gains achieved at the cost of the heroic efforts and selfless labor of each people are the common internationalist duty of the socialist countries,

consistently and steadfastly favoring the strengthening of the unity and solidarity of all countries of the socialist commonwealth, based on the community of their social systems and ultimate goals,

firmly resolved strictly to observe the obligations stemming from the May 14, 1955, Warsaw Treaty of Friendship, Cooperation and Mutual Aid,

stating that economic cooperation between the two states facilitates their development, as well as the further improvement of the international socialist division of labor and socialist economic integration within the framework of the Council for Mutual Economic Aid,

expressing the firm intention to promote the cause of strengthening peace and security in Europe and throughout the world, to oppose imperialism, revanchism and militarism,

guided by the goals and principles proclaimed in the United Nations Charter,

taking into account the achievements of socialist and communist construction in the two countries, the present situation and the prospects for all-round cooperation, as well as the changes that have taken place in Europe and throughout the world since the conclusion of the Treaty of Dec. 12, 1943,

have agreed on the following:

Art. 1.—In accordance with the principles of socialist internationalism, the High Contracting Parties will continue to strengthen the eternal, indestructible friendship between the peoples of the Union of Soviet Socialist Republics and the Czechoslovak Socialist Republic, to develop all-round cooperation between the two countries and to give each other fraternal assistance and support, basing their actions on mutual respect for state sovereignty and independence, on equal rights and noninterference in one another's internal affairs.

Art. 2.—The High Contracting Parties will continue, proceeding from the principles of friendly mutual assistance and the international socialist division of labor, to develop and deepen mutually advantageous bilateral and multilateral economic, scientific and technical cooperation with the aim of developing their national economies, achieving the highest possible scientific and technical level and efficiency of social production, and increasing the material well-being of the working people of their countries.

The two sides will promote the further development of economic ties and cooperation and the socialist economic integration of the member-countries of the Council for Mutual Economic Aid.

Art. 3.—The High Contracting Parties will continue to develop and expand cooperation between the two countries in the fields of science and culture, education, literature and the arts, the press, radio, motion pictures, television, public health, tourism and physical culture and in other fields.

Art. 4.—The High Contracting Parties will continue to facilitate the expansion of cooperation and direct ties between the bodies of state authority and the public organizations of the working people, with the aim of achieving a deeper mutual familiarization and a closer drawing together between the peoples of the two states.

Art. 5.—The High Contracting Parties, expressing their unswerving determination to proceed along the path of the construction of socialism and communism, will take the necessary steps to defend the socialist gains of the peoples and the security and independence of the two countries, will strive to develop all-round relations among the states of the socialist commonwealth, and will act in a spirit of the consolidation of the unity, friendship and fraternity of these states.

Art. 6.—The High Contracting Parties proceed from the assumption that the Munich Pact of Sept. 29, 1938, was signed under the threat of aggressive war and the use of force against Czechoslovakia, that it was a component part of Hitler Germany's criminal conspiracy against peace and was a flagrant violation of the basic norms of international law, and hence was invalid from the very outset, with all the consequences stemming therefrom.

Art. 7.—The High Contracting Parties, consistently pursuing a policy of the peaceful coexistence of states with different social systems, will exert every effort for the defense of international peace and the security of the peoples against encroachments by the aggressive forces of imperialism and reaction, for the relaxation of international tension, the cessation of the arms race and the achievement of general and complete disarmament, the final liquidation of colonialism in all its forms and manifestations, and the giving of support to countries that have been liberated from colonial domination and are marching along the path of strengthening national independence and sovereignty.

Art. 8.—The High Contracting Parties will jointly strive to improve the situation and to ensure peace in Europe, to strengthen and develop cooperation among the European states, to establish good-neighbor relations among them and to create an effective system of European security on the basis of the collective efforts of all European states.

Art. 9.—The High Contracting Parties declare that one of the main preconditions for ensuring European security is the immutability of the state borders that were formed in Europe after the second world war. They express their firm resolve, jointly with the other member-states of the May 14, 1955, Warsaw Treaty of Friendship, Cooperation and Mutual Aid and in accordance with this treaty, to ensure the inviolability of the borders of the member-states of this treaty and to take all necessary steps to prevent aggression on the part of any forces of militarism and revanchism and to rebuff the aggressor.

Art. 10.—In the event that one of the High Contracting Parties is subjected to an armed attack by any state or group of states, the other Contracting Party, regarding this as an attack against itself, will immediately give the first party all possible assistance, including military aid, and will also give it support with all means at its disposal, by way of implementing the right to individual or collective self-defense in accordance with Art. 51 of the United Nations Charter.

The High Contracting Parties will without delay inform the United Nations Security Council of steps taken on the basis of this article, and they will act in accordance with the provisions of the United Nations Charter.

Art. 11.—The High Contracting Parties will inform each other and consult on all important international questions affecting their interests and will act on the basis of common positions agreed upon in accordance with the interests of both states.

Art. 12.—The High Contracting Parties declare that their obligations under existing international treaties are not at variance with the provisions of this Treaty.

Art. 13.—This Treaty is subject to ratification and will enter into force on the day of the exchange of instruments of ratification, which will be conducted in Moscow in a very short time.

Art. 14.—This Treaty is concluded for a period of 20 years and will be automatically extended every five years thereafter, if neither of the High Contracting Parties gives notice that it is denouncing the Treaty 12 months before the expiration of the current period.

Signed in Prague on May 6, 1970, in two copies, one each in the Russian and the Czech languages, both texts having equal force.—[Signed] For the Union of Soviet Socialist Republics, L. BREZHNEV and A. KOSYGIN; for the Czechoslovak Socialist Republic, G. HUSÁK and L. STROUGAL.

DOCUMENT 11

"COMBAT FRATERNITY"

GENERAL S. SHTEMENKO

JANUARY 24, 1970

Moscow: *Krasnaya Zvezda*—first paragraph is the newspaper's introduction
[translation revised by Michael Berman]

❦

The author of this article—Army Gen. S. Matveyevich Shtemenko—was chief of the Operations Directorate and Red Army deputy chief of the General Staff during the Great Patriotic War. In the postwar years S. M. Shtemenko worked as USSR Armed Forces chief of General Staff, chief of the Main Ground Forces Staff, and in other high military posts. In August 1968 he was appointed chief of staff of the Joint Armed Forces of the Warsaw Pact member-states. Every time I enter the building where the command and staff of the Joint Armed Forces of the Warsaw Pact member states are situated, I see the flags of the seven fraternal countries standing in the vestibule. On the wall next to them are the words of Vladimir Ilich: "To you has fallen the great honor of defending with gun in hand our sacred ideas and . . . implementing in deeds the international brotherhood of peoples."

With these words V. I. Lenin in August 1918 addressed the soldiers and officers of the Warsaw Revolutionary Regiment—formed mainly from Polish volunteers—who were being sent to the front. And now Ilich's words express the very essence of the relations existing between the soldiers of the armies of the socialist countries united by the Warsaw Pact. The Leninist idea of the international brotherhood of the peoples unites them in a single combat family.

This fraternity has long-standing traditions. A glorious page in the history of international proletarian solidarity was written by the participation of tens of thousands of soldier-internationalists in armed defense of the world's first worker and peasant state in the years of the Civil War and foreign military intervention. Shoulder to shoulder with Soviet soldiers with gun in hand they promoted the Leninist behest that a revolution is only worth its salt if it knows how to defend itself.

Our people have not forgotten the feats of their brothers abroad; nor have they remained in their debt. In defending Great October's achievements we have fought for the consolidation of mankind's brightest ideals. As genuine internationalists Soviet soldiers fought in the thirties in Spain, China, and Mongolia. The internationalism of our peoples showed itself particularly clearly in the years of the Great Patriotic War. We went into battle against Hitler's invaders and the Japanese militarists not only for our motherland's honor, freedom, and independence but also to deliver the peoples of other countries from their hated foreign yoke.

In this respect we must not forget that Polish and Czechoslovak soldiers fought together with Soviet soldiers against the common enemy on USSR territory and that in the final stages of the war, units of the Bulgarian and Rumanian armies joined them. In the battles to liberate Budapest, the Hungarian Budayskiy Volunteer Regiment worked valiantly together with Red Army soldiers. During my service on the General Staff at that time I had occasion to deal directly with questions concerning foreign formations and units and the organization of their combat application. I am therefore well aware of the considerable contribution they made to the struggle against Hitler's hordes.

After defeating world imperialism's shock forces during World War II, the Soviet Army honorably fulfilled its noble liberation mission. This to a decisive degree aided the success of the popular democratic revolutions in several European and Asian countries.

V. I. Lenin perspicaciously predicted that the peoples setting out on the socialist path of development "would perforce need a close military and economic alliance; otherwise the capitalists . . . would crush and suppress us one at a time." Indeed, the most aggressive circles of modern imperialism, primarily in the United States and the Federal Republic of Germany, are nurturing the most perfidious plans vis-à-vis the socialist countries. As the CPSU Central Committee theses for Vladimir Ilich Lenin's birth centenary stress, they have not abandoned hopes of restaging the historic battles of the 20th century, obtaining revenge, and thrusting socialism from the heights of world influence.

In the face of imperialism's aggressive strivings and the danger of a military attack, the European socialist countries rallied together in an indestructible combat alliance in order, in concert and by collective efforts, to defend the great revolutionary achievements of their peoples. The Warsaw Pact concluded in May 1955 became the expression of that alliance. Its present members include Bulgaria, Hungary, the GDR, Poland, Rumania, the Soviet Union, and Czechoslovakia. The Warsaw Pact, embodying the combat brotherhood of the peoples and the armies of the states forming it, is a firm fortress reliably counterposing the aggressive NATO bloc, an indestructible barrier to West German revanchists, and the guarantor and effective instrument of peace and security in Europe and throughout the world.

The combat community of the socialist states embodied in the Warsaw Pact, has firm economic, political, and ideological foundations. From the economic standpoint their fraternal cooperation is based on socialist production relations and on the advantages of the international socialist division of labor. It is not fortuitous that all the Warsaw Pact member countries are at the same time members of CMEA. Uniformity of social and state system among socialist countries serves as the political base for our combat alliance. Finally, the ideological basis of our unity lies in the community of the Marxist-Leninist world outlook, proletarian internationalism, and the friendship of peoples.

The fraternal peoples have one common aim: to build communism and socialism. The soldiers of the Warsaw Pact member-states' armed forces also have a single common aim: the reliable defense of the peoples' revolutionary achievements and of their peaceful constructive labor. That is why the CPSU and the Marxist-Leninist parties of the other socialist countries collectively and unanimously determine the tasks for further strengthening our community's defense might. I had occasion to be present at the Budapest meeting of the Political Consultative Committee of the Warsaw Pact member states last March, in whose work the leaders of the communist and workers parties and the government heads of the fraternal countries participated. There, in an atmosphere of unity and cohesion, very important decisions were adopted directed toward further strengthening the defense of the socialist countries belonging to the pact in the interests of peace and security in Europe and throughout the world. And this is only one example. Guided by the Leninist doctrine on the defense of the socialist revolution and socialism's achievements, the fraternal parties show daily concern for strengthening the defense capability of their countries and of the entire socialist community as a whole.

As a result of this concern the Warsaw Pact member states now possess more than first-class national armies. For the collective defense of the socialist cause they have created mighty Joint Armed Forces. Allocated to them from the national armies by the decisions of their governments are formations and units, and also control and rear organs. The Joint Armed Forces now include ground forces, air and naval forces, and also air defense forces. They have an advanced organization and are equipped with the most modern combat equipment. The fact that the nuclear missile might of the Soviet Armed Forces is standing guard for the socialist community's security is of exceptionally great importance.

The high combat efficiency and combat-readiness of the troops allocated to the Joint Armed Forces are above all insured by the high level of political consciousness of their personnel, who are educated in the spirit of the Leninist ideas of socialist patriotism and proletarian internationalism. At the same time it should be stressed that unified principles and methods of instruction and troop education lie at the basis of the training of the Joint Armed Forces, along with the retention of national traits and specific features by each army. We have identical views on conducting modern operations and combat. We share very important standards whose main ideas of regulations, leadership, and directions coincide and which have absorbed the rich combat experience of the Soviet Army accumulated in the years of the past war and in the postwar period, as well as the experience of the friendly armies. The common viewpoint both on questions of military art and generally on all the fundamental problems of military organizational development is determined by the unity of the tasks and goals of the fraternal socialist countries and of their armed defenders, and by the Marxist-Leninist methodology which is common to us all.

The troop contingents allocated by Warsaw Pact member-states for the Joint Armed Forces engage in daily combat and political training according to the plans of the national commands. However, the final decisions on the various issues concerning joint operations of the allocated, mutual assistance, and the exchange of experience are effected according to the plans of the joint command. A particularly important role is played here by troop and command-staff exercises.

A number of such exercises have been carried out recently, during the course of which many matters of combat interaction were worked out, the skill of the commanders and staffs was sharpened, the combat-readiness of the units and formations was improved, and the military skill of the personnel was heightened. At the same time, as practice shows, these exercises are becoming a true school of socialist internationalism. Further improvement of the Warsaw Pact mechanism is of great importance for the steady growth of the defense might of our socialist military coalition. The communist and workers parties of the fraternal countries are showing constant concern in this respect. The Budapest meeting of the Political Consultative Committee, which I have already mentioned, approved a provision on the Committee of Defense Ministers of Warsaw Pact Member-States, a new provision on the Joint Armed Forces and the Joint Command, and other important documents.

At present the command and staff of the Joint Armed Forces are hard at work putting the decisions made in Budapest into practice. A session of the Military Council of the Joint Armed Forces was held on 9–10 December last year in Moscow. It was devoted to an examination of ways of further improving the training of troops and staffs and strengthening the control organs of the Joint Armed Forces. A session of the Committee of the Defense Ministers of the Warsaw Pact Member-States took place two weeks later. This meeting examined the state of the allied armies and measures for strengthening the defense of the Warsaw Pact countries in connection with the aggressive aspirations of NATO's leading circles.

As long as the threat of military attack by imperialism continues to exist, the patriotic and international duty of the soldiers of the USSR Armed Forces and of all the fraternal armies consists of raising still higher our community's defense capability and of daily heightening their combat-readiness. This is the fundamental principle and the law of the life and activity of the Joint Armed Forces and of all armies of the Warsaw Pact member countries.

The armed defenders of socialism's great achievements well understand their duty and are conscientiously executing it. Proof of this is the enormous political upsurge with which the soldiers of all the fraternal armies are preparing to greet the Vladimir Ilich Lenin centennial. They are striving to study still more fully and more profoundly the ideological heritage of the great Lenin, to implement his undying teaching still more persistently, and to celebrate his glorious jubilee with practical deeds.

Soldiers of the Warsaw Pact member-states armed forces stand in indestructible formation. Proud of their international mission, bequeathed by Ilich, they will always be worthy of it.

Our combat fraternity is invincible!

DOCUMENT 12

COMMUNIQUÉ OF THE CONFERENCE OF FOREIGN MINISTERS
OF WARSAW PACT MEMBER-STATES
CONDENSED TEXT

Pravda, June 24; *Izvestia,* June 25, quoted from *CDSP* 22, no. 25
(July 21, 1970): 19

A conference of the Foreign Ministers of the Warsaw Pact member-states was held in Budapest on June 21 and 22. . . .

At the conference, which was held in a spirit of friendship and mutual understanding, there was an exchange of opinions on certain urgent problems in the development of the situation in Europe.

The Ministers affirmed their governments' conviction that an all-European conference would make an important contribution to achieving detente, strengthening security and broadening peaceful cooperation in Europe. In this connection, special attention was devoted to questions of stepping up preparations for an all-European conference.

There was an exchange of information on the bilateral and multilateral contacts and consultations that have been held in recent months between the interested states on questions of convening an all-European conference.

The governments of the countries represented at the conference took note of the broad and, on the whole, favorable response to thir proposals, put forth in Prague in October, 1969, a response that attests to the realism and vitality of these proposals, which are consistent with the interests of safeguarding security and developing cooperation in Europe; also, the governments examined with due attention the considerations expressed on this score by various parties. They concluded that favorable conditions are being created at present for placing the preparation of the all-European conference on a practical basis.

The conference stressed the desirability of direct participation by interested states at every stage of preparations for, and organization of, an all-European conference, in such forms as are deemed expedient, including appropriate preparatory meetings between representatives of these states.

Taking this into consideration, the Ministers reached an agreement on further important steps to ensure the convocation, fruitful work and success of an all-European conference. They are directed in particular toward reaching agreement on an agenda acceptable to all interested states and on methods for preparing an all-European conference, on which work could be started without delay.

The participants in the conference assume that in the process of preparing and organizing the conference, all interested countries will act in a spirit of cooperation in examining constructive proposals, in order to help find solutions acceptable to all the participants in an all-European conference. . . .

A corresponding document was unanimously approved and will be conveyed to the governments of all interested states.

DOCUMENT 13

MEMORANDUM ON QUESTIONS RELATED TO THE CONVOCATION
OF AN ALL-EUROPEAN CONFERENCE
COMPLETE TEXT

Pravda and *Izvestia,* June 27, quoted from *CDSP* 22, no. 26
(July 28, 1970): 27

The governments of the People's Republic of Bulgaria, the Hungarian People's Republic, the German Democratic Republic, the Polish People's Republic, the Socialist Republic of Rumania, the Union of Soviet Socialist Republics and the Czechoslovak Socialist Republic deem it necessary to bring to the attention of the interested states their considerations, which in their opinion would serve the interests of the preparation and convocation of an all-European conference on questions of security and cooperation in Europe.

They note with satisfaction that during bilateral and multilateral consultations and an exchange of opinions the positions of the interested states grew closer on a number of important questions related to the all-European conference. The results of the consultations and the exchange of opinions show that the proposals made in Prague in October, 1969, created the basis for transferring, already in the immediate future, the preparation of the all-European conference to a practical foundation and, along with bilateral talks, to multilateral forms of preparing the all-European conference. The direct participation of the interested states is desirable at every stage of the preparation and organization of the all-European conference in the forms that will be deemed expedient, including appropriate preparatory meetings between representatives of these states.

The question of the makeup of the conference participants has been clarified —all European states may take part, including the G.D.R. and the F.R.G.— on an equal footing with each other and on the basis of equal rights with the other European states—and also the U.S.A. and Canada. The initiative of the government of Finland to hold the conference in Helsinki is being greeted favorably. It is understood that convocation of the conference should not be made dependent on any preconditions.

In many countries the opinion is shared that a successful first all-European conference—the preparation, organization and convocation of which must be the result of a contribution by all the interested states—would facilitate joint consideration in the future of other European problems, particularly the problem of creating a stable European security system, and that in this connection it would be advantageous to hold a number of all-European conferences and to create an analogous body of all interested states on questions of security and cooperation in Europe.

Continuing is the discussion of questions of the content of the work of the all-European conference and its agenda. The two items proposed in Prague for the conference agenda meet the interests of safeguarding security and developing cooperation in Europe and are questions on which there is a possibility of achieving wide agreement. These proposals have not raised fundamental objections. At the same time, a number of states are advocating an extension of the conference agenda.

Guided by a desire to reach agreement on an agenda for the all-European conference that is acceptable to all the interested states, the governments of the People's Republic of Bulgaria, the Hungarian People's Republic, the German Democratic Republic, the Polish People's Republic, the Socialist Republic of Rumania, the Union of Soviet Socialist Republics and the Czechoslovak Socialist Republic propose to include in the all-European conference also the question of creating a body on questions of security and cooperation in Europe.

The governments that have adopted the present memorandum believe that the interests of detente and security in Europe would be served by consideration of the question of reducing foreign armed forces on the territory of European states. In order to create as quickly as possible the most favorable conditions for discussing the appropriate questions at the all-European conference and in the interests of productive consideration of the question regarding a reduction of foreign armed forces, this question could be discussed in the body whose creation at the all-European conference is proposed, or in another form acceptable to the interested states.

Moreover, they believe that it would be possible to discuss, within the framework of the second item of the agenda proposed in Prague, questions of the environment, and also to enlarge this item by including in it a provision on the development of cultural ties.

Thus, the following questions could be submitted for the consideration of the all-European conference:

—the safeguarding of European security and renunciation of the use of force or the threat of its use in interstate relations in Europe;

—expansion on an equal basis of trade, economic, scientific, technical and cultural ties, directed toward the development of political cooperation between the European states;

—creation at the all-European conference of a body for questions of security and cooperation in Europe.

The governments of the People's Republic of Bulgaria, the Hungarian People's Republic, the German Democratic Republic, the Polish People's Republic, the Socialist Republic of Rumania, the Union of Soviet Socialist Republics and the Czechoslovak Socialist Republic express the hope that the proposals contained in the memorandum, which take into account the opinions expressed by many interested states, will meet with favorable response from the governments concerned. These proposals are directed particularly toward reaching agreement on an agenda acceptable to all the interested states and on methods of the preparation of the all-European conference, which may be begun already in the immediate future.

The governments issuing the present memorandum are convinced that the convocation of an all-European conference—resulting from the joint efforts of all interested states—would be an important contribution to the achievement of rapprochement, the strengthening of security and the furthering of peaceful cooperation in Europe.

DOCUMENT 14

TREATY OF FRIENDSHIP, COOPERATION, AND MUTUAL AID
BETWEEN THE UNION OF SOVIET SOCIALIST REPUBLICS
AND THE SOCIALIST REPUBLIC OF RUMANIA
COMPLETE TEXT

Pravda, July 8, 1970, quoted from *CDSP* 22, no. 28 (August 11, 1970): 8–9

The Union of Soviet Socialist Republics and the Socialist Republic of Rumania,

being profoundly convinced that the eternal and inviolable friendship, fraternal mutual assistance and close and comprehensive cooperation between the Union of Soviet Socialist Republics and the Socialist Republic of Rumania, based on the immutable principles of socialist internationalism, correspond to the fundamental interests of the peoples of the two countries and of the entire socialist commonwealth,

proceeding from the desire constantly to develop and strengthen the relations of friendship between the Soviet and the Rumanian peoples, relations that are deeply rooted in the historical past and were cemented in the common struggle against Hitlerism and raised to the highest level in the years of the construction of socialism and communism, and to develop comprehensive fraternal cooperation between their two neighboring and friendly states,

recognizing that the international solidarity of the socialist states is based on their common social system, on the unity of basic goals and aspirations and on the common interests of the struggle against imperialism and reaction,

fully determined tirelessly to strengthen the unity and solidarity of the socialist countries and unswervingly to observe the commitments envisaged in the Warsaw Treaty of Friendship, Cooperation and Mutual Aid of May 14, 1955, for the period that the treaty—which was concluded in response to the NATO threat—is in effect,

expressing their firm desire to promote the consolidation of peace and security in Europe and throughout the world and the development of cooperation with European and other states regardless of their social systems, and to oppose imperialism, revanchism and militarism,

guided by the goals and principles of the United Nations Charter,

considering that the Treaty of Friendship, Cooperation and Mutual Aid between the Union of Soviet Socialist Republics and the Rumanian People's Republic of Feb. 4, 1948, which formulated important goals and principles, laid a firm foundation for the development of relations of fraternal friendship and comprehensive cooperation between the two countries,

taking into account the experience and achievements of the two states in the construction of socialism and communism, the present stage and possibilities of the development of political, economic and cultural cooperation between the Soviet and the Rumanian peoples, as well as the changes that have occurred in Europe and the world over,

have decided to conclude the present treaty and for this purpose have agreed about the following,

Art. 1.—The High Contracting Parties, in accordance with the principles of socialist internationalism, will continue to strengthen the eternal and indestructible friendship between the peoples of the two countries and to promote cooperation between the Union of the Soviet Socialist Republics and the Socialist Republic of Rumania in the political, economic, scientific, technological, and cultural fields, on the basis of fraternal assistance, mutual advantage, respect for sovereignty and national independence, equality, and noninterference in each other's internal affairs.

The two sides will intensify their exchange of experience in the various fields of socialist and communist construction.

Art. 2.—The High Contracting Parties, proceeding from the principles underlying relations between socialist states, the principles of mutual assistance and international socialist division of labor, will continue to develop and deepen mutually advantageous economic, scientific and technological cooperation, to expand cooperative production and scientific and technological ventures, and will also promote the development of economic ties and cooperation with other countries of the socialist camp within the framework of the Council for Mutual Economic Aid.

Art. 3.—The High Contracting Parties will continue to promote and expand cooperation between their two countries in the fields of science, education, literature and art, the press, radio and television, health, tourism, physical education and other fields.

Art. 4.—The High Contracting Parties, convinced that the unity and cohesion of the socialist states are the prime source of the strength and invincibility of the world socialist system, which is the decisive force in the development of modern society, will steadfastly advocate the development of friendship and cooperation between the socialist states and the strengthening of their unity in the interests of socialism and peace.

Art. 5.—Consistently adhering to the policy of the peaceful coexistence of states with different social systems, the High Contracting Parties will take steps to protect international peace and the security of the peoples from the encroachments of the aggressive forces of imperialism and reaction, to resolve disputed issues between states by peaceful means, to achieve general and complete disarmament and the final abolition of colonialism in all its forms and manifestations, and to support countries that have liberated themselves from colonial rule and are advancing along a path of strengthening their independence and sovereignty.

Art. 6.—The High Contracting Parties will jointly strive to improve the situation and to maintain the peace in Europe, to promote cooperation and good-neighbor relations between European states on the basis of the principles of sovereignty and national independence, equality, mutual advantage, and noninterference in each other's internal affairs, and to establish an effective system of European security.

The two sides will take steps to establish good-neighbor relations and to promote mutual understanding and cooperation in the Balkan peninsula and in the Black Sea area.

Art. 7.—The High Contracting Parties state that one basic prerequisite for ensuring European security is the inviolability of the European state boundaries that were established after the second world war.

The two sides express their firm determination, in keeping with the Warsaw Treaty of Friendship, Cooperation and Mutual Aid of May 14, 1955, to take, together with the other treaty member-states, all measures necessary to preclude aggression on the part of any forces of imperialism, militarism and revanchism, to ensure the inviolability of the Warsaw Treaty member-states' borders and to repel the aggressor.

Art. 8.—Should one of the High Contracting Parties be subjected to an armed attack by some state or group of states, the other party, by way of exercising its inalienable right of individual or collective self-defense, and in accordance with Art. 51 of the United Nations Charter, will immediately render it all-round assistance with all the means at its disposal, including the armed force necessary to repel the armed attack.

The sides will immediately inform the United Nations Security Council of the measures taken on the basis of Art. 51, and will act in accordance with the provisions of the United Nations Charter.

Art. 9.—The High Contracting Parties will consult each other on all important international questions that touch on the interests of the two countries, in order to coordinate their positions.

Art. 10.—The High Contracting Parties state that their commitments under existing international treaties are not in contradiction with the provisions of the present treaty.

Art. 11.—The present treaty is subject to ratification and takes effect on the day that the instruments of ratification are exchanged; said exchange is to take place in the city of Moscow as early as possible.

The treaty is concluded for a period of 20 years and will be automatically extended for consecutive periods of five years' duration each, provided neither of the High Contracting Parties denounces the treaty by giving notice 12 months prior to the expiration date of the corresponding term.

Signed in Bucharest on July 7, 1970, in two copies, one each in the Russian and the Rumanian languages, both texts having equal force.—[Signed] For the Union of Soviet Socialist Republics, A. KOSYGIN; for the Socialist Republic of Rumania, I. G. MAURER.

DOCUMENT 15

STATEMENT ON QUESTIONS OF THE STRENGTHENING OF SECURITY AND THE DEVELOPMENT OF PEACEFUL COOPERATION IN EUROPE

COMPLETE TEXT

Pravda, December 4, 1970; *Izvestia,* December 4, 1970, quoted from *CDSP* 22, no. 49 (January 5, 1971): 2–3.

The People's Republic of Bulgaria, the Hungarian People's Republic, the German Democratic Republic, the Polish People's Republic, the Socialist Republic of Rumania, the Union of Soviet Socialist Republics and the Czechoslovak Socialist Republic, all represented at the Berlin Conference of the Political Consultative Committee of the Warsaw Treaty Member-States, have considered the situation that is taking shape in Europe.

The conference noted with satisfaction that the efforts exerted by the socialist countries effectively promote the normalization of the situation on the European continent and the practical implementation of the principles of the peaceful coexistence of states with different social systems. It was stated that recently tendencies toward a detente and extensive good-neighbor cooperation have been making more and more headway in relations among European states.

The states represented at the conference welcome this progress in European affairs, which corresponds to the interests of all European countries, large and small, and to the safeguarding of lasting peace throughout the world. They intend to continue to facilitate the expansion and deepening mutually advantageous relations with other states of Europe that on their part are ready to pursue a policy of the easing of international tension. Once again, it was noted that in relations among all states it is strictly necessary to observe the principles of independence, sovereignty, territorial integrity, equality and noninterference in the internal others.

The participants in the conference emphasized the great international importance of the conclusion of the treaty between the U.S.S.R. and the F.R.G. and the initialing of the treaty between the P.P.R. and the F.R.G. Recognition of the existing situation in Europe that has come about as a result of the Second World War and postwar developments, the inviolability of the present borders of European states, observance of the principle of settling disputes exclusively by peaceful means without resorting to force or the threat of its use—all this has enormous significance for the fate of European peace, for the peaceful future of the European peoples. The entry into force of these treaties will correspond to the vital interests of all states and peoples.

The participants in the conference unanimously expressed solidarity with the peace-loving policy of the German Democratic Republic. The entire course of European development indicates that without the participation of the G.D.R. it is possible to build the edifice of lasting peace in this area. The establishment of equal relations between the German Democratic Republic and other states that as yet have not established such relations, including relations between the G.D.R. and the F.R.G. based on the generally recognized norms of international law, and the admission of the G.D.R. to the United Nations and other international organizations as an equal member are vital requirements of our time and would be a weighty contribution to the cause of European international security.

The states represented at the conference wholly support the just demand of the Czechoslovak Socialist Republic that the F.R.G. recognize the Munich Agreement as invalid from the outset, with all the consequences stemming therefrom. F.R.G.'s clear and definitive dissociation from this diktat which embodied the Hitlerite policy of plunder, would facilitate the normalization of the situation in Europe and the development of the F.R.G.'s relations with the socialist countries.

It was noted at the conference that preconditions are taking shape for the settlement of other problems existing in Europe, and in this connection the hope was expressed that the talks now under way on West Berlin will be concluded by the achievement of a mutually acceptable agreement that corresponds to the interests of a detente in the center of Europe, as well as to the requirements of the population of West Berlin and the legitimate interests and sovereign rights of the G.D.R.

The participants in the conference expressed their confidence that the convocation of an all-European conference on questions of security and cooperation would be a major step on the path to the consolidation of peace in Europe.

Thanks to the preparatory work that has already been done, sufficient preconditions for holding such a conference have now been created. The agenda has largely been outlined, the participants in the conference have been determined, and a broad basis has been laid for mutual understanding and for ensuring that the conference will have positive results. The reaching of agreement on all questions connected with the convocation of the conference at present requires, along with bilateral contacts, the holding of multilateral consultations with the participation of all interested states. Many European states have already spoken out in favor of this.

The participants in the conference welcomed the new initiative of the government of Finland on holding preliminary meetings of representatives of all interested states in Helsinki on questions connected with the convocation of an all-European conference. The states represented at the conference announced their agreement to take part in such meetings, which would be called upon to facilitate practical preparations for an all-European conference.

There are no reasons whatever for delaying the convocation of the conference or for making any kind of preliminary conditions. The movement for security and cooperation on the European continent is becoming ever broader and more inclusive. The socialist states participating in the conference are fully resolved to do anything in their power so that the will of the European peoples for peace will be implemented.

The participants in the conference stated that the opponents of an easing of tension and peaceful cooperation in Europe have not ceased their dangerous activity. In this connection, attention was drawn to the stepped-up activity of the aggressive circles of NATO, the provocational actions of revanchist and militarist forces in the F.R.G. and the incessant attempts from outside to retard the development of favorable processes on the European continent. Firm confidence was expressed that the peace-loving forces of Europe will be able to surmount the obstacles created by the opponents of peace and, through joint efforts, will accomplish the task of ensuring a dependable peace in this part of the world.

The participants in the conference reaffirmed the positions on questions of European security, the easing of tension and disarmament that were set forth in the Bucharest Declaration of July 5, 1966.

The participants in the conference expressed the determination of their countries' parties and governments to continue to carry out concerted joint actions in the international arena in the interests of safeguarding dependable security in Europe aand throughout the world. To this end, each of them will continue an active policy of peace, the easing of tension and broad international cooperation.—[The statement is signed by Zhivkov for Bulgaria, Kádár and Fock for Hungary, Ulbricht and Stoph for the G.D.R., Gomułka and Cyrankiewicz for Poland, Ceaușescu and Verdet for Rumania, Brezhnev and Kosygin for the U.S.S.R. and Husák and Strougal for Czechoslovakia.] Berlin, Dec. 2, 1970.

POSTSCRIPT

The pattern of politics has as little concern for the demands of publishing as a printer's production schedule has for the rhythm of political life. Therefore I was not surprised when the barometer of European détente soared during May and June 1971—only sorry to have to deal with such encouraging events as an afterthought.

In mid-May, Senator Mike Mansfield's resolution for a mandatory cut in US forces in Europe came on the heels of a dollar crisis in which the NATO allies had paid little heed to Washington's economic difficulties. It was an embarrassing combination for the Nixon administration. Although Mansfield's resolution lost, he had made his point. The resolution undoubtedly affected at least the timing of Brezhnev's May 14 speech calling for talks on mutual and balanced reduction of forces (MBFR). It simultaneously increased American enthusiasm for that suggestion.

On June 4 the NATO Lisbon communiqué noted progress in the negotiations on Berlin. Although still tying the European Security Conference to Berlin, its tone gave much more cause for optimism than that of the December meeting. Thus, even if it is no longer "likely" that an ESC will occur by the end of 1971, multilateral preparations for such a conference and/or MBFR negotiations might in fact be under way by the end of the year.

Throughout East Europe, events are still in motion. Gierek seems to have consolidated his regime in Poland. His major rival, Moczar, has fallen from sight, although one should not necessarily assume that his former backing will not revive as supporters of the loosely defined "neo-partisans" should the economic situation worsen. In Czechoslovakia Husák, with obvious Soviet support, continues to hold his somewhat tenuous line against the more dogmatic factions of the KSČ. Ceauşescu's trip to China has once again dispelled the myth of Bucharest returning to a Warsaw Pact fold, while Kádár's Hungary has not strayed from its steady, quiet path toward reform.

Indeed the major question mark concerns what has long been the most predictable member of the Warsaw Pact: East Germany. When Walter Ulbricht stepped down as first secretary of the SED in early May, much of the political analysis said "of course." He was old, clever, and had hand picked his successor. Now no one is so sure. Ulbricht did not speak to the East German Communist Party Congress at the end of June. Honecker attacked the former leader's style of rule as one that had not paid sufficient attention to the norms of collective leadership. He spoke with much enthusiasm of the Soviet Union and with some slight sign of conciliation on Berlin.

Speculation began to buzz as to whether Moscow might have gotten rid of Ulbricht because the grand old man of East German Communism had blocked Russian plans for détente by balking on Berlin. It is far too soon to hazard any safe guesses about what happened in the internal politics of the GDR. Yet one should be cautious about assuming that Honecker's behavior while securing his position says much about the way he will jump if pushed. He may, it is true, be more vulnerable to Soviet pressure than Ulbricht because he does not have Walter Ulbricht's long-standing prestige in the international Communist movement. But the new leader of the SED certainly did not speak on the side of moderation throughout 1969–1970. What is more to the point, however, is that the Soviet leaders may be more willing to come to an agreement over his head than they would have been while Ulbricht held the reins of power.

These are all variations on what at this moment seems a reasonably steady note of détente and relaxation of tensions. If this environment continues, it can only work in favor of decentralizing trends in Europe, that is, toward a Europe in which, as a leading Yugoslav theoretician once put it, "there is no justification at all for the view that small nations must jump into the mouth of this or that shark" (Moshe Pijade, *Borba,* July 9, 1949).

Robin Alison Remington
Belgrade, Yugoslavia
June 28, 1971

BIBLIOGRAPHY

Aćimović, Ljubivoje. "Cohesion and Conflict in Relations Among the East European Countries." *International Affairs* (Belgrade 1970).

———. "Die blockfreien Länder und die europäische Sicherheit." *Europa-Archiv* 3–4 (December 10, 1969): 815–822.

Ágoston, István. *Le Marché Commun Communiste: Principles et pratique du COMECON*. Geneva: Librairie Droz, 1965.

Ambroz, Oton. "The Doctrine of Limited Sovereignty: Its Impact on East Europe." *East Europe* 18, no. 5 (May 1969): 19–24.

Andras, Charles. "The Evolution of the Warsaw Pact's Approach to European Security." *Radio Free Europe* (August 1968).

The Anti-Stalin Campaign and International Communism: A Selection of Documents. New York: Columbia University Press, 1956.

Batov, General P. "Reliable Shield for the Security of the Nations." *Soviet Military Review*, no. 7 (July 1965): 32–35.

Beer, Francis A., ed. *Alliances: Latent War Communities in the Contemporary World*. New York: Holt, Rinehart and Winston, Inc., 1970.

Ben, Phillippe. "Le Começon, Homme Malade de l'Europe de l'Est." Third in the series "La Roumanie entre Moscou et Pékin" in *Le Monde*, December 3, 1963.

Bender, Peter. "Inside the Warsaw Pact." *Survey* 74–75 (Winter–Spring 1970): 253–268.

Bezymensky, L. "The Geneva Conference." *New Times* 45 (November 1955): 7–11.

Birnbaum, Karl E. *Peace in Europe: East-West Relations 1966–1968 and the Prospects for a European Settlement*. London: Oxford University Press, 1967.

———. "Ways Toward European Security." *Survival* 10, no. 6 (June 1968): 193–199.

Brandt, Willy. *A Peace Policy for Europe.* New York: Holt, Rinehart and Winston, 1968.

———. "German Policy Towards the East." *Foreign Affairs* 46, no. 3 (April 1968): 476–486.

Breyere, Siegfried. "Warsaw Pact: Landing Craft." *Military Review* 47, no. 5 (May 1967): 106–108. (Translated from *Soldat und Technik,* December, 1966.)

Bromke, Adam. *Poland's Politics: Idealism vs. Realism.* Cambridge, Mass.: Harvard University Press, 1967.

Brown, J. F. *The New Eastern Europe.* New York: Praeger, 1966.

———. "Rumania Steps Out of Line." *Survey* 49 (October 1963): 19–35.

Brzezinski, Z. K. "Organization of the Communist Camp." *World Politics* 13, no. 2 (January 1961): 175–209.

———. *The Soviet Bloc: Unity and Conflict.* Cambridge, Mass.: Harvard University Press, 1967 (3rd. ed.).

Brzezinski, Zbigniew, and Samuel P. Huntington. *Political Power: USA/ USSR.* New York: The Viking Press, 1967.

Burton, John W. *Conflict and Communications.* London: Macmillan, 1969.

———. *Systems, States, Diplomacy, and Rules.* Cambridge, Eng.: Cambridge University Press, 1968.

Campbell, John C. "European Security. Prospects and Possibilities for East Europe." *East Europe* 19, no. 2 (November 1970): 2–8.

Chalfont, Lord. "Value of Observation Posts in NATO and Warsaw Pact Areas." *European Review* 16, no. 4 (1966).

Chou En-lai. "Speech to the Twenty-second Party Congress." *Peking Review* 4, no. 43 (October 27, 1961): 9.

Clemens, Walter C. "The Changing Warsaw Pact." *East Europe* 17, no. 6 (June 1968): 7–12.

———. "The Future of the Warsaw Pact." *Orbis* 11, no. 4 (Winter 1968): 996–1033.

Clews, J. C. *Communist Propaganda Techniques.* New York: Praeger, 1964.

Committee of the Judiciary, U.S. Senate, 84th Cong., 2nd Session, Internal Security Subcommittee Hearings, part 29, June 8–29, 1956. "Scope of Soviet Activity in the U.S." Washington, D.C.: Government Printing Office, 1957.

Cornides, Wilhelm. "German Unification and the Power Balance." *Survey* 58 (January 1966): 140–148.

Cramer, Dettmar. "Die DDR und die Bonner *Ostpolitik.*" *Europa-Archiv* 25 (March 10, 1970): 167–172.

Crankshaw, Edward. *The New Cold War: Moscow v. Peking.* Baltimore, Md.: Penguin special, 1963.

Croan, Melvin. "Bonn and Pankow. Intra-German Politics." Survey 67 (April 1968): 77–89.

Csizmas, Michael. "Das militärische Bundnissystem in Osteuropa." *Allgemeine Schweizerische Militärzeitschrift,* 10 and 11 (October–November 1967): 675–682.

———. "Military Cybernetics in Eastern Europe." *Military Review* 47, no. 9 (September 1967): 20–26.

ČSSR: The Road to Democratic Socialism (Facts on Events from January to May 1968). Prague: Praguepress, 1968.

Dallin, David J. *Soviet Foreign Policy After Stalin.* Philadelphia: Lippincott, 1961.

Deutsch, Karl. "The Growth of Nations: Some Recurrent Patterns of Political and Social Integrations." *World Politics* 5, no. 2 (January 1953): 161–195.

——— and Morton Kaplan. "The Limits of International Communism" in James N. Rosenau ed., *International Aspects of Civil Strife.* Princeton, New Jersey: Princeton University Press, 1964.

Devlin, Kevin. "The New Crisis in European Communism." *Problems of Communism* 17, no. 6 (November–December 1968): 58.

Dinerstein, Herbert S. "The Transformation of Alliance Systems," *The American Political Science Review* 59, no. 3 (September 1965): 589–602.

———. *War and the Soviet Union: Nuclear Weapons and the Revolution in Soviet Military and Political Thinking.* New York: Praeger, 1959.

Draper, Theodore. "The Dominican Crisis—A Case Study in American Policy." *Commentary* 40, no. 6 (December 1965): 33–68.

Duchene, François. "SALT, the *Ostpolitik,* and the Post-Cold War Context." *The World Today* 26, no. 12 (December 1970): 500–511.

Duevel, Christian. "Ideological Acrobatics on Sovereignty." *Radio Liberty Research* CRD 361/68 (October 7, 1968).

———. "Radio Moscow Issues Warning to Rumania." *Radio Liberty Information Bulletin* 2280 (July 8, 1966).

———. "Rumania's Position After the Moscow 'Summit' Meeting." *Radio Liberty Information Bulletin* 1568 (August 7, 1963).

Dziewanowski, M. K. *The Communist Party of Poland: An Outline of History.* Cambridge, Mass.: Harvard University Press, 1959.

———. "Communist China and Eastern Europe." *Survey* 77 (Autumn 1970): 59–74.

———. "The 1970 Rumanian-Soviet Treaty" East Europe 20, no. 1 (January 1971): 19–22.

Ermarth, Fritz. "The Warsaw Pact and Its New Commander." *Radio Free Europe Research Report* (July 3, 1967).

————. *Internationalism, Security, and Legitimacy: The Challenge to Soviet Interests in Eastern Europe, 1964–1968.* RAND RM 5909–PR, March 1969.

Farrell, Barry. "Foreign Policy Formation in the Communist Countries of Eastern Europe." *East European Quarterly* 1, no. 1 (March 1967): 39–86.

Fejtö, François. *Behind the Rape of Hungary.* New York: McKay, 1957.

Fischer-Galati, Stephen. *The New Rumania: From a People's Democracy to a Socialist Republic.* Cambridge, Mass.: The MIT Press, 1967.

Garder, Michael. *A History of the Soviet Army.* New York: Praeger, 1966. Revised version of the original French edition, *Histoire de l'armée sovietique.* Paris, 1959.

————. "Le potential militaire des satellites de l'URSS." *Revue Militaire Générale* (June 1965): 124–131.

————. Der Warschauer Pakt im System der sowjetischen Aussenpolitik. Eine Darstellung aus französischer Sicht." *Europa-Archiv* 21, no. 24 (December 25, 1966): 895–904.

Garthoff, Raymond L. "The Military Establishment." *East Europe* 14, no. 9 (September 1965): 2–16.

————. *Soviet Strategy in the Nuclear Age.* New York: Praeger, 1962 (revised ed.).

Gasteyger, Curt. "Probleme und Reformen des Warschauer Pakts." *Europa-Archiv* 22, no. 1 (January 10, 1967): 1–10.

Griffith, W. E. *Albania and the Sino-Soviet Rift.* Cambridge, Mass.: The MIT Press, 1963.

————, ed. *Communism in Europe, Volumes I and II.* Cambridge, Mass.: The MIT Press, 1964 and 1965.

————. *Sino-Soviet Relations 1964–1965.* Cambridge, Mass.: The MIT Press, 1967.

————. *The Sino-Soviet Rift.* Cambridge, Mass.: The MIT Press, 1964.

————. "The November 1960 Meeting: A Preliminary Reconstruction." *The China Quarterly* 11 (July–September 1962): 48.

Gelberg, Ludwik, *Układ warszawski.* Warsaw: Panstwowe Wydawnictwo Narrkowe, 1957.

Gryzbowski, Kazimierz. *The Socialist Commonwealth of Nations: Organizations and Institutions.* New Haven: Yale University Press, 1964.

Guédon, Commandant. "Le Service militaire dans les pays du bloc Sovietique." *Revue de défense nationale* (April 1964): 626–641.

Haigh, Patricia. "Reflections on the Warsaw Pact." *The World Today* 24, no. 4 (April 1968): 166–172.

Hassner, Pierre. "Change and Security in Europe." *Adelphi papers,* 45–46. London: ISS, February 1968 and July 1968.

Heinman, Leo. "Peking's Adriatic Stronghold." *East Europe* 13, no. 4 (April 1964): 15–17.

Herrick, R. Waring. "Warsaw Pact Restructuring Strengthens Principle of National Control." *Radio Liberty Research Bulletin* no. 10 (2540), March 11, 1970).

———. "Soviet Foreign Policy and the German Question." *Radio Liberty Research* (January 12, 1970).

———. "Moscow Summit Sanctions Controlled Steps Toward Bilateral Détente with Bonn." *Radio Liberty Research* (December 15, 1969).

Hilsman, R. "Coalitions and Alliances" in W. W. Kaufman ed., *Military Policy and National Security,* 1956.

Hinterhoff, Eugene. "Die Potentiale des Warschauer Paktes." *Aussenpolitik* 8 (August 1965): 535–547.

———. "The Warsaw Pact." *Military Review* 42, no. 6 (June 1962): 89–94.

Hoeffding, Oleg. *Recent Efforts Toward Coordinated Economic Planning in the Soviet Bloc.* Santa Monica, Calif.: The RAND Corporation (August 7, 1959).

Hudson, G. F., Lowenthal, Richard, and MacFarquhar, Roderick. *The Sino-Soviet Dispute.* New York: Praeger, 1961.

Hunter, Robert. *Security in Europe.* London: Elek Books, 1969.

Institute for the Study of the USSR (Munich). *Biographic Directory of the USSR.* New York: Scarecrow Press, 1958.

Ionescu, Ghita. *The Breakup of the Soviet Empire in Eastern Europe.* Baltimore, Md.: Penguin special, 1965.

———. *Communism in Rumania, 1944–1962.* London: Oxford University Press, 1964.

Jaster, R. S. "CEMA's Influence on Soviet Policies in Eastern Europe." *World Politics* 14, no. 3 (April 1962): 505–518.

Johnson, J. Arthur. "Rumanian–Soviet Polemics: An Escalation of Pressures on Bucharest?" *Radio Free Europe Research Report* (April 22, 1970).

Johnson, Ross. *The Warsaw Pact "European Security" Campaign.* RAND R–565–PR, Santa Monica, California: November 1970.

Jurek, Marian, and Edward Skrzypkowski. *Układ warszawski* Warsaw: Wydawnictwo Ministerstwa Obrony Narodowej, 1970.

Kaiser, Karl. *German Foreign Policy in Transition.* London and New York: Oxford University Press, 1968.

Kaser, Michael. *COMECON: Integration Problems of the Planned Economies.* London: Oxford University Press, 1965.

Keckemeti, Paul. *The Unexpected Revolution.* Stanford, Calif.: Stanford University Press, 1961.

Keohane, Robert O. "Lilliputians' Dilemmas: Small States in International Politics." *International Organization* 23, no. 2 (1969): 291–310.

Khrushchev, N. S. "Nasushchnye voprosy razvitia mirovoi sotsialisticheskoi sistemy." *Kommunist* 12 (August 1962): 3–27.

Király, General Béla. "Budapest 1956—Prague 1968." *Problems of Communism* 17, nos. 4–5 (July–October 1969): 52–60.

———. "Hungary's Army: Its Part in the Revolt." *East Europe* 7, no. 6 (June 1958): 3–15.

———. "Hungary's Army Under the Soviets." *East Europe* 7, no. 3 (March 1958): 3–14.

———. "Why the Soviets Need the Warsaw Pact." *East Europe* 18, no. 4 (April 1969): 8–17.

Klaiber, Wolfgang. "Security Priorities in Eastern Europe." *Problems of Communism* 19, no. 3 (May–June 1970): 32–44.

Kolkowicz, Roman. "Spezifischer Funcktionswandel des Warschauer Paktes." *Aussenpolitik* 20, no. 1 (January 1969): 5–23.

———. "The Warsaw Pact: Entangling Alliance." *Survey* 70–71 (Winter–Spring 1969): 86–101.

———, ed. *The Warsaw Pact: Report on a Conference on the Warsaw Treaty Organization Held at the Institute for Defense Analysis May 17–19, 1967.* IDA: Research Paper P–496 (March 1969).

Korbel, Josef. "West Germany's *Ostpolitik:* I. Intra-German Relations." *Orbis* 13, no. 4 (Winter 1970): 1050–1072.

Konstantinov, F. T., ed. *Sodruzhestvo stran sotsialisma.* Moscow: Akad. nauk, 1958.

Korbonski, Andrzej. "COMECON." *International Conciliation,* No. 549 (September 1964).

———. "The Warsaw Pact." *International Conciliation,* No. 573 (May 1969).

Korovin, E. "Law of the Jungle Versus the Law of Nations." *New Times* 11 (January 1, 1957): 15–17.

Kotyk, Václav. "Některé otázky dějin vztahů socialistických zemí" (Some Aspects of the History of Relations Among Socialist Countries). *Československý časopis historický* 4 (1967): in *Czechoslovak Press Survey,* No. 1973, RFE/233 (October 30, 1967).

Lachs, M. "O varshavskom dogovore i severoatlanticheskom pakte." *Mezhdunarodnaia zhizn'* 2 (1956): 113.

————. "Varshavskii dogovor i problema kollektivnoi bezopasnosti v Evrope." *Mezhdunarodnaia zhizn'* 10 (1955): 52–62.

Lambeth, Benjamin S. *Soviet Views on European Security 1965–1970: An Annotated Bibliography of Selected Soviet Sources.* Cambridge, Mass.: M.I.T. Center for International Studies, C/71–2, March 1972.

Lasky, Melvin J. *The Hungarian Revolution.* New York: Praeger, 1957.

"Leninism or Social Imperialism?" *Peking Review* 13, no. 17 (April 24, 1970): 10.

Legvold, Robert. "European Security Conference." *Survey* 76 (Summer 1970): 41–52.

Lendvai, Paul. "How to Combine Detente with Soviet Hegemony?" *Survey* 77 (Autumn 1970): 74–92.

Leonard, Wolfgang. *The Kremlin Since Stalin.* New York: Praeger, 1962.

"Les pays communistes après la crise Tchecoslovaque." Series in *Le Monde,* February 11–19, 1969.

Lesnevskii, Colonel S. "Voevoe sodruzhestvo vooruzhennykh sil sotsialisticheskikh stran." *Kommunist vooruzhennykh sil* 10 (May 1963): 73.

Liska, George. *Nations in Alliance: The Limits of Interdependence.* Baltimore, Md.: The Johns Hopkins Press, 1968.

Littell, Robert, ed. *The Czech Black Book.* New York: Praeger, 1969.

Loeber, Dietrich Andre. "The Legal Structure of the Communist Bloc." *Social Research* 27, no. 2 (Summer, 1960): 183–202.

London, Kurt, ed. *Eastern Europe in Transition.* Baltimore, Md.: Johns Hopkins Press, 1966.

Lowenthal, Richard. "The Sparrow in the Cage." *Problems of Communism* 17, no. 6 (November–December 1968): 2–28.

Mackintosh, J. M. *Strategy and Tactics of Soviet Foreign Policy.* London: Oxford University Press, 1963

————. "The Evolution of the Warsaw Pact." *Adelphi Papers* 58, London: ISS, June 1969.

"The Military Establishments II." *East Europe* 17, no. 5 (May 1958): 3–11.

Miller, Dorothy. "Kassel and Thereafter." *Radio Free Europe Report* (May 29, 1970).

————. "Some Political Aspects of the 13th SED CC Plenum." *Radio Free Europe Research Report* (June 18, 1970).

Modelski, George. *The Communist International System.* Princeton University: Center for International Studies, 1960.

Molotov, V. M. "Report on the International Situation." (February 8, 1955), quoted from *NEWS, Supplement* 4 (February 16, 1955): 10.

Monat, Pawel and Dille, John. *Spy in the U.S.* New York: Harper and Rowe, 1961.

Monin, M. "Ukreplenie voennogo sotrudnichestva—internatsional'nyi dolg bratskikh Marksistsko–Leninskikh partii." *Kommunist vooruzhennykh sil* 9 (May 1969): 9–17.

Montias, John Michael. *Economic Development in Communist Rumania.* Cambridge, Mass.: The MIT Press, 1967.

"Moscow's Allies on the Defensive." *The Interpreter* (December 1968): 5–10.

Moskovskoe soveshchanie evropeiskikh stran po obespecheniu mira i bezopastnosti v Evrope. Moscow: Gospolitizdat 1954. English versions in *New Times* 49 (December 4, 1954), Supplement: 3–72.

Moyne, Claudia W. *European Security—A Bibliography of Some Western Sources.* Cambridge, Mass.: M.I.T. Center for International Studies, C/71–73, March 1971.

Neuberger, Egon. *Soviet Bloc Economic Integration: Some Suggested Explanations for Slow Progress.* Santa Monica, California: RAND Memorandum, July 1963.

On Events in Czechoslovakia: Facts, Documents, Press Reports and Eyewitness Accounts (Soviet White Book). Moscow: 1968.

Pavlov, O. "Proletarian Internationalism and Defense of Socialist Gains." *International Affairs* (Moscow) 10 (October 1970): 11–16.

Pavlov, V. and Gorelov, G. "The Socialist States Struggle for European Security." *International Affairs* (Moscow) 2 (February 1967): 17–19.

Pergent, J. "Le pacte de Varsovie et l'inventaire des forces de l'Est." *Est et Ouest* 19, no. 387 (July 1967): 16–19.

Pool, Ithiel de Sola et al. *Satellite Generals: A Study of Military Elites in the Soviet Sphere.* Stanford, Calif.: Hoover Institution Studies, Stanford University Press, 1955.

Pryor, Frederic L. *The Foreign Trade System of the European Communist Nations.* Ph.D. Dissertation, Yale University, 1961.

———. *The Communist Foreign Trade System.* Cambridge, Mass.: The MIT Press, 1963.

Ra'anan, Uri. *The USSR Arms the Third World: Case Studies in Soviet Foreign Policy.* Cambridge, Mass.: The MIT Press, 1969.

Ray, Hemen. "China's Initiatives in Eastern Europe." *Current Scene* 7, no. 23 (December 1, 1969): 1–17.

Reitz, Col. James T. "The Satellite Armies." *Military Review* 45, no. 10 (October 1965): 28–35.

Remington, Robin Alison. *The Changing Soviet Perception of the Warsaw*

Pact. Cambridge, Mass.: M.I.T. Center for International Studies, C/67–24, November 1967.

———. "Czechoslovakia and the Warsaw Pact." *East European Quarterly* 3, no. 3 (September 1969).

———. The Growth of Communist Regional Organization 1949–1962. Ph.D. Dissertation, Indiana University, April 1966.

———. *Winter in Prague: Documents on Czechoslovak Communism in Crisis:* Cambridge, Mass.: The MIT Press, 1969.

Ritvo, Herbert, ed. *The New Soviet Society: Final Text of the Program of the Communist Party of the Soviet Union. New Leader* paperback, 1962.

Robinson, William F. "Czechoslovakia and Its Allies." *Studies in Comparative Communism* 1, nos. 1 and 2 (July–October, 1968): 141–170.

Różański, Henryk. "Budowa Komunizmu w ZSRR a rozwój współpracy gospodarczej państw socjalistycnych." *Nowe drogi* 12, no. 151 (December 1961): 99.

Roy Chowdbury, Subrata. *Military Alliances and Neutrality in War and Peace.* Bombay: Orient Longmans, 1966.

Sanakoyev, Sh. "Proletarian Internationalism: Theory and Practice." *International Affairs* (Moscow) 4 (April 1969): 9–15.

———. "Socialist Foreign Policy and the Community of Fraternal Countries." *International Affairs* (Moscow) 10 (October 1968): 71–81.

——— and Kapchenko, N. "Triumph of the Principles of Proletarian Internationalism." *International Affairs* (Moscow) 8 (August 1969): 32–39.

Schmidt, Helmut. "Implications of the Brezhnev Doctrine." *Vorwärts,* February 13, 1969; *The German Tribune* no. 5 (April 22, 1969): 1–7.

Schonherr, Siegfried. "Über den Zusammenhang zwischen Wirtschaft und Landesverteidigung beim Aufbau des entwickelten gesellschaftlichen Systems des Sozialismus in der DDR." *Wirtschaftswissenschaften* 8 (August 1969): 1161–1175.

Senin, M. "Peace in Europe and Consolidation of the Socialist Countries." *International Affairs* (Moscow) 8 (August 1965): 3–11.

Shelling, Thomas, C. *The Strategy of Conflict.* New York: Oxford University Press, 1963.

Shirk, Col. Paul R. "The Warsaw Treaty Organization." *Military Review* 49, no. 5 (May 1969): 28–37.

Shulman, Marshall D. "The Communist States and Western Integration." *International Organization* 17, no. 3 (Summer 1963): 649–662.

Sitkovskiy, E. P. "Marksizm-Leninizm—edinoe internatsional'noe uchenie rabochego klassa." *Filosofskie nauki* no. 1 (1970).

Skilling, H. Gordon. *The Governments of Communist East Europe.* New York: Crowell, 1966.

Smith, Canfield F. "The Rocky Road to Communist Unity." *East Europe* 18, no. 2 (February 1969): 3–10.

Sokolovskii, V. C., ed. *Soviet Military Strategy.* New Jersey: Prentice-Hall, 1963.

Staar, Richard F. "The East European Alliance." *United States Naval Institute Proceedings* 90, no. 9 (September 1964).

———. *The Communist Regimes of Eastern Europe: An Introduction.* Stanford, California: Hoover Institution on War, Revolution, and Peace, 1967.

———. "What Next in East European Intrabloc Relations." *East Europe* 18, nos. 11–12 (November–December 1969): 19–28.

Taborsky, Edward. "Czechoslovakia: The Return to Normalcy." *Problems of Communism* 19, no. 6 (November–December 1970): 31–41.

"Treaty on Relations Between the Union of Soviet Socialist Republics and the German Democratic Republic." *United Nations Treaty Series* 266, no. 3114: 201.

Tunkin, G. I. "New Measures for Security of Peace–Loving Countries." *International Affairs* 5 (May 1955): 5–11.

———. "O nekotorykh voprosakh mezhdunarodnogo dogovora v sviazi s varshavskim dogovorom." *Sovetskoe gosudarstvo i pravo* 1 (1956): 98–104.

———. "Parizskie soglashenia i mezhdunarodnoe pravo." *Sovetskoe gosudarstvo i pravo* 2 (1955): 13–22.

Tykociński, Władysław. "Poland's Plan for the 'Northern Tier.'" *East Europe* 15, no. 11 (November 1966): 9–16.

USSR Delegation. "Basic Principles of a Treaty Between the Alignments of States Existing in Europe." (Proposal) *New Times* 31 (July 28, 1955): 13.

USSR Delegation. Draft, "General European Treaty of Collective Security in Europe," Article 14, *New Times* 31 (July 28, 1955): 8–9.

U.N. Report Supplement of the Special Committee on the Problem of Hungary, General Assembly Records: 11th Session, Supplement 18 (A/3592). New York, 1954.

Váli, Ferenc A. *Rift and Revolt in Hungary.* Cambridge, Mass.: Harvard University Press, 1961.

Vasilyev, Lt. Col. N. "Brotherhood in Arms." *Soviet Military Review* 61, no. 1 (January 1970): 30–34.

"Velikoe edinstvo sotsialisticheskich stran nerushimo." *Kommunist* 16 (November 1956): 3–13.

Voenno-morskoy mezhdunarodno-pravovoy spravochnik. Moscow: Voennoe izdatelstvo, 1966.

von Krannhals, Hans. "Command Integration Within the Warsaw Pact." *Military Review* 41, no. 5 (May 1961): 40–52 (translated from *Wehrwisgenschaftliche Rundschau*, 1961).

von Laeuen, Harald. "Osteuropa unter dem Zugriff der Hegemonialmacht." *Europa-Archiv* 20 (October 25, 1968): 738–743.

von Paschta, Thaddäus. "Das System der sowjetischen Militärberater in den Satellitenstaaten." *Wehrkunde* (September 1962): 496–500.

Voprosy vneshnei politiki, stran sotsialisticheskogo lageria. Moscow: Izd-vo mezhdunarodnykh otnoshenii, 1958.

Vúkadinović, Radovan Dr. *Odnosi medju evropskim socijalističkim dravama —SEV i Varšavski ugovor.* Zagreb: Školska knjiga, 1970).

Wagenlehner, G. "Die sowjetische Rechtfertigung der Intervention in der CSSR." *Osteuropa* 18, no. 10–11 (October–November 1968): 758–768.

"The Warsaw Pact: Arms and Equipment." *Military Review* 45, no. 10 (October 1965): 36–37 (translated from *Soldat und Technik* [March 1965]).

The Warsaw Pact: Its Role in Soviet Bloc Affairs. Report of the Subcommittee on National Security and International Operations to the Committee on Government Operations, United States Senate, 89th Cong., 2nd Session, Washington, D.C.: U.S. Government Printing Office, 1966.

"Western and Eastern Europe: The Changing Relationship," *Adelphi papers* 33 London: ISS March 1967.

Wettig, Gerhard. "Die europäische Sicherheit in der Politik des Ostblocks 1966." *Osteuropa* 17, no. 2–3 (February–March 1967): 94–113.

———. "Der Einfluss der DDR auf die Deutschlandpolitik der Warschauer-Pakt Staaten." *Aus Politik und Zeitgeschichte,* Beilage zur Wochenzeitung *Das Parlament,* B 43/69 October 25, 1969: 3–24.

Whetten, Lawrence L. "The Role of East Germany in West German–Soviet Relations." *The World Today* 25, no. 12 (December 1969): 507–520.

———. "Recent Changes in East European Approaches to European Security." *The World Today* 26, no. 7 (July 1970): 277–289.

Wolfe, Thomas W. *Soviet Power and Europe: 1945–1970.* Baltimore, Md.: Johns Hopkins Press, 1970.

———. *Soviet Strategy at the Crossroads.* Cambridge, Mass.: Harvard University Press, 1964.

———. "The Warsaw Pact in Evolution." *The World Today* 22, no. 5 (May 1966): 191–198.

Woźniak, Marian. "The Soviet Presence in Legnica." *East Europe* 18, no. 3 (March 1969): 19–22.

Yakubovsky, I. "Bastion mira i bezopasnosti narodov," *Voennoistorichesky zhurnal* 3(March 1971): 20–31.

————. "Na strazhe mira i sotsialisma." *Voenno-istoricheskii zhurnal* 5 (May 1970): 17.

Zasedania politicheskogo konsul'tativnogo komiteta, uchrezdennogo v sootvetstvii s varshavskim dogovorom. Moscow: Gospolitizdat, 1956.

Zauberman, A. "Economic Integration: Problems and Prospects." *Problems of Communism* 8, no. 4 (July–August 1959): 23–29.

Zhukov, G. "Pact of Peace and Security." *International Affairs* 3 (March 1958): 111–113.

Zhukov, G. P. *Varshavskii dogovor i voprosy mezhdunarodnoi bezopasnosti.* Moscow: Cotsekgiz, 1961.

Zinner, Paul E., ed. *National Communism and Popular Revolt in Eastern Europe: A Selection of Documents on Events in Poland and Hungary February to November 1956.* New York: Columbia University Press, 1956.

————. *Revolution in Hungary.* New York: Columbia University Press, 1962.

SUBJECT
INDEX

NAME
INDEX